THE
THURTELL-HUNT
MURDER CASE

Albert Borowitz

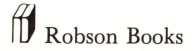 Robson Books

First published in Great Britain in 1988 by Robson Books Ltd,
Bolsover House, 5 – 6 Clipstone Street, London W1P 7EB.

British Library Cataloguing in Publication Data

Borowitz, Albert
 The Thurtell-Hunt murder case.
 1. Hertfordshire. Weare, William, d.1823.
 Murder
 I. Title
 364.1'523'094258

ISBN 0-86051-483-8

Printed in Great Britain by St. Edmundbury Press Ltd,
Bury St. Edmunds, Suffolk.

For Thurtell's compatriots
Alex Auswaks
Christianna Brand
Jonathan Goodman
Richard and Molly Whittington-Egan

CONTENTS

Acknowledgments   xi
Note on the Regency   xiii

Introduction   1
Chapter One   Bruisers and Blacklegs   6
Chapter Two   The Gas Went Out   13
Chapter Three   The Swell Yokel   19
Chapter Four   The Road Menders' Discoveries   31
Chapter Five   Revelations at the Artichoke   52
Chapter Six   The White-Faced Horse   65
Chapter Seven   The Rumormongers   79
Chapter Eight   The Second Solicitor   94
Chapter Nine   The Fairness of Mr. Justice Park   103
Chapter Ten   Egan's Interviews   135
Chapter Eleven   A Trout in the Milk   142
Chapter Twelve   Another Kean   166
Chapter Thirteen   The New Drop   182
Chapter Fourteen   The Fatal Effects of the Fast Life   198
Chapter Fifteen   Probert's Mare   210
Chapter Sixteen   The Survival of Hunt   222
Chapter Seventeen   A Return to Hertfordshire   234
Chapter Eighteen   Blockheads in a Dark Lane   250

Notes   277
Selected Bibliography   289
Index   297

ILLUSTRATIONS

following page   120
John Thurtell's Scissors
Plan of Gill's Hill Cottage
Gill's Hill Cottage
The Recovery of the Body
Pond at Gill's Hill Cottage
The Conspirators Divide the Spoils
The Burial of Weare
The Gig in the Lane
John Thurtell
Joseph Hunt
William Probert
Thurtell's Execution
The Gallows and Drop
Playbill for *The Gamblers*
Playbill for *The Hertfordshire Tragedy*
Contemporary Broadside
Probert's Confession, a Catchpenny Pamphlet
Hunt's Farewell to England
Gill's Hill Lane in 1960

MAPS

Contemporary Map   38
Vicinity of Gill's Hill Lane   238

CHART

Murder Route and Chronology   243

ACKNOWLEDGMENTS

For archival data and materials and copies of newspapers and pamphlets, I am greatly indebted to the Archives Office, New South Wales; the Bodleian Library; the British Library; the Mitchell Library, Sydney; the National Library of Australia; the Public Record Office, London; and the Registry of Births, Deaths and Marriages, New South Wales. I also acknowledge the expert assistance of Barbara Gillen and Jean Richards for guiding me through the labyrinths of English and Australian record offices. Thanks, as always, are due to the staff of the Cleveland Public Library, who have become used to my exotic requests for dust-covered, noncirculating tomes from the stacks and for interlibrary loans.

Special gratitude is due the Reverend David Wallace-Hadrill and the Aldenham School for a personally guided tour of the murder site and for the loan of a unique collection of Thurtell-Hunt ephemera. I am also greatly indebted to Judith Bailey for her painstaking and creative editing of the manuscript and to Diane Kastelic for her preparation of the map of the murder scene that accompanies Chapter Seventeen.

I reserve my last tribute for my wife, Helen, who has learned more about boxing and gambling than she could have reasonably anticipated when we exchanged our vows.

NOTE ON THE REGENCY

———

The term *Regency* is used broadly in this book, as in Donald Low, *Thieves' Kitchen: The Regency Underworld* (London, 1982), to refer to the period from 1800 to 1830. It accordingly includes the reign of George IV, his regency of 1811–1820, and the previous decade. This extensive definition appears appropriate in studies of early nineteenth-century England's underworld activities, public amusements, and social attitudes, all of which changed more slowly than the names and titles of its rulers.

THE
THURTELL-HUNT
MURDER CASE

INTRODUCTION

British historian G. M. Trevelyan has described the Thurtell-Hunt murder case as the event that created the greatest popular interest between the adultery trial of Queen Caroline and the Reform Bill of 1832.[1] What strange allure is there in this crime, committed for the most sordid of motives and unprofitably at that, which gave it rank with royal scandal and constitutional upheaval? It will be the purpose of this first full-length historical study of the case to rediscover the sources of John Thurtell's fierce grip on the post-Regency imagination and to measure the even more remarkable impact his crime has had on British literature over a period of more than a century and a half.

It is no surprise that the case was, in Thackeray's phrase, a "god-send" to journalists.[2] Murder was rare, and rarer still was a murder of such incredible brutality, committed on the very fringe of the metropolis. The scenes and circumstances of the crime and of the disposition and recovery of the body were melodramatic in the extreme, and the sheer narrative drive of the case would have won it a secure place in public favor. From early on, though, there was a general sense that something more was involved, that the unfolding details of the news stories were nightmarishly reflecting the excesses of the Regency.

Foremost among the figures in the social landscape the case revealed was John Thurtell himself, prodigal son of a prominent Norwich merchant, who came to London and plunged eagerly into the sporting and gambling underworld of the city. His fall from respectability through evil acquaintance gave his crime the quality of a cautionary tale, and its setting amid boxing circles and in gambling "hells" implicated in his ruin two of the unlawful pleasures of the Regency. Thurtell was personally known to journalists as a boxing promoter and an amateur boxer, and he was also a gambler distinguished more for avidity than shrewdness. When it was reported that the murder victim was a swindling gambler who had cheated Thurtell at cards, the Hogarthian moral pointed by the tale seemed complete: forbidden urban entertainments in which social barriers were disregarded led inevitably to loss of restraint, followed by deception, revenge and expiation.

The close association of John Thurtell with boxing and gambling gave his case a special appeal to two constituencies—the broad ranks of those who shared his passions and the rising pre-Victorian moralists who favored stronger enforcement of legal prohibitions of these amusements. The Thurtell case stirred a debate (never yet stilled) as to whether boxing is an inhumane expression of violence or a useful channel for inborn aggression. The uneasiness Thurtell's fate inspired on this question was at least as deep as that aroused in recent years by hooliganism at British soccer matches. The revulsion to gambling stirred by the Thurtell case has also persevered, but cyclically. The Victorians shut down the gambling houses; in modern London they are open for business again (but please call them clubs).

The Thurtell case afforded fresh confirmation of one of the worries that united opponents of prizefighting and gambling—that both activities were inextricably tied to professional crime. The same ruffians who fixed boxing matches and jostled or robbed the respectable fans at ringside were likely to preside over crooked card games or roulette wheels in the gambling houses. In Thurtell's case the public was treated to the spectacle of the biter bit; the murderer, notorious as a fight fixer himself, had played pigeon to the card sharper with whom he evened the score through murder. As the rumors of the unsavory connections of Thurtell and his accomplices multiplied, the public preoccupation with the underworld ramifications of the case grew. The press speculated that the murder was a gangland killing and hinted darkly of a "hit" list that contained the names of many victims whose lives had been spared only by Thurtell's arrest. Although a well-organized underworld had existed in London since Elizabethan times and had been brought to new heights of efficiency by Jonathan Wild in the early eighteenth century, the Thurtell case is an important benchmark in rising urban fears of the criminal mob. Unwittingly, Thurtell and his confederates confirmed this historical role by inventing for their murder a strategy that has become a signature of the modern gangland slaying.

All these features of the Thurtell-Hunt case were bound to hold the public's attention, but the furor was whipped up to a higher pitch by the unprecedented scope of coverage in the rapidly growing popular press; the crime lays fair claim to being the first English example of what Richard Altick has called the "early murders for the million."[3] The extravagance of the pretrial newspaper reports, in which no rumor, however wild, was deemed unfit to print, was matched by the prodigious efforts of the other hawkers of crime—the chapbook publishers and the proprietors of melodrama theaters. As the building frenzy threatened to turn the coming trial into a meaningless footnote to the judgment the public was already being invited to make, Thurtell's lawyers invoked the aid of the courts and the case moved into still another arena of controversy: how were England's cherished rights of freedom of speech and press to be reconciled with claims to a fair trial by an unprejudiced jury? In issuing an injunction against certain publications and a stage depiction of the crime, the Court of King's Bench, braving howls of outrage from the press, opened the modern era of battle between the public's right to "know" and the defendant's need for silence. Ironically, it was the very concern for isolation of the prisoners from outside communications (with fancied gangster allies) that led overzealous local magistrates to restrict the access of legal advisers, producing yet another controversy whose resolution makes the case an important chapter in the development of the right to counsel.

The social and legal impact of the case entitled it to permanent recognition in crime history, but what stamps it as unique is its rich legacy to English literature. Called the "most literary murder," the Thurtell-Hunt case is England's closest parallel to the patricide of Beatrice Cenci in its unflagging fascination for generations of writers who have continued to rework its themes and to reinterpret its principal personalities.⁴ Why has this been so? Thurtell, it is true, had a certain advantage over other criminals who might flatter themselves with aspirations to immortality: he knew a number of writers, including William Hazlitt, who described him in an essay written before the murder; Pierce Egan, who was to interview him in prison; and George Borrow, a fellow resident of Norwich to whom he had reportedly given sparring lessons. But, as shown in the final chapter of this book, many writers who did not know him or who lived in later eras—have also reflected the influence of Thurtell and his crime.

It is risky to attempt to identify the qualities in a murder case that are likely to lay the foundation for a perennial literary tradition like those associated with the Cenci and Thurtell cases. Certain common elements, though, can be identified in the two murders. A crucial requirement seems to be a central figure indelibly striking in appearance and personality. Beatrice Cenci's immortality was assured in large measure by her traditional identification with a portrait attributed to Guido Reni, and John Thurtell's strong, almost simian features were imprinted on the public mind and memory by the illustrations of the popular press. Thurtell's personality had as its mainspring an irresistible drive to dominate and intimidate, but during his trial and execution, this powerful man showed surprising admixtures of warmth, fortitude, eloquence, and a capacity to inspire love. People began to see what in other circumstances he might have been.

A second factor that probably contributes to literary longevity of a crime is the presence of very concrete, visually stimulating images associated with the commission of the crime and its aftermath. The Cenci affair was virtually ready-made for the stage with the scenes of Beatrice's isolation in a remote castle and the incestuous assaults of her father (probably an invention of her defense counsel). In the Thurtell case, unforgettable images cluster in profusion around a murder that is itself astounding for its ferocity: a ghostly horse leading a doomed man in a gig down a lonely lane; water burial of the corpse; an uncanny nocturnal exhumation in a country churchyard; the murder conspirators being spied upon by a sleepless wife.

A third element that may enhance the appeal of a criminal case to the literary imagination is the interplay between the compelling images of the case and broader concepts and issues.[5] In the Cenci case the domestic drama in the Castle of Petrella where Beatrice was imprisoned by her father lent itself to interpretation as a symbol of oppression by parents or by the old and powerful. Similarly, the unusual literary response to the Thurtell case may have been heightened by the more general significance given the melodramatic physical details of the crime by their association with recognizable features of Regency life. The complexity and diversity of Thurtell-inspired literature demonstrates the limitless adaptability of the theme of willful pursuit of pleasure. In the broad stream of this tradition there has been room for every viewpoint: for Pierce Egan, the Regency sports scribe who was as fight-mad as Thurtell but was constrained to sigh in public over a comrade gone wrong; for Bulwer Lytton, who used the case to launch the moralistic sensation mongering of the "Newgate novel"; and for two great Victorians, Dickens and Carlyle, who saw in Thurtell's fate a just reward for soulless materialism and superficiality. Perhaps the most notable literary reincarnation of Thurtell's crime was in the writings of Carlyle. Here image and symbolic meaning are perfectly fused by the conversion of the gig driven by one of Thurtell's accomplices into a central concept in Carlyle's indictment of bourgeois values.

Chapter One

BRUISERS AND BLACKLEGS

Bareknuckle boxing shared certain traits with two of the other ruling pleasures of Regency England, gambling and whoring: it was carried on in open violation of criminal laws, and its celebrants paid no respect to the class distinctions that were generally observed by the rigidly stratified society of the period. It would be comforting to be able to record that the banning of prizefights was due to humane aversion to the brutality of the sport, in which a round ended only with a knockdown or a fall and the bout went on until one of the "bruisers" was so badly beaten or exhausted that he could not "come up to the scratch" in the half-minute interval allowed between rounds. However, tradition offers a less inspiring explanation for boxing's prohibition. In 1750 the duke of Cumberland heavily backed Jack Broughton, the "father of the Science of the Art of Self-Defence," against Jack Slack, a butcher from Bristol, then England's second largest city and a breeding ground of great boxers. The fight took place at the London mecca of the sport, the New Amphitheatre in Oxford Street, which Broughton had built at the suggestion of his many admirers in 1743. The champion was so sure of himself that he did not train seriously, and the betting fraternity regarded the relatively unknown challenger just as lightly, quoting odds at ten to one in favor of Broughton.[1]

In the early going Broughton performed as expected, knocking Slack all over the ring, but after about two minutes the butcher suddenly jumped in and landed a desperate blow between the champion's eyes. Pierce Egan in *Boxiana* describes what followed:

Broughton now appeared like one stupid, and it was two or three minutes before this circumstance was discovered by the spectators, whose attentions were attracted by the strange and unusual manner in which Broughton appeared to *feel* for, instead of boldly facing and attacking his man: at length his patron, the Duke of Cumberland, earnestly exclaimed, "What are you about, Broughton? You can't fight—you're beat!" To which question Broughton instantly replied: "I can't see my man, your Highness. I am blind, but not beat; only let me be placed before my antagonist and he shall not gain the day yet."[2]

But Broughton was not destined to be a second Samson; Slack followed up his advantage and obtained a victory after fourteen minutes. The duke of Cumberland, having lost thousands of pounds on Broughton, was furious and made no secret of his conviction that he had been cheated. The duke's outrage over his disastrous bets is commonly credited for Parliament's passage, soon after Broughton's defeat, of an act outlawing prizefights.

Whatever role the duke of Cumberland may have played in the parliamentary action, his close association with the Broughton-Slack fight illustrates the early dependency of pugilism on aristocratic support. Prizefights were arranged by noble patrons who raised funds for the stakes and supported their favorite boxers during training. As can be seen from the duke's inconsolable pining for his lost pounds, the betting motive was, from the very infancy of professional boxing, well mixed with love of the sport. However, the mode of sponsorship changed in 1814 with the organization of the Pugilistic Club. This new group, financed by the subscriptions of members who included not only noblemen but other respectable boxing enthusiasts, established codes of conduct for prizefights, hired pugilists to maintain order at ringside, and provided modest purses that were often bolstered by side stakes. The supplementary stakes, and private wagers as well, were customarily arranged in the various haunts of the fight crowd (or the Fancy, as it came to be called); favorite gathering places were the "sporting" pubs including many, like London's Castle Tavern, that were operated by retired boxers.[3]

Even in the heyday of aristocratic control of prizefights, critics of "boximania" carped at the Fancy's disregard of customary barriers between social classes. The passion for boxing as an amateur ath-

letic skill and a spectator sport raged as strongly in Oxford and
Eton as in city and country taverns; it was a common frenzy that
united the public school with the public house. The professional
boxers themselves were recruited mostly from the urban working
class, and their ranks were swollen in the period of economic depression following the Napoleonic Wars. Occasionally a champion
aspired to climb a rung or two on the social ladder. "Gentleman"
John Jackson, the son of a successful builder, cut a plausible figure
in Regency drawing rooms and taught the fine points of boxing to
the nation's nobility (including Lord Byron) in his training rooms
in Bond Street. However, his claim to gentlemanliness was suspect
at best, for he had won the championship in 1795 from Daniel
Mendoza by holding Mendoza by his long hair while punching
him senseless. Social acceptability of boxers had its limits, though;
while some noblemen paid court to Gentleman John, others were
outraged when George IV forgot proprieties to the point of hiring
a contingent of eighteen leading pugilists to guard the approaches
to Westminster Hall on the occasion of his coronation in 1821.[4]

The jostling and intermingling of the various ranks of society
were even more in evidence at ringside. To some, the extinction of
all class boundaries in the gatherings of the Fancy seemed a healthy
sign of democracy. Indeed, the duke of Clarence (the future William IV) was said to have rebuked a nobleman looking down his
nose at the crowds assembled at Moulsey Hurst, the favorite fight
locale of the Pugilistic Club: "Be pleased to recollect, my lord, that
we are all Englishmen here; and as for places we must do the best
we can for ourselves."[5] But Washington Irving, writing in England
under the pseudonym Geoffrey Crayon, took a darker view of the
ill-assorted mobs of the Fancy in his story "Buckthorne": "What, in
fact, is the Fancy itself, but a chain of easy communication, extend-
ing down from the peer to the pick-pocket, through the medium
of which a man of rank may find that he has shaken hands at three
removes, with the murderer on the gibbet?"[6]

England's ardor for gambling had long preceded its love affair
with boxing. Concern with the social costs of gambling had motivated a series of statutory prohibitions and restrictions dating back
to the reign of Henry VIII. The earliest of these enactments reflected a belief of England's lawgivers that gaming might perhaps

be a tolerable diversion for the leisured class but that it should be strictly barred to workers, who could ill afford their losses and might be turned from the path of labor and thrift by the hope for easy money. Under a law of 1541, no apprentice, servant or artisan was permitted to play at tennis, bowls, cards, dice, quoits, or "any other unlawful game," except at Christmas. A series of later statutes from the reign of Queen Anne through the years of George IV authorized suits against gamblers for the recovery of losses at play, banned certain gambling games, and proscribed the keeping of common gaming houses and gambling in public places.[7] Despite the breadth of the later legislation, the primary worry of public officials in the early nineteenth century was over the spread of the gambling itch from the aristocracy and the armed forces to the lower orders. This preoccupation is evident in the discussion of gaming houses in John Wade's *Treatise on the Police and Crimes of the Metropolis* (1829):

> To the military and naval officer, in time of peace, the chances of the tables serve in lieu of the vicissitudes and stimulus of actual warfare. To the nobility, gentry, and great moneyed classes, it forms a species of traffic or barter; their incomes vastly exceed their wants, and staking the surplus on the cast of a die, even if lost, is mere child's play with counters, which deprives them only of that for which they had no indispensable use, neither abridging their comforts nor luxuries, nor incapacitating them for the discharge of the few duties society has left them to perform.
>
> Unfortunately, the passion does not stop here; it has extended through every grade and class in the community; is found not only at every watering-place, but at every inn, publican's, and almost every private house in the metropolis, and seems the natural offspring or accompaniment of immense wealth and luxury.[8]

The effect of governmental pressure was not to destroy the compulsion to gamble but to drive gambling into places of secrecy, including aristocratic clubs such as White's (where members bet on anything from the dates of future marriages and births to developments in the European wars) and the clandestine gambling houses mentioned by Wade. How, in fact, could Parliament have hoped to eradicate a gambling instinct so deep and all-pervasive that, like the ancient Germans of Tacitus, Englishmen would bet their lives when all else was lost? A startling instance of such a wager was reported in the *Annual Register* for 1812. In April of that year a police officer came upon two men on a wall and shortly thereafter saw the taller of them hanging by his neck from a lamppost attached to the wall; the man was saved when the handkerchief by which he was dangling gave way and he fell to the ground. At an examination at Bow Street police station, the following facts were established about the two men: "They had been together on Wednesday afternoon, tossed up for money, and afterwards for their clothes; the tall man, who was hanged, won the other's jacket, trousers, and shoes; they then tossed up which should hang the other, and the short one won the toss."[9]

The law enforcement problem was aggravated after the French Revolution by a vast increase in gaming attributed by Wade to the introduction of many novel games of chance by continental immigrants. The number of London's gaming houses, or "hells," had increased from about five prior to the revolution to at least twenty-two by 1821; in the following year a concerted program of prosecutions resulted in the imprisonment and fining of seven or eight gaming-house keepers, but the gambling fever remained unabated. Most of the hells, located in St. James's Street and other addresses in the West End, featured the French games that were greatly in vogue—rouge et noir, roulette, and hazard. All these games were operated on a "bank" principle under which the house made its profit by reserving a point or ball that, when it turned up, entitled the bank to sweep the bets from the table.

But the "blacklegs," the swindlers of the gambling profession, knew how to alter the odds in their own favor. The proprietors of the hells were a heterogeneous group who by no means felt bound by the honorable rules that governed the betting book at White's Club; among them were "persons of the very highest rank in the state, not excepting some of orthodox habits, from the top of nobility down to the very lowest of the low, the scum and outcast of society, all commingled and identified in one ruinous vice; all following the same criminal pursuits, and each one endeavouring, by every means in his power, to ruin his fellow."[10] Some of the principal blacklegs among them are known today principally by the nicknames given them by their underworld cronies: the Leviathan, the Black Dwarf, the Hebrew Star, the Four German Barons, Coax-

ing Tom, and Captain Whimper. These worthies had mastered the
time-honored arts of fraudulent card play and their dice, if not
loaded, were "cogged," that is, dropped into "cramped" dice boxes
designed to hold them fast so that they could be thrown with the
desired faces upward. The sharpers had also invented a device to
control the action of roulette tables with a hidden spring operated
by the foot. Outraged by this new swindling technique, the author
of an antigambling tract, *The Gambler's Scourge,* wrote of roulette
(or roly poly, as the English called it): "Of all the infamous games
ever introduced in this country for the purpose of fraud and robbery, this is decidedly the most abominable. It is disgraceful to the
police of the metropolis, that these gangs of French sharpers are
allowed to pursue their destructive plans with impunity." [11]

What made matters worse in the eyes of fulminating enemies of
gambling was that many a crook had cheated the master he had
formerly served. This horrifying lesson was taught in "The Gamblers: A Moral Poem," included in *The Gambler's Scourge:*

> Behold Lord ——— in affable discourse
> With one who saddled once his Lordship's
>   horse!!
> Now, by a system of deceptive vice,
> False cards, false character, and loaded dice,
> He lends the Peer, by adverse fortune cross'd,
> Part of the money which his Lordship lost.
> . . . .
> The humble waiter at the ——— Hotel
> Now sups with noble gamblers at Pall Mall.
> He, who once filled a servant's wretched place,
> Elbows my Lord, and tipples with his Grace.
> He, who wash'd glasses ere superiors drank,
> Assumes equality with men of rank! [12]

Certain gambling establishments specialized in preying on the
fashionable youth of London. A "dandy hell," conducted at the
corner of Bennett Street, St. James's by a former clergyman of the
Church of England, employed a number of ruined gamblers as
"recruiting officers," under the captaincy of the infamous Black
Dwarf. These men "frequent the fashionable coffee-houses at the
west-end, insinuate themselves into the society of young men of
fashion, introduce them to the houses, and are paid a bonus by the

proprietors, great, in proportion to the sum their victim has been robbed of."[13]

The activities of the blacklegs, however, were by no means restricted to the gambling houses. They were to be seen at country fairs and race meetings fleecing unwary "pigeons" or "flats" with their rigged gambling devices, and they also became adept at drugging or poisoning racehorses. In the years after the Napoleonic Wars, prizefighting was to become another victim of the gambling underworld; more and more frequently shady promoters and their confederates arranged "crosses," that is, fixed boxing matches so that the favorite would fall as the result of an imaginary blow or inexplicably fail to rise in time from his second's knee, which served in place of a stool in the interval between rounds. By the 1820s even the fighter who had fairly vanquished his opponent in the ring was regularly suspected by the public of having participated in a cross. In less than a decade, the blacklegs had made the entire fight crowd as skeptical as the duke of Cumberland.

Chapter Two

THE GAS WENT OUT

Tom Hickman, better known to the boxing world as the Gas-light Man, strutted around the ring sucking an orange. With a toss of his head he spat out the skin and at insultingly short range stared down his hulking opponent Bill Neat. The familiar confidence and swagger of the "Gas" did not sway the onlookers; the odds, which had run as high as seven to four in Hickman's favor at the London gathering places of the Fancy were now being quoted on the ground at five to four in favor of Neat.[1]

Though the Hickman-Neat match, held at the Hungerford Downs racetrack on December 11, 1821, had been ballyhooed in the press as "the Great Fight for the Championship of England," English boxing was in an interregnum, and the title was hotly disputed by a number of aspirants. The fighting days of the old champion Tom Cribb were over, though he deferred his formal retirement until the next year. Cribb favored Tom Spring as his successor, but the Fancy bluntly rejected the notion of a transferrable championship; the crown, a journalist wrote, could only be won "by force and arms" in the ring.

In London the backers of the Gas-light Man were strident in the assertion that their man would own the title outright once he put Neat away, and they felt certain he would do that in short order. Gas was a compactly built middleweight in a sport that was becoming a preserve of giants. His height was five feet, nine and a half inches, but Neat was close to six feet tall and outweighed the Gas fourteen stones to twelve (196 pounds to 168). But Gas was convinced that his demonstrated ring prowess rendered these physical disadvantages of no account, and the chorus of adulation from the London Fancy supported his own boast that he could beat any fighter in the land. Hickman's meteoric rise on the London prize-fighting scene seemed to bear out his claims to supremacy. Born in Worcestershire in 1795, he made the neighborhood boys victims of his skill at brawling while still "at a tender age." He put together a string of boxing successes in the provinces and then moved to London, where his employment at a gasworks on the South Bank gave him his nicknames, the "Gas-light Man," the "Gas-Man," the "Gas," and even, in a dreadful punning reference to Goliath, the "Man of Gas." His first local triumphs included spontaneous set-tos with some fellow workers at the gasworks; on another occasion he was haled before the magistrate at Union Hall Police Court, South-wark, for administering a sound thrashing to seven iron founders on Tooley Street. When the magistrate compared Hickman's mod-est size with that of the enormous complainants, he dismissed the charge as incredible.[2]

Beginning in 1819, he fought four bouts with respected profes-sional opponents and won them all—in an aggregate time period of less than forty-five minutes. In his second match with George Cooper, the Gas put his adversary out of action in three minutes, for Hickman's method was "more ferocious than scientific." In *The Fancy* his unsubtle approach to ring battles is described: "Although he stands well up to his man, and bores away at him even before he gets warm, yet it cannot be denied, that he is then watching an opportunity for doing execution, and his favourite hit is on the jaw-bone. . . . he seems desirous of making his blows *tell* upon the head or trunk, and unlike the *mere sparrers* he defends himself not at all."[3]

Out of the ring Hickman was fond of fun and even fonder of drink, good-natured, and friendly, but it was observed that "re-proof renders him irritable and unruly." In one of his unpredict-able fits of violence, perhaps brought on by too much "blue ruin" (gin), the Gas-Man assaulted the master of ceremonies at the Fives Court, one of London's arenas for exhibitions of sparring with gloves on; the old man died a day or two later. Another of his less agreeable traits was his overweening sense of invulnerability, which led him to taunt opponents in the ring and to make cocksure predictions of victory in upcoming fights. At a recent appearance at the Fives Court he had bragged that "the Gas should never go out."

The Gas-Man's opponent, Bill Neat, hailed from Bristol, which prided itself on its fabled ring champions, including Tom Cribb and Jem Belcher. Indeed, Neat, like all Bristolians, was fighting under Belcher's yellow colors. Belcher had popularized the practice (later embodied in the 1838 boxing rules) that each fighter should have a colored handkerchief tied around one of the ring stakes and that the winner should claim both. Jem's yellow handkerchief, which came to be known as the "yellowman" or "Belcher," was not only adopted by the bruisers of his city but graced "the bosoms of some of our most elevated and beautiful country-women."[4]

The powerful Neat had had only one contest before his appearance on the national boxing scene: in a large malt room at Bristol, he had undertaken to put his big opponent Churchill out of action in ten minutes. Although he punished Churchill severely, Neat lost his wager against the clock. In 1818 he caught the eye of the London Fancy by decisively defeating one of their favorites, Tom Oliver, after twenty-eight rounds. Despite his triumph, Neat appeared "little more than a novice respecting scientific boxing." However, he possessed a devastating punch that no teaching could achieve: "One hit from his right hand, given in proper distance, can gain a victory; but three of them are positively enough to dispose of a giant."[5] It was no wonder that top billing had been given to the match of the Bristol powerhouse with the bull-like Gas-Man.

Since prizefighting was illegal, bouts were generally staged far from London at locations announced only shortly in advance so that local magistrates could less readily interfere. However, London boxing devotees who could not make the sixty-mile journey to Hungerford for the Hickman-Neat fight had one prime consolation: they could read a ringside account of the action by Pierce Egan.[6] Probably born in Ireland in 1774, Egan suffered years of obscurity in London as a compositor and proofreader for printing houses, a hack writer, and an anonymous contributor of sporting articles to various newspapers; in 1812 he won fame overnight when George Smeeton published the first volume of Egan's history of British pugilism, *Boxiana*. From this point on, any boxing match of importance was recounted by this widely acclaimed

"Xenophon of the Ring" in a style that uniquely blended mock-epic grandiloquence with sporting jargon and underworld slang, or "flash." Egan's celebrity was widened in 1820 with the publication of the first monthly number of *Life in London; or, The Day and Night Scenes of Jerry Hawthorn, Esq., and His Elegant Friend Corinthian Tom, Accompanied by Bob Logic, the Oxonian, in Their Rambles and Sprees Through the Metropolis.* It was this work, illustrated by George and Robert Cruikshank, that gave the world Tom and Jerry (who, through no fault of theirs, later bestowed their names on an American drink and a tiresome duo of cat and mouse). In its installments, which created an immediate sensation among England's reading public, the raffish gentleman, or "Corinthian," Tom initiates his provincial cousin Jerry into varied scenes of the high and low life of the metropolis—from the fashionable assemblies at Almack's Ballroom to the taverns frequented by the Fancy, the underworld, and the poor. Literary purists railed against Egan's "vulgar" style, in which the mixture of high-flown effusions with urban slang mirrored the conglomerate, unbounded vitality Egan found so attractive in London life and in the gatherings of the Fancy. The public paid no heed to those who inveighed against the Tom and Jerry fever; *Life in London* and its many imitations exhausted edition after edition, and theatergoers flocked to stage productions of *Tom and Jerry,* the most successful of which was the adaptation by W. T. Moncrieff that opened at the Adelphi in November, 1821.

The renowned Egan, when he went to Hungerford in December, 1821, to cover the Hickman-Neat bout, found that he himself would face a redoubtable challenger—the essayist and critic William Hazlitt. Although in all his forty-three years Hazlitt had never seen a boxing match, he had decided to chronicle the monumental encounter of the Gas-light Man with Bill Neat in an essay for the *New Monthly Magazine.*[7] His first step after conceiving this project was quite adroit considering that he was a neophyte; to learn where the fight was to be held, he called at one of the popular London resorts of the Fancy, the Hole in the Wall, Chancery Lane, a pub operated by a retired boxer, Jack Randall. It took some courage for Hazlitt to enter the pub, for the gin-sodden Randall had "threatened once upon a time to kick [him] out of doors for wanting a mutton-chop at his hospitable board." Learning the location of the

bout by eavesdropping on a conversation, Hazlitt, after some mis-
adventures, caught the Bath mail coach for Newbury, which was
nine miles from Hungerford. When he arrived at the town the
beds in every inn were full, but he was lucky to spend the night in
the kitchen of the Crown listening to the amusing nonstop tirades
of "a fine fellow, with sense, wit, and spirit, a hearty body and a
joyous mind, free-spoken, frank, convivial—one of that true English breed that went with Harry the Fifth to the siege of Har-
fleur." When the day dawned, he paid a visit to the barber and
walked with his friend Joe Parkes, a London solicitor, to Hungerford, where at last "on a gentle eminence, we saw the ring, surrounded by covered carts, gigs, and carriages, of which hundreds
had passed us on the road." As the time drew near, a bustle running through the crowd announced the entry of Neat, who "rolled
along, swathed in his loose greatcoat, his knock-knees bending
under his huge bulk; and with a modest, cheerful air, threw his hat
into the ring." From the other side "there was a similar rush and an
opening made, and the Gas-man came forward with a conscious
air of anticipated triumph, too much like the cock-of-the-walk."[8]

Now the supercilious Gas Man was in the ring and stared his fill
at his giant foe; the fight was to begin. The ring-wise Pierce Egan
describes the highlights of the first round:

> The Gas, on placing himself in attitude, surveyed his opponent from
> head to foot, and Neat was equally on the alert. Hickman kept dodging
> about in order to get an opening to plant a determined hit; but Neat was
> too leery to be had upon this suit, and whenever the Gas moved, he like-
> wise altered his position. . . . Hickman . . . attacked Neat with great ac-
> tivity, and the result was, the Bristol hero went down (more from a slip
> than the severity of the blow) between the legs of Hickman—the Cock-
> nies shouting for joy, and the regular Fanciers declaring "it was all right,
> and that Gas would win it easy."[9]

The tide turned for Neat in the third round, and at the same time
Hazlitt's description began to surpass that of his veteran rival Egan:
"The Gas-man aiming a mortal blow at his adversary's neck with
his right hand, and failing from the length he had to reach, the
other returned it with his left at full swing, planted a tremendous
blow on his cheek-bone and eyebrow, and made a red ruin of that
side of his face. The Gas-man went down, and there was another

shout—a roar of triumph as the waves of fortune rolled tumultu-
ously from side to side. This was a settler." About the twelfth
round it seemed to Hazlitt that the fight must be as good as finished. His impression of the scene is beyond the literary powers of
Egan. "I never saw anything more terrific," he wrote, "than [Hick-
man's] aspect just before he fell. All traces of life, of natural expression, were gone from him. His face was like a human skull, a
death's-head spouting blood. The eyes were filled with blood, the
nose streamed with blood, the mouth gaped blood. He was not like
an actual man, but like a preternatural, spectral appearance, or
like one of the figures in Dante's 'Inferno.'"[10] The Gas Man fought
on, but after the eighteenth round, the bout, which had lasted
twenty-three and a half minutes, was all over; Hickman remained
insensible when the end of the half-minute interval was called. Despite his boast at the Fives Court, the Gas had at last gone out.

On the way down to Newbury from London, Hazlitt had sat on
the coach box opposite a man whom the essayist identified as "Tom
Turtle the trainer." His conversation, as Hazlitt recalled it, had distinct limits: "My friend the trainer was confined in his topics to
fighting dogs and men, to bears and badgers; beyond this he was
'quite chapfallen,' not a word to throw at a dog, or indeed very
wisely fell asleep, when any other game was started." "Turtle" told
his fellow passenger about the boxer's training regime: "A yolk of
an egg with spoonful of rum in it is the first thing in a morning,
and then a walk of six miles till breakfast. This meal consists of a
plentiful supply of tea and toast and beefsteaks. Then another six
or seven miles till dinner-time, and another supply of solid beef or
mutton with a pint of porter, and perhaps, at the upmost, a couple
glasses of sherry." Hazlitt, for his part, had made free with his dis-
approval of Hickman's arrogance. "A boxer was bound to beat his
man," he had ventured, "but not to thrust his fist, either actually or
by implication, in every one's face. Even a highwayman, in the way
of trade, may blow out your brains, but if he uses foul language at
the same time, I should say he was no gentleman. A boxer, I would
infer, need not be a blackguard or a coxcomb, more than another." But "Turtle" made no reply, for having exhausted his category of pugilistic training methods, he had fallen asleep.[11]

Chapter Three

THE SWELL YOKEL

———

The name of the trainer who bored William Hazlitt unmercifully was not "Tom Turtle" as the essayist recalled; it was John Thurtell. Eric Watson, who has sketched Thurtell's early life in his introduction to a volume in the Notable British Trials series, states that John was born on December 21, 1794, one of the many children of a prosperous merchant of Norwich.[1] Watson appears to be in error in giving the father's name as John, Sr., for contemporary records and biographical sources identify him as Thomas. The senior Thurtell was a prominent member of the Whig party in Norwich; he became a member of the Common Council in 1812, alderman and sheriff in 1815, and mayor in 1828. He is remembered to have been "a somewhat tempestuous character, or at least to have often been at the centre of a storm." During his mayoralty, the ceremony of swearing in the sheriffs was the scene of great uproar between the contending Whig and Conservative factions; the windows of the courtroom had been screwed tight to prevent intrusion of outside agitators "but the court was so crowded and the heat so intolerable that [Thurtell] ordered the windows to be broken and proceeded with the business." On another occasion, the town assembly on Guild Day was disturbed by a fierce quarrel between Thurtell and another politician. At the end of his year as mayor, he complained bitterly of the insults he had received: "I have been attacked by a bulldog and the yap has been constantly barking at my heels and language has been applied to me that would disgrace Billingsgate itself."[2] It is tempting to speculate that Thomas endowed his son John with some of his own incendiary nature.

Though little is known of John's relations with his father, contemporaries agreed that he was, in Pierce Egan's words, "the favourite son of a doating mother." According to Watson, young John may have attended Norwich Public School, where he must have proved an indifferent scholar, at least in spelling, if we are to judge from letters written in his adult years. There is no evidence that in his childhood he gave any signs of hostility or unruliness, except that the Norwich-born author George Borrow in *Romany Rye* recalled John's relatively harmless (and possibly apocryphal) prank of tying a canister to the tail of the butcher's dog.[3]

When he was fourteen John Thurtell joined the naval service, receiving a commission on May 8, 1809, in Company 99 of Marines, headquartered at Chatham. A month later he was transferred to the *HMS Adamant,* the fifty-gun flagship of Rear Admiral Sir Edmund Nagle. After cruises in the Downs, off the Nore, and as far as the mouth of the Zuyder Zee, the ship was ordered to North Britain where she lay moored for several years in Leith Roads and rarely put to sea. In July, 1810, Thurtell suffered the only blot on his naval record: he was peremptorily discharged at the personal order of Nagle's successor, Rear Admiral William Otway, for some misconduct the nature of which is unknown. The offense must have been minor, though, for on November 7, 1811, Thurtell joined another ship, the seventy-four-gun *Bellona* commanded by Captain J. E. Douglas and later by Captain George Mackinlay. Despite its warlike name, the *Bellona* saw little more action than the *Adamant.* In early 1813 the ship proceeded to St. Helena to pick up a convoy of East Indiamen returning from the Orient with cargoes of silk and spice. When Thurtell's name became notorious a decade later, it was often asserted that he and his shipmates of the *Bellona* participated in the storming of the port of San Sebastián. Eric Watson, however, found that on August 1, 1813, when San Sebastián fell, a muster of the ship was called at St. Helen's on the Isle of Wight and that it cruised near San Sebastián a few days after hostilities had ended. In early September the *Bellona* chased a brig of war and schooner; the brig escaped, but the unarmed schooner was captured as a prize of war. These bloodless encounters with the enemy were apparently the only basis for Thurtell's later claims of gallantry under fire.[4]

In June, 1814, Thurtell resigned his commission as second lieutenant and returned to Norwich, perhaps to live at the family
home two miles south of the city near Harford Bridge. When he
reached age twenty-one in the following year, his father set him up
in business as a manufacturer of bombazine, a twilled or corded
dress fabric, in partnership with John Giddens. He seemed to be
settling into his family's conventional mold, for the young business-
man was soon courting a Quaker girl of whom his parents ap-
proved. However, a stronger passion was not long in asserting
its mastery—a love for boxing. He formed a friendship with the
fighter Ned "Flatnose" Painter who, after his defeat of Tom Spring
in August, 1818, moved to Norwich where he presided over the
Anchor Pub in Lobster Lane. It was apparently during this same
period that Thurtell met George Borrow and may have taught him
a little sparring. The teenaged Borrow looked upon Thurtell with
understandable awe. Jack stood almost five feet, ten inches, and
had a iean athletic build; his pale, pockmarked face with protrud-
ing lips and massive jaw was rather hard, but still he struck many
observers as resembling a "gentlemanly farmer."[5]

Within a year or two, Jack Thurtell was more and more distracted from his business by the siren call of London and its boxing and gambling hangouts, and his Quaker sweetheart was replaced in his affections by a Norwich girl named Mary Dodson,
celebrated more for beauty than for virtue. In London's sporting
circles, Jack made the acquaintance of Pierce Egan, who would
later record his first impression of the young provincial:

> I first became acquainted with John Thurtell by his occasional visits to
> the metropolis, about the years 1818 or 1819, by accidentally meeting
> with him amongst other sporting characters, at the various houses in
> London, kept by persons attached to the sports of the field, horse-
> racing, and the old English practice of boxing. He was well known to be
> the son of Alderman Thurtell, of Norwich, a man of great respectability,
> of considerable property, and likewise possessing superior talents. John
> Thurtell was . . . viewed as a young man of integrity.[6]

Jack's London reputation for integrity was quickly and irretriev-
ably lost. He made one of his journeys to the city to collect several
thousand pounds for goods sold to a reputable London firm,
money he was obligated to pay to creditors of his partnership. In-

stead, on his return home, he gave out the story that "he had been attacked and cruelly beaten by footpads [street robbers]: but after a most desperate resistance on his part, he was compelled, at the hazard of his life, to part with his property to the robbers." Though he exhibited bruises, a black eye, and cuts on his head, his skeptical creditors insisted that Thurtell had made up his tale to deprive them of their property, and all his melodramatic accounts of the scuffle on the road "could not remove the impression from their minds, that they had been cheated and imposed upon." Its credit hopelessly undermined, the Thurtell-Giddings firm announced bankruptcy in February, 1821. Insolvency, in fact, appeared to be a contagious disease among the younger Thurtells for Jack's brother Tom, who had first tried his hand at farming with his father's financial support, failed as a "licensed victualler" in October, 1821. The long-suffering Alderman Thurtell was son Tom's largest creditor in the bankruptcy settlement that followed.[7]

Fleeing Norwich in disgrace, Jack Thurtell moved to London, where he briefly operated the Black Boy Pub, Long Acre, in the name of his little brother Henry, who, perhaps because of his tender years, was one of the few members of his generation of Thurtells who had not yet gone bankrupt. Jack was regarded as a good-humored and sociable innkeeper, but the principal attraction of the place was "the handsome Miss D.," who served as barmaid. Miss D. made a less favorable impression, however, on some who met her when she came down to Wade's Mill to join Thurtell who was observing the training of the boxer Martin: "The . . . woman was about 22 years of age, a fine full figure; her face rather plain than otherwise, and slightly freckled." She conducted herself at times with great propriety but occasionally indulged in vulgar anecdotes, "nor would the presence of the other sex occasion any hesitation in her manner or call the slightest tinge of modesty to her cheek." Her favorite amusement, however, was the innocent diversion of swinging; Thurtell had a rope fixed up in a shed and frequently took time out from the training sessions to give his darling a swing.[8]

As Thurtell's life, like a Hogarthian cautionary tale, continued a downward progress into London's underworld, he found new companions to mark the extent of his fall. Among his haunts were the

Brown Bear in Bow Street, a favorite drinking place of the Fancy, and the Army and Navy Tavern. Somewhere in the course of his pub crawling, he came upon a fellow bankrupt named William Probert. A powerful man of colossal build, the black-haired, swarthy Bill Probert had a general appearance that observers, if they meant to be kind, called "neither prepossessing nor repulsive." Born about 1789 to a respectable farming family of Herefordshire, this slovenly giant made his first appearance on the London scene in 1813 as clerk to a wine merchant and later in the same year confirmed his destined place in the world of alcoholic beverages by marrying Elizabeth Noyes, the "elderly ugly daughter" of a former brewer. With the proceeds of a generous dowry Probert established himself in business as a wine merchant, maintained an elegant residence and drove around town in a tilbury attended by a liveried servant. These signs of prosperity were false, for by late 1819 he was bankrupt with debts of fourteen thousand pounds, and he flirted with criminal proceedings by refusing to answer questions of the bankruptcy commissioners and hiding assets from his creditors. (His solicitor in the bankruptcy, John Noel, would meet him again in an even more critical juncture of his life.) While confined as a debtor in the King's Bench prison, he robbed the till of the prison coffeehouse and was committed to the House of Correction at Brixton, where he underwent the punishment of the treadmill. It was also said that while at the King's Bench prison he had seduced the wife and the daughter of one of its most unfortunate inmates. In 1823 Probert was still far from disillusioned with the profit potential of alcohol; he was rumored to be operating an illegal still near his cottage in Radlett, Hertfordshire.[9]

A somewhat less well delineated figure who crossed Thurtell's path was Joseph Hunt, manager of Jack's beloved Army and Navy Tavern. Little is known about Joe Hunt's early years except that he was born in 1797 and that before he met Thurtell he had been confined for a time in London's Newgate Prison. For the past several years, Pierce Egan later recalled, Hunt had been well known around Charing Cross among the stagecoach men and was somewhat contemptuously regarded as a good-natured fool. Joe was married to a respectable woman; he dressed in a very flashy style and sported large whiskers and a luxuriant moustache; his conversation was ignorant and sometimes disgusting; and his principal social asset was a vocal talent that he shared with his brother who was a singer at Covent Garden. Hunt enjoyed only a brief tenure at the Army and Navy Tavern, where he failed to pay suppliers and left a pile of debts on his departure.[10]

Thereafter, Hunt had no visible means of support. It was suspected that he became a hanger-on of a gang of blacklegs who preyed on their innocent victims in London's gambling hells. The gang leader was reputed to be a shadowy underworld figure named Lemon or Lemming; one of his lieutenants was a man named William Weare, who had been a waiter at the Globe Tavern in Fleet Street and later at a gaming house, "where by assiduity and enterprise he got forward as an official, and ultimately as an independent player."[11] He now was well launched on a professional career as a gambler and billiards player, and he commonly attended races, fights, and other sporting occasions as the operator of an even-odd table. Harboring an incurable mistrust of banks, Weare was accustomed to carry large amounts of cash—as much as two thousand pounds—on his person in the form of bank notes.

John Payne Collier, who knew Weare well from hundreds of billiards games, wrote of him in *An Old Man's Diary:* "He was a regular blackleg, and was content to do business in a small way, if he could get no larger prey. So, as he was a good player he used to earn a few shillings from me, who never risked more."[12] Pierce Egan wrote that Weare was also slow and cautious in his play at the gambling tables and was thought to have been very successful from his "systematic" methods. His systems were apparently not unduly scrupulous, for Egan also opined that "no spider darted with more eagerness on a poor fly, than did Weare pounce upon the unwary." Egan thought that the gambler's look was cunning and hard; his cheekbones stood out so prominently and his chin was so small and pointed that the lower part of his face was precisely triangular. Diminutive in stature and proud of his well-knit figure, Weare was remarkably neat in his dress. Second only to his love for gambling was his fondness for the sports of the field; he used to keep fine hunting dogs in his lodgings at Lyon's Inn.[13]

Jack Thurtell was no match for Lemon, Weare, and their blackleg allies at the gambling table. In Pierce Egan's view, "Thurtell, like a number of other foolish young men from the country, flattered himself that he was a knowing, clever fellow. It was on this rock that he split." In short order, the all too obvious aspiration of the provincial Thurtell to acquire the veneer of the fast sporting set won him a derisive nickname, the "Swell Yokel." Viewed as a betting man, wrote Egan, "Thurtell was considered a complete novice among the sporting people; and whatever knowledge he might have possessed of book-keeping . . . acquired at school, his betting-book has often proved the source of laughter among his companions." Unsurprisingly, Thurtell suffered a series of losses to his crooked adversaries. Ignoring his landlord's caution not to play with them since he was inexperienced, he lost about three hundred pounds to Lemon and one of his henchmen. The sharpers, ostensibly to soothe his anger at his losses, invited him to the boxer Jack Martin's training sessions at Wade's Mill, but they actually had new chicanery in mind; Weare was brought along as the "plant" who pretended to be a flat, or pigeon, an easy target for more experienced players. Pitted against Thurtell, Weare allowed him to win at first but finally bilked him of another three hundred pounds. It was common talk in the gambling hells that Thurtell had been cheated again in London. It was also rumored that the gang attempted to pacify the gullible Thurtell by letting him share in the betting on a boxing match they had rigged, but they had wounded his pride even more indelibly than his pocketbook.[14]

Thurtell's happier times were spent in the world of boxing. He was one of the promoters of the great fight between Ned Painter and Tom Oliver at North Walsham near Norwich in July, 1820, and took great pride in the crowd of thirty thousand persons from all social ranks who witnessed the bout. Even this high point in Jack's association with the Fancy was marred by displays of the hot temper for which acquaintances had dubbed him the "Bully" and "Old Flare." A few days after a Norwich sporting dinner held in connection with the Painter-Oliver fight, Jack beckoned a gentleman down from the roof of a stagecoach and beat him unmercifully because he thought he recognized the man as a pickpocket who had attempted to steal his watch at the dinner. During the same dinner, Jack had had an argument with the fighter Abraham Belasco, who reproached him with attempting to bribe his brother Israel to fight a cross. Enraged, Thurtell offered to pay Josh Hudson, a great boxer present at the dinner, five pounds if he would trash Abe Belasco, who responded by calling Thurtell a rascal and saying "that he should live to see him hanged." Even moments of charity could erupt in displays of Thurtell's famous rage. Although the law against prizefighting was strictly enforced in the cities, sparring exhibitions in which gloves were worn were held at urban locales (such as London's Five Court and Royal Tennis Court) and often presented benefits for a professional fighter who would appear with another ring celebrity in the featured bout. On one occasion Thurtell volunteered to arrange a benefit in a provincial town for the fighter Jack Carter, whom he had met by chance about sixty miles from London and found to be in great distress. Carter wanted some novelty for the program, since benefits by their frequency were beginning to bore the public. Thurtell suggested that they advertise an appearance by the popular boxer Jack Martin, a baker who was punningly called the Master of the Rolls; he offered to impersonate Martin whom nobody knew in the vicinity. The deception worked and produced a full house, but when a Londoner in the audience complained of the imposture, Thurtell bullied him into acknowledging his "mistake." "Do you think sir," he said to the terrified man, "that one, two upon your nose would convince you of your error before this company; if not, sir, you shall have three, four." Thurtell's penchant for beating or bullying persons uninitiated in the art of boxing was not matched, however, by his courage in the ring. His sparring exhibition with Carter, in which the beneficiary of his charity must have treated him gently, was his only match with a famous boxer. On one occasion, he challenged Tom Belcher to a fight for five hundred pounds a side, but he remained silent when the great veteran invited him to a sparring match at the Fives Court.[15]

Among all these turbulent scenes, however, Pierce Egan was able to recall a few moments of unalloyed kindness and sympathy—when Thurtell raised a subscription for an ailing sportsman or burst into tears in composing a quarrel between two friends or in taking leave of another friend who was at the point of death. Egan was also impressed by the respect Thurtell showed for the giants of the ring. When he acted as a second to Martin in his bout with Jack Randall, the "Nonpareil," Thurtell asked Egan as a personal favor that his name not be mentioned in the journalist's account of the fight and said that "in the situation he filled in the prize ring he might be designated as an amateur." [16]

When the Gas-Man was defeated by Bill Neat in December, 1821, at Hungerford Downs, the Londoners who had backed the loser (including Thurtell) were pretty thoroughly cleaned out. Eric Watson speculates that this disaster caused Jack Thurtell to renounce his interest in boxing. [17] By the following year Jack was deeply involved with his brother Tom and Bill Probert in more dubious activities. It is astounding that Tom was still on speaking terms with his brother, who in April, 1822, had had him thrown into prison because of a trifling debt. Tom's nature, if not forgiving, must have been submissive, for when, through the influence of Probert, unaccountably still employed in the wine and spirits trade, Tom became the licensee of the Cock Tavern, Haymarket, he hired his brother Jack as manager. As a sideline the Thurtells decided to embark on Probert's favorite method of fraud, the "long firm" scheme, in which goods are bought for credit and sold for cash and then the promissory notes given to the suppliers are dishonored at maturity. Towards the end of the year they raised loan capital for their venture, including five hundred pounds lent by the unsuspecting Alderman Thurtell, and bought a stock of bombazine, Norwich crepes, and other silk goods. Like many ambitious entrepreneurs, they soon opted for diversification and decided to supplement their frauds on creditors with arson and a false insurance claim. For the purpose of the new conspiracy, Tom, before Michaelmas, had leased part of the premises of a wine merchant in Watling Street as a warehouse for the bombazine goods, but the bulk of the stock was actually taken elsewhere and quickly sold for cash at a deep discount below its cost through a confederate, John Borthwick Snowden. The inventory supposedly located at Watling Street was insured before any purchase for nearly two thousand pounds in December, 1822, and the premises were completely destroyed by fire on January 26, 1823.

Preparations for the arson were apparently masterminded by Jack Thurtell. Until shortly before the fire he had been sleeping at the warehouse with Mary Dodson, and his only tangible activity in behalf of the business venture was to engage a carpenter named Davison to make certain structural alterations to the premises that struck the workmen as distinctly odd: a glass window that gave light to the lobby was blocked up and a door was built three steps up the stairs leading to the Thurtells' premises above. These alterations would have hampered the operations of the warehouse but were very well suited to their intended purpose of preventing the light of a fire from coming under prompt observation by neighbors and other tenants. As soon as this work was done, Thurtell and Mary found another place to sleep and were safely away at the time of the fire.

The County Fire Office, with whom Tom Thurtell's warehouse had been insured, understandably disputed liability. Tom filed suit against its managing director Barber Beaumont and others and the case was tried before a jury at the Guildhall on June 25, 1823, with Mr. Justice James Alan Park presiding. During the course of the trial Park was angered by an insistent challenge to one of his evidentiary rulings by defense counsel Serjeant Taddy, and it seemed to some observers that the judge took his revenge by delivering a summation to the jury that was unfavorable to the insurance company. The judge had some harsh words for the other side as well; he told the jury that the brazen manner in which John Thurtell had given testimony suggested that "he was in the lowest state of degradation in point of moral feeling." This unflattering character sketch did not, however, carry the day for the defendants; the jury promptly returned a verdict requiring them to pay the plaintiff nineteen hundred pounds. From this brief moment of triumph the affairs of the Thurtell brothers went swiftly downhill. Outraged at the verdict, Barber Beaumont refused to pay the judgment and at once procured an indictment against the Thurtells for conspiracy to defraud the County Fire Office. With the expected bonanza deferred, the brothers were unable to keep the wolf from the door of the Cock Tavern; the butcher who had supplied the Cock cut off credit in early 1823, and they had to sell their wine cellar to meet the pressing demands of creditors. At last they absconded from the Cock not only to escape its final collapse under a mountain of unpaid bills but to avoid arrest on the conspiracy charge, which appeared imminent because of their inability to raise bail. They hid from Beaumont and the authorities in temporary lodgings at the Coach and Horses, Conduit Street, kept by Charles Tetsall, a friend of Probert.[18]

Jack Thurtell's recent calamities—the bets lost on Hickman, the failure of the Cock Tavern, and the arson prosecution—were accompanied, perhaps brought on or exacerbated, by an observable disintegration of his personality. Pierce Egan felt that Thurtell was sometimes bitter over recollections of his respectable origin and family. Egan pointed, for example, to Thurtell's complaint about a personal item inserted in the *Weekly Dispatch* by the boxer Josh Hudson. In a letter to the editor Hudson related that Thurtell, in a conversation with a promoter who proposed a match between Hudson and Martin for a hundred guineas, had asserted that Hudson knew nothing of the art of boxing; the offended boxer therefore now publicly challenged either Thurtell or Martin to a bout within two months. In a postscript he got off a low blow at Thurtell's origin: he had once had the honor to fight a "gent" and in this instance would prefer that Thurtell accepted the challenge instead of Martin since he knew that Thurtell was a "gent" by birth. Thurtell, incensed, sent Hudson's letter off to his solicitor for advice as to whether it was libelous. Egan generalized from this incident and other examples of erratic behavior on the part of his friend Jack: "It is decidedly the opinion of Thurtell's most intimate friends, that his conduct for the last two years, had been more like a madman than of a rational being; indeed, I have no doubt, at times, he felt keenly his degradation in society; and that it operated very forcibly upon his feelings."[19]

More and more, Jack's famous temper would flare at random. Shortly after the fire he assaulted with a candlestick his new landlady, Amanda Gwillim, who rented apartments in a disreputable house in Garlick Hill, and he was also brought up before a police magistrate (but discharged) on a complaint of having assaulted a man who he thought was not treating two prostitutes with the courtesy they deserved.[20] At the same time he continued to brood over his mounting grievances—against his adversaries in his bankruptcy case, in which, unlike his partner Giddens, he had failed to obtain a discharge; against a young Londoner named Woods, who was paying suit to Probert's attractive sister-in-law Caroline, whom

Jack now fancied as a more respectable successor to Mary Dodson; and against his dangerous enemy Barber Beaumont. But of all those who had done him wrong, he could least forgive William Weare, who in cheating him at cards had not only stolen his money but had made him the laughingstock of London's gamblers. This was an injury that his ever more fragile self-esteem could not bear. To his friend Hunt, he talked of all his enemies and of wild plans for revenge, but it seemed to Joe that it was William Weare who was mainly on Thurtell's mind.

Chapter Four

THE ROAD MENDERS' DISCOVERIES

———

Charles Nicholls, a placid sort of man, would not hurry himself, even for murder. On Tuesday, October 28, 1823, Nicholls, a farmer of Battlers Green in the parish of Aldenham, went calling on the Watford magistrates, who sat every Tuesday at the Essex Arms Inn.[1] Without ceremony he told them his business. On Saturday morning another farmer of the same parish, Philip Smith of Kemp Row had paid him a visit and had told a hair-raising story. About eight o'clock on Friday night Smith, accompanied by his wife and child, was driving a donkey chaise home from Battlers Green along a road to the highway lying between Radlett and High Cross (near Kemp Row). The country road Smith was taking was separated by a field from Gill's Hill Lane, a byway that picked its narrow and tortuous course between the Radlett–High Cross road and Loom Lane, which connected Battlers Green on the west to the Elstree-Radlett highway on the east. Smith, like most local residents, had taken little notice of the uninviting Gill's Hill Lane, whose twisting path, sharply banked on each side, resembled, in the eyes of one contemporary, a "dismal ravine"; its very approach looked "as if one were threading the mazes of those subterranean labyrinths, in which banditti were used to dwell. Beneath hedges which meet over head, and through which there is hardly one point of escape, it twines along for about three quarters of a mile, at the end of which it assumes a character even more dark and gloomy."[2] Since the lane was seldom traveled, Smith was startled to hear the noise of another carriage coming down it towards Battlers Green, and his surprise turned to alarm when shortly afterwards the report of a pistol sounded from the same direction, followed by deep groans, which continued for a minute or two and then died away. He and his wife were frightened and quickened their homeward pace.

Later on Saturday, Nicholls went into Gill's Hill Lane to check on the progress of the two laborers, John Herrington and Richard Hunt, who were working under his supervision repairing the lane, which had not been attended to for four decades. Much to his surprise, Herrington handed him a pistol and a small knife that he had just found under a hedgerow along the lane. The workman told Nicholls that at break of day he had seen two men come down the lane from Gill's Hill; passing him and his fellow worker, they went to a spot near which the pistol and knife were later found and searched about in the hedges for about five minutes, as if they were looking for something they had lost.

Nicholls gave the two weapons to the magistrates and particularly called their attention to the grisly features of the pistol—the bloodstains, the hair that stuck to it in many parts, and a quantity of human brains that filled nearly the whole barrel. If the farmer expected praise for his disclosure, he was disappointed. Smith or the two laborers should have notified the authorities on Saturday of the discovery of the weapons, and the magistrates demanded to know why Nicholls had delayed his report until their next regular session. Not waiting for an answer, they swung into action. They immediately dispatched Constable Henry Simmonds of Watford to the Bow Street police office in London with instructions to show the pistol to the sitting magistrate there, to tell him what had transpired, and to request that he send one of his runners to Watford as soon as possible.[3]

The Bow Street Runners, a plainclothes detective police force founded by novelist Henry Fielding in 1749 during his service as magistrate, had scored an enviable string of successes against organized crime in London. It was natural for the inexperienced Watford authorities to look to them for assistance, particularly since the scene of the crime was less than fifteen miles north of the metropolis.[4]

The prompt summons for help from Bow Street did not, however, mean that the Watford magistrates intended to stand about with their arms folded. Two of the magistrates who had heard Nicholls' report, Robert Clutterbuck and John Finch Mason, set out by different routes to the Nicholls' house to begin their own investigation into the apparent murder. Clutterbuck, accompanied by the magistrates' clerk (and author of one of the principal accounts of the case) George Henry Jones, went to the spot where the pistol had been found. It was plain enough that some person had been killed in this part of the lane, for the ground and hedges were saturated with blood. The victim had obviously been dragged through the hedge into the adjoining plowed field, as they noted from the appearance of the bank of the lane, the hair found sticking to the boughs and lower parts of the hedges and the blood with which they were covered, and the heavy trampling of the ground of the neighboring field. When Clutterbuck and Mason arrived at Nicholls' house, they subjected him to further questioning. What they were told gave them more grounds for irritation that the farmer had so long delayed his report. Nicholls now related that on Sunday evening his neighbor living at Gill's Hill Cottage, William Probert, and James Heward, Probert's landlord, had come to his house. Nicholls asked Probert whether someone at Gill's Hill Cottage had fired off a pistol in the lane on Friday evening. Probert, inquiring when the shot had been heard and being told it was eight o'clock, remarked defensively that it could not have been his doing. Nicholls had thought that since Probert had a good deal of company that night someone must have fired off the pistol in a frolic to frighten some of his companions returning home and that the person Smith had heard groaning might have been a traveler thrown from a gig when his horse was startled by the noise.[5]

Clutterbuck and Mason were not as inclined as the easygoing Nicholls to assume that Probert and his mysterious guests were innocent merrymakers. Their suspicion deepened when they learned that Probert was to give up possession of his cottage on the following day and that at the very moment a caravan loaded with goods ready for town stood in his yard. They went immediately to the cottage, accompanied by Constable Charles Foster and two or three others, arrested Probert and searched the house and grounds.

Probert's home was located in Hertfordshire about three miles north of Elstree and to the west of the highway (Watling Street) leading to St. Albans. Probert had told his cronies that he operated an illegal still in his neighborhood, and if that was his purpose in settling there, he had chosen well. Villages and farmhouses in the area were widely separated, and the fields were intersected by narrow, crooked lanes fringed on both sides by thick shaggy hedges. Probert could hardly have found a better place for clandestine activity. Clutterbuck, who was an expert topographer, took careful note of the layout of the property, to which he was to return many times for the purpose of producing an accurate ground plan of the place, measuring distances by chain and reducing them on the plan to precise scale. The cottage was located on the eastern side of Gill's Hill Lane close to its junction with the Radlett–High Cross road and about a half a mile from the center of the village of Radlett. Clutterbuck observed that Gill's Hill Lane and Probert's cottage could be reached without passing through Radlett; the southern end of the lane could be reached by turning up Loom Lane from the Elstree-Radlett highway, or by taking the road across Letchmore Heath and then turning right at Battlers Green into Loom Lane. Alternatively, one could enter the northern end of Gill's Hill Lane near Probert's cottage by following the road Philip Smith had taken from Battlers Green and turning right into the High Cross–Radlett road.

The main entrance into Probert's property was through folding gates leading from Gill's Hill Lane; adjoining the gateway were very high wooden palings that prevented any view of the premises from the lane. When Clutterbuck and his arresting party passed through the entrance they found themselves in a dilapidated stable-yard heaped with dung and straw. From here a small wicket gate led off to the left into a garden immediately in front of the cottage. The house was approached by a gravel path on the left of the wicket and by another more circuitous path that skirted a part of the shrubbery and emerged opposite the parlor door. Clutterbuck's aesthetically trained eyes rebelled against the ruinous state of the cottage, whose sorry exterior of lath and whitewashed plaster was only imperfectly masked in front by latticework against which prior owners had trained some vines. Though built on a rise commanding a fine view of the countryside, the building was extremely confined and uncomfortable; by far the most commodious room was the kitchen, the parlor having apparently been added as an afterthought. Whatever charm the property possessed was boasted by its rear gardens, whose principal feature was a pond narrower and shallower near the house, and at its far end thickly surrounded with shrubs and weeping willows. The banks of the pond, covered with green turf, were approached from among the trees and hedges of the garden by two serpentine walks.[6]

When their inspection was over, the arresting party returned with their prisoner to the Nicholls house, which the magistrates had made their temporary headquarters for the investigation. The details of their first questioning of Probert are not known, but it is obvious that the magistrates wanted to know the identity of his recent visitors. Probert told them that Tom Thurtell had arrived from London to visit his young daughters who were staying at Gill's Hill Cottage; Constable Foster was dispatched to the cottage with others and arrested Tom in bed.

About two o'clock in the morning of Wednesday, October 29, while Probert's questioning was continuing, Constable Simmonds returned from London, accompanied by one of the preeminent detectives of Bow Street, George Thomas Joseph Ruthven. In 1820 Ruthven had made his name by arresting the Cato Street conspirators who had plotted the murder of Lord Castlereagh and other ministers. By the time the questioning ended at three o'clock, Bill Probert had identified Jack Thurtell and Joe Hunt as his weekend visitors; the magistrates gave Ruthven a warrant for their arrest and in the meantime committed Probert and Tom Thurtell to St. Albans Gaol for further examination.

Ruthven arrested Hunt at his lodgings at 19 King Street, Golden Square. A search of the apartment turned up a double-barreled gun, a mahogany backgammon board containing two dice boxes and a pair of dice, a large sponge, a shooting jacket with a whistle fixed to one of the buttonholes, a variety of shooting paraphernalia, and a traveler's carpetbag containing several shirts marked with the letter *W*. Thurtell was apprehended by Ruthven at the

Coach and Horses. Public house wit Renton "Lord Chief Baron"
Nicholson, in his autobiography, claimed to have received Ruthven's
account of this arrest from his own lips:

> "After it had been ascertained that it was human blood and human
> hair on the pistol, and Hunt and Probert were in custody, I left in order
> to secure John Thurtell. I found him at the Coach and Horse, Conduit
> Street, Hanover Square. I said,—
>
> "'John, my boy, I want you.'
>
> "'What for, George?' said he.
>
> "I replied, 'Never mind; I'll tell you presently.'
>
> "Thurtell had been anticipating serious proceedings against him for
> setting his house on fire in the city, by Mr. Barber Beaumont, on behalf
> of the County Fire Office. It was highly probable that he suspected I
> wanted him on that charge. He, however, prepared to accompany me.
> My horse and chaise were at the door. He got in, and I handcuffed him
> to one side of the rail of my trap. I drove on towards Hertford. On the
> road nothing could be more chatty and free than the conversation on
> the part of Thurtell. If he did suspect where I was going to take him, he
> played an innocent part very well, and artfully pretended total igno-
> rance. We had several glasses of grog on the road. When we arrived I
> drove up to the inn where Probert and Hunt were, in the charge of the
> local constables.
>
> "'Let us have some brandy and water, George,' said Thurtell, after he
> had shaken hands with his associates. I went out of the room to order it.
>
> "'Give us a song,' said Thurtell; and Hunt, who was a beautiful singer,
> struck up,—
>   'Mary, list, awake!'
>
> "I paused, with the door in my hand, and said to myself, 'Is it possible
> that these men are murderers?'"[7]

The evidence Ruthven found on Thurtell's person and apparel
was grimmer than the tone of Nicholson's memoir. The cuffs of
Thurtell's coat were heavily bloodstained on the inside. His waistcoat pocket seemed to have had a bloody hand thrust into it, and
the edges of his hat were marked with blood. Thurtell's right hand
was scratched and bruised and his upper lip was swollen and lacer-
ated as if it had received a violent blow. In one pocket of Thurtell's
coat the detective found a small screw-barreled pistol, and in his
waistcoat pocket a pearl-mounted three-bladed pocket knife, a
pistol key, and ten small lead slugs.[8]

At five o'clock the following afternoon Ruthven brought Jack
Thurtell and Hunt to the magistrates' headquarters at the Essex

Arms Inn in Watford, where the examination was to continue in earnest. But before the proceedings began, Clutterbuck, who was still resting at his home from his exertions of the day before, received two unexpected visitors: John Noel, a London solicitor, and William Rexworthy, keeper of a billiard hall in Spring Gardens. Noel told the magistrate that as he was preparing to go to a London theater that afternoon he was told that one of the patrols on the Edgware Road had brought word of a murder of an unknown victim in Hertfordshire. The solicitor had reason to think that the victim was his client, William Weare of Lyon's Inn. It had come to his knowledge from Rexworthy that Weare had made an engagement a few days before to go on a shooting excursion into Hertfordshire with a man named John Thurtell. Weare had not returned to London; his chambers were locked up; and Noel had been unable to obtain any news of him in several of his haunts in London. Clutterbuck rushed over to the Essex Arms Inn with his London visitors.[9] As the evening drew on, Noel shouldered his way into the position of counsel for the investigation; either Clutterbuck and his colleagues had been strongly impressed by the newcomer, or Watford was suffering from that rarest of communal ailments—a lawyer shortage.

William Rexworthy was called as first witness in the hearings. He testified that on Thursday evening, October 23, between eight and nine o'clock, he had seen John Thurtell at his London billiard rooms in conversation with Weare. After Thurtell left, Weare told Rexworthy that he was to accompany his friend the next day into Hertfordshire for a few days' shooting. Between one o'clock and three on the following afternoon, Weare called on Rexworthy and informed him that he was on his way to meet Thurtell in Edgware Road. Although the witness did not say so, the magistrates could fairly have concluded that some uneasiness had induced Weare to advise Rexworthy of his plans. Before the witness left the stand, he was shown the penknife found by Ruthven on Thurtell's person at the time of his arrest; he confirmed that it had belonged to Weare.

The magistrates then heard testimony from a series of witnesses as to the time and place of the murder and the discovery of the pistol and knife. The earliest evidence in chronological order was that of James Freeman, a laborer of Aldenham Parish. About eight

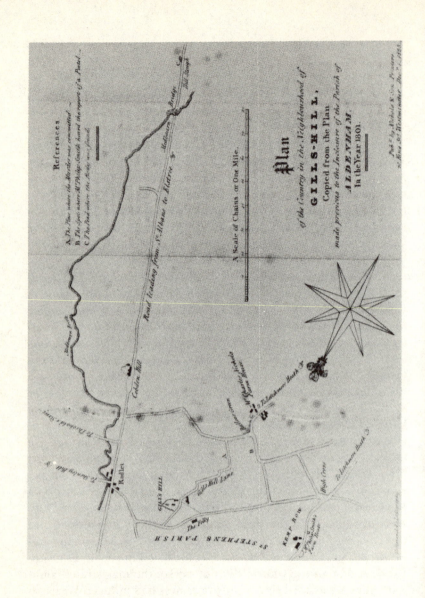

Plan

of the Country in the Neighbourhood of

GILLS-HILL,

Copied from the Plan

made previous to the Inclosure of the Parish of

ALDENHAM,

In the Year 1801.

A Scale of Chains or One Mile.

References

A The Place where the Murder was committed —
B The Spot where Mr Philip Smith heard the report of a Pistol —
C The Pool where the Bodie was found —

o'clock on the evening of Friday, October 24, he was walking from his house called the Folly along a path leading diagonally from the High Cross–Radlett road to Gill's Hill Lane. When he came to the gate opening into the lane, a one-horse carriage with two men in it passed him and stopped; one of the men got down. Freeman ventured a friendly observation: they must have driven the horse very fast, for he was very much out of wind. He received no reply but, nothing daunted, added the less controversial observation that it was a very dark night, and this time had only a curt answer. The man who had alighted got back up on the whip side of the carriage and drove off. About the same hour, Freeman's wife Elizabeth was walking in the opposite direction along Gill's Hill Lane and encountered two persons in a gig. Soon afterwards she met her husband, who turned back and went home with her. On Sunday, she saw William Probert's servant boy, James Addis, and asked him whether the gentlemen who had been visiting had met with any accident on Friday. The boy had replied, "They came home very dirty, and one of them had a few spots of blood upon him, and the horse was a little grazed."

Philip Smith gave his account of hearing the pistol shot followed by groans. It was then the turn of the two laborers to tell for themselves their tale of the discovery of the weapons. John Herrington said that while he was working with Richard Hunt on the resurfacing of Gill's Hill Lane about six o'clock on Saturday morning, October 25, he saw two men, one tall and wearing a white hat, and the other middle sized with large black whiskers. Both passed him without a word and when they had gone on about a distance of ten poles, they stopped by the side of the left-hand hedge and stooped down and "grabbled" as if looking for something they had lost. After about five minutes they went a little farther up the lane and then turned back. As they passed by, they told Richard Hunt that their gig had capsized the night before. To Richard Hunt's questions, the tall man said he had hurt himself only a little and that the gig had not gone over nor had the horse fallen. Later the same morning Herrington strolled along the lane while eating breakfast. When he came to the spot where the two men had been searching he noticed a small knife with an open blade and afterwards, returning to the same spot, he came upon the pistol; he turned over both weapons to Nicholls about ten that morning. Around noon the two mysterious gentlemen reappeared in the lane, neatly dressed and now both wearing black hats. They both looked hard at the spot where he had found the knife and pistol, but he kept silent. They had come this time in a gig drawn by an iron gray horse with the tall man driving. Herrington now knew who the tall man was: he had identified him as John Thurtell, who had been presented to him in the custody of the constable.

Richard Hunt confirmed this testimony adding that the tall man had said of the lane, "It is a damned nasty dark place; it is as dark as a grave." The stranger had added that he had not hurt himself in his accident but had lost a silk handkerchief and a small pen-knife, both of which he had found. Richard Hunt had been skeptical, observing to the stranger, "It is a very queer thing to me, sir, that you should be capsized and your gig not fall." The tall man and his shorter companion had also been seen between six and seven o'clock on Saturday morning, October 25, by William Bulmer, who was at work in Probert's garden. As the men drove off in a gig about nine o'clock that morning, Bulmer had noticed that their horse "had a white face." He was the first witness to observe the face that, more than any other, was to stamp its image unforgettably on the murder case.[10]

The magistrates then questioned two of Probert's servants about their master's weekend visitors. Susan Anne Woodruff, Probert's maid, said that her master came home about nine o'clock Friday evening in the company of two other gentlemen with whom he sat up all night. The guests left the cottage on Saturday morning a little after six o'clock and were gone about half an hour; they then returned and took their departure about ten. On the next day her mistress' brother, Mr. Noyes and three other men came to the cottage. Two of these guests left with the servant boy James Addis on Monday morning about seven, and the third guest left with Mr. Noyes and her mistress' sister, Anne Noyes, later the same day. The servant boy, James Addis, was able to identify one of the Friday visitors as John Thurtell, who had arrived alone in a dark green rig drawn by a black and gray horse. When Thurtell drew up he was driving in the direction of Radlett. Thurtell told the boy that he did not want anything taken out of the carriage. When

Addis ran the gig into the coachhouse, the visitor's instructions began to intrigue him for there appeared to be something heavy in
the bottom of the vehicle. He noted that the visitor had brought
with him a carpetbag and a double-barreled gun. It was Thurtell's
clothes, however, that caught the attentive young boy's eye: he
wore a pair of Wellington boots covered with mud, and his coat
and trousers were dirty. Addis thought he saw spots of blood on
the skirts of Thurtell's greatcoat and his suspicion was confirmed
afterwards when he saw him sponging his clothes. About a quarter
of an hour after Thurtell's arrival, Probert came home with another guest who sported large whiskers. Addis recalled seeing this
gentleman on Saturday morning rubbing Thurtell's coat with a
sponge (the magistrates would have been forgiven for thinking
that the boy had sponges on the brain or that he had confused two
of the visitors). On Monday morning, October 27, Addis went to
London with Thomas Thurtell. He didn't know where he was
going more than five minutes before his departure; on arriving in
London he was first taken to Saint Clement's Church in the Strand
and afterwards to the Coach and Horses in Conduit Street, where
he was left to fend for himself in the taproom.[11]

The magistrates' clerk George Jones recorded in his notes that,
after testimony from Officer Ruthven as to Jack Thurtell's arrest,
Thurtell, Hunt, and Probert were called for examination after
having been cautioned against self-incrimination. None of the
principal accounts of the case, however, report the substance of
Probert's testimony, and it is doubtful that he can have made
any disclosures helpful to the investigation; he cannot have been
pleased to recognize in the cross-examiner Noel his former bankruptcy attorney. Hunt took a somewhat subtler course than the re-
calcitrant Probert, providing the magistrates with a fair amount of
detail about the trio's movements over the weekend but always
taking care to steer clear of peril. He was, he began, a dealer and a
professional singer. He knew William Probert extremely well but
had never been at his cottage until last Friday evening. Earlier on
that Friday he had received an invitation from Probert to dine with
him and Thurtell at the Coach and Horses. After dinner Probert
turned to him and said: "Hunt, I have often spoken to my wife of
your singing, and I should like for you to go down with me for a

day or two to my cottage." Pardonably flattered, he had agreed and they left together that evening in a gig for Hertfordshire. In Oxford Street, Hunt purchased a loin of pork for supper, and they stopped at several inns along the way to drink brandy and water. When they arrived at Probert's cottage they drove into the yard and found that Thurtell and the servant boy Addis were in the stable. Thurtell, Hunt explained, had started from Conduit Street in another gig about a quarter of an hour before them. Hunt was introduced to Mrs. Probert and her sister Anne Noyes, whom he entertained after supper for about two hours singing several songs. He slept on a sofa in the parlor and recollected that Thurtell remained in the room with him through the night.[12]

In response to questions from Noel, Hunt stated that he had arrived at Probert's cottage about ten o'clock at night and that no one was waiting in Gill's Hill Lane for him and Probert when they drove up. He had never left the cottage on Friday evening after his arrival, and no one went out in the course of the evening. On the next morning he arose at seven. He denied that his boots or shoes had been brushed on Saturday morning or that he ever used a sponge on any clothes. At seven o'clock in the morning he, together with Probert and Thurtell, had gone for a stroll through the field and had broken into Gill's Hill Lane over a hedge; they did not meet anyone during the walk. Questioned about the alleged capsizing of the visitors' gig, Hunt said he had not heard of any accident happening to either of the Thurtells. He did hear Jack Thurtell say that he had scratched his hands going through briars; he had shown Hunt his hands after breakfast when he made that remark. It was obvious to the magistrates that Hunt was not above casting at least some suspicion on Thurtell and that he was most anxious to bracket Thurtell more closely with Probert than with himself, but they could get nothing more out of him at the moment. He had made no mention of murder or of the missing Weare.[13]

When Thurtell followed Hunt to the stand, it was immediately apparent that he had adopted quite different tactics: he would deny all. He had no appointment with any gentleman to go down to Hertfordshire Friday night, he asserted, and he did not pick anyone up on the road. He had never told anyone he would take him for a day's shooting in the country. He conceded that he had walked with Probert and Hunt on Saturday morning in Gill's Hill Lane for about ten minutes, stating that they all wore black hats. Despite his journey up from London and his Saturday stroll, his clothes and boots were not so dirty as to require brushing while he was at Probert's. The scratches on his hands to which Hunt had testified were caused "partly by some brambles while he was shooting, and partly by the bite of a dog. He never said anything to Mr. Hunt about his hands being scratched."[14]

Noel's questioning now took a more dangerous turn. Had the witness ever carried pistols? Thurtell said at first that he never had any, but pressed to recall that Ruthven had found a pistol in his pocket on his arrest, Thurtell claimed that he had found it on a bank near Probert's house on Sunday morning (a safe day and a half after the crime). Noel pretended to be satisfied with the answer and appeared to change the subject:

Q. Do you know Mr. Weare?
A. I do.
Q. Do you know where he is?
A. I do not.
Q. When did you see him last?
A. On Tuesday, last week, was the last time.
Q. Did you see him last Friday?
A. No, I did not.
Q. Did you not meet him by chance on Friday in the Edgware Road?
A. No I did not.

Noel then abruptly turned back to the question of the pistol:

Q. Now, Mr. Thurtell, you have said you found this pistol near Probert's; what would you say when I told you I can produce the fellow to it, found within a few yards of the same spot?
A. I know nothing about that.

Treasuring the melodrama of the moment, Noel slowly unwrapped the bloody pistol that had been found in Gill's Hill Lane and forced it on Thurtell's unwilling sight. The witness' composure immediately faded. According to one of the journalists present, "his countenance and manner underwent a change too striking to escape the notice of the most careless observer. His complexion, naturally sallow, assumed a deadly pale, and he appeared to shudder and shrink backwards at the sight of the weapon." Noel then laboriously compared the two pistols. Each was of the same size and had "Hill, London" engraved on it. The two weapons were numbered 2 and 3 and resembled each other in every detail.[15]

Hoping to drive through the breach in Thurtell's defenses that had been caused by the sight of the damning weapons, Noel returned to the charge: "I can tell you Thurtell, Mr. Weare is not to be found." But Jack had found the resources for another denial, "I am sorry for it; but I know nothing about him."[16]

Noel then had Hunt recalled to the stand to see what effect the matching pistols would have on this more talkative witness. As the weapons again made their telling point, Noel made a frank appeal for a confession, suggesting to Hunt that "persons who made a true and full confession of all they knew were generally admitted evidence for the Crown" and were granted immunity from prosecution. When the witness stubbornly maintained that he knew nothing of the crime, Noel's tone became shrill: "Mr. Hunt, Mr. Weare has been murdered, and we only want to know where the body is, and if you know, for God's sake tell us." When Hunt renewed his denials, Magistrates Clutterbuck and Mason concluded that he needed time for personal reflection: "You had better retire and consider the offer made to you, and recollect your perilous situation." The witness was then escorted from the room by Ruthven and Officer John Upson. Noel and other emissaries came to him in relays but were unsuccessful in their efforts to obtain a confession. Noel told Joe that he had been positively assured by the magistrates that if he would tell them where the body of Weare was to be found, his life would be spared. Officer Upson, leaving the legalities to the solicitor, appealed directly to Hunt's love for his mother and wife. When Noel saw that the mention of his family greatly affected him, he quickly seized this advantage, asserting that Joe had a chance of saving himself and for the sake of his family should avail himself of the magistrates' offer. He improvised an enlargement of the magistrates' protection: "I am authorized to say that the Magistrates will not only admit you as a witness for the Crown, but take care that you are not treated as the other prisoners; you will merely be confined until the trial, and after you have given your evidence you will be discharged."[17]

The double attack of lawyer and policeman finally overthrew Joe Hunt's defenses, and he asked Noel to advise the magistrates that he was prepared to make a statement. Readmitted to the hearing room, he dictated to the clerk Jones and signed a detailed account of the crime. Destined to become the great confessor of the Thurtell-Hunt murder, Hunt had composed what was to be only the first of several versions of the killing of William Weare.[18]

One night at Rexworthy's billiard rooms Jack Thurtell had told Hunt he wanted to see Weare privately. He called Weare out of the room and was absent for about twenty minutes. Shortly after his return Thurtell and Hunt left together, and as they made their way up the Haymarket, Jack said "that Mr. Weare had behaved extremely ill to him, for he and a man of the name of Leman or Lemon had won 300 pounds of him at blind hookey." ("Blind hookey" was one variety of a category of card games known as "banker and broker" in which the players cut the pack for the highest card. To the compulsive gambler, it provided the thrill of quick abandonment to pure chance, while the professional crook found easy means to improve the odds by legerdemain.) When Thurtell discovered he had been robbed by false cards, he accused Weare of foul play, but received a cool affront from the gambler: "You dare not say a word, for you know you have defrauded your creditors of that money." To make matters worse, Thurtell, when he later asked Weare for a loan of five pounds, was advised, "Go and rob for it as I do." Jack told Hunt that sooner or later he would be revenged.

On Thursday night, the night before the murder, Thurtell asked Hunt to call on him on Friday morning. When Joe turned up, Jack took him for a walk; when they got into Marylebone High Street, Thurtell stopped at a pawnbroker's shop and purchased the pistols that were now in the possession of the magistrates. He paid one pound, five shillings, for them. After dinner at the Coach and Horses, Thurtell asked Hunt to get him a horse and gig immediately, "for he had to meet a gentleman who was going into the country with him, on a shooting excursion." (Hunt took care to emphasize that the name of the companion had not been confided to him.) Jack gave him one pound, ten shillings, for the hire of the horse and carriage, but the canny Hunt was able to save five shillings in his negotiations. Following Thurtell's instructions, he did not tell the livery stable proprietor, Mr. Probett, where the horse was being taken, and for some reason Probett assumed that his customer's destination was Dartford.

When the rented horse and carriage came to Thurtell's door about 7:45 P.M., Jack had a new story ready for Probert, who was with him: in consequence of the arrest warrants being issued against him and his brother Tom for conspiracy to defraud the County Fire Office, he wanted to lie low for a while at Probert's cottage in Hertfordshire. Bill suggested that they go together, but Jack rebuffed him, saying that he had to pick up a gentleman at Paddington Gate; he immediately drove off taking a greatcoat he had borrowed from Tom. (Note that the hours Hunt was fixing in his narrative would place him in London at the time of the murder.) Probert said that he did not like traveling up to Gill's Hill Lane by himself and would be glad if Hunt would join him for a pleasant evening or two; he had accepted.

At this point in the narrative, Hunt gave his first outline of one of the crucial lines of evidence in the case—the bibulous journey he and Probert had made into Hertfordshire. Not giving their throats even the slightest chance to run dry, they had stopped for a glass of brandy and water at the Red Lion Pub operated by Mr. Harding at the Hyde along Edgware Road in the northwestern outskirts of London. Afterwards they made two more stops for refreshment and the amount of intake steadily increased: first at Mr. Clarke's White Lion, in the village of Edgware, where they had two glasses of brandy and water and finally at Mr. Field's establishment, called the Artichoke, which lay just north of Elstree on the high road (Watling Street) leading to Radlett and Gill's Hill Lane, where they brought their consumption up to three glasses each.

In this first confession, it was Joe Hunt's story that he and Probert had stayed together during the whole journey. From the Artichoke they had proceeded directly to Gill's Hill Cottage, where they came upon Thurtell. He had startling news for them: "I have settled that bastard that robbed me of 300 pounds." When Probert asked what he meant, Jack added, "I mean to say, I have blown his brains out, and he lies behind a hedge in the lane." Probert tried to assure himself that his friend was pulling his leg: "Nonsense, you have never been guilty of a thing of that kind, John Thurtell; if you have, and near my cottage, my character and my family are ruined forever; but I cannot believe that you have been guilty of so rash an act." Recalling his duties as host, he asked Hunt to take the pork loin into the cook. Joe did so, and before he accompanied the other men into the parlor, he seconded Probert's effort to get Jack to admit he had been joking: "You are jesting about killing a man tonight." The response was chilling: "Aye, but I have, and no one else but Weare that robbed me of my 300 pounds." Probert was so upset that he could think of no remedy but his favorite brandy. He said that unless they had some refreshments together his senses would totally leave him. They had a glass apiece, and then the servant brought in the pork chops. Hunt recalled the details of the repast: "Mr. Probert and I ate two each, John Thurtell declined eating any, as he complained of being very sick." Perhaps the magistrates were intended to read good appetite as a barometer of innocence.

After supper Jack called his two friends away from Mrs. Probert and Anne Noyes and showed the men a "very handsome gold watch with a gold face," asking whether now they believed him. He added that he would show them "where he lies stiff enough," but when they showed little enthusiasm for viewing a fresh corpse Jack assured them that they would not see the body for it was in a sack.

About one o'clock in the morning Probert had a private conference with Hunt. Do you think Thurtell has been guilty, he asked. Hunt thought it looked rather suspicious; how otherwise to account for the gold watch? Joe couldn't face going to bed with his fears and asked Probert to sit up with him all night in the parlor. But Thurtell wouldn't leave them alone. About three he invited them again to "come and look at him; he is a bloody rogue, and I have had my revenge." Jack then walked about the garden until four o'clock and, finally giving up on his cowardly friends, told them that if they declined to help him fetch the body he would go himself. About ten minutes afterwards he left the cottage and while he was gone, Probert's terror mounted: what should he do if Thurtell's account was true, and besides, the uxorious giant added, "What will my wife think of my not going to bed?" Before Joe could give him family counseling, Thurtell returned saying that the "bastard" was so heavy he could not carry him, but since they would not help him he would have to put a bridle on his horse and throw the corpse across its back. After he brought the horse out of the stable and bridled him, Probert implored him not to bring a dead man near his premises. Jack had replied: "What bloody stuff you talk; I shall bring him and throw him into your fish pond." This was not a response calculated to calm the householder's fears, and he and Hunt had the brandy out again in a trice, this time taking only a "small glass."

About 5:15 or 5:30 A.M. Thurtell had come into the parlor again and reported that he had thrown Weare into the fishpond. Probert insisted on his removing the body immediately. His courage somewhat restored by his anger, Probert, accompanied by Hunt, strode off to the pond where they saw the feet of a man projecting upwards from the water. Thurtell calmly fetched a line, which he threw across the corpse's feet so as to keep them underwater, saying that Probert should not be alarmed for he would not want him brought into any trouble, "since he was a family man"; only let him remain here tonight and Thurtell would get him safe away.

On Monday night, when Hunt was back in London, Tom Thurtell had asked him to go to Probert's to tell Bill that they had been unable to obtain bail in the County Fire Office prosecution. Jack Thurtell, who was standing by, said that he would accompany Hunt and take "that man away from Probert's premises." Hunt told him not to expect any assistance from him. When they arrived at Probert's cottage, Hunt stated his business about Tom's bail difficulties and after a few minutes Thurtell called Probert out. Bill returned alone after ten minutes and Thurtell joined them about a half hour later asking them to put his horse in the gig and take him to the side gate, which they did. As they waited at the gate Thurtell approached them carrying over his shoulder a male corpse, the head plunged into a sack and the feet hanging out. Probert refused to help him put the corpse in the gig, again blaming his formidable wife: "I cannot stop any longer, for my wife will think it strange my stopping so long." Thurtell put the corpse into the carriage unassisted and tied the feet to the dashing iron. He politely offered Hunt a seat between him and the corpse but when Joe declined, said he would pick him up on the road after he had disposed of the body.

At this juncture in his narrative, Hunt drew a deep breath for he had come through hazardous territory. He had admitted only hiring a horse and carriage for Thurtell and an unnamed companion, but had steadfastly denied any prior knowledge of the murder or any assistance in disposition of the body. He had also been extremely protective of Probert in his confession, attributing to him no more than an understandable anxiety to have the unwelcome corpse removed from his property. Now the most important revelation lay ahead: Thurtell, Joe continued, had overtaken him on the road and told him that he had disposed of the corpse "in a small muddy marsh about four feet deep. The marsh is about a mile on this [the Radlett] side of Field's Artichoke on the left side of the road." Hunt concluded by offering to conduct the authorities to the spot where the body could be found.

However, before a search party could be organized, the courtroom echoed to the first volley on a new battlefront of the murder case. A journalist who had attended the hearing and taken notes of the proceedings for the London newspapers was about to leave the hearing room to make arrangements for following the authorities in search of the body when he was called back by Clutterbuck, the senior magistrate. Clutterbuck told him that he was perfectly at liberty to publish all the proceedings with the exception of Hunt's "confession," which the magistrates desired should not be published, as they considered such a publication would be exceedingly improper. The reporter said he was very sorry to find himself compelled to state that he must refuse compliance with this order. Clutterbuck, unruffled, attempted to persuade the reporter that the confession would prejudice the accused persons before trial and that it must not be published. The journalist responded that he was unwilling to prejudice any man, particularly when he was laboring under so heavy an accusation, and that if he thought the publication of the confession would injure the accused he would greatly regret it, "but he had a duty to perform, and must endeavor to execute it to the best of his judgment and ability. He had attended for the purpose of reporting the whole of the proceedings, and he felt himself bound to do so."

John Noel jumped into the fray again, warning the reporter that he would be acting in contempt of the Court of King's Bench, which had decided many times that magistrates had the power to order a reporter to leave the examination place and, if they allowed one to remain, had the power to prohibit publication of any part of the proceedings. (The *Times* later commented dryly: "We should like to know where this 'learned Theban' has found these repeated decisions.") Cutting short the reporter's attempted response, Clutterbuck stated flatly that the magistrates had thought fit to prohibit the publication of the confession, and he ordered the reporter to give up his notebook before he left the room. But the journalist stood his ground, saying that compliance with the order was perfectly out of the question. For a moment it looked as if the magistrates would resort to physical compulsion. Clutterbuck said he would order a constable to take the notebook, the reporter repeated that he would not give it up, and the magistrate looked towards a constable and began to raise his hand. Ultimately, the reporter, preferring not to undergo the indignities of a police search, took his notebook from his pocket and placed it on the table before him, requesting it to be understood that he was surrendering it under coercion.[19] The magistrates, however, had won only a temporary victory, for the full text of the confession appeared in the *Times* and other London newspapers on November 1.

After this interruption, Hunt directed a group of searchers headed by Ruthven to the pond where Weare's body lay concealed. On approaching the pond, which lay on the left (eastern) side of the road from Radlett to Elstree, Hunt put his hand out of the carriage in which he was riding with Ruthven and said, "That is the place." He had pointed to a pond that local inhabitants called the Hill Slough. Lying a little north of the Artichoke, it was fed by the waters of a small brook. The slough was bounded by a hedge and jutted into the road, which was defended by a slight railing. Within its waters were many shallows and clusters of rushes, and there was only one small space that appeared to suit the murderers' purposes. The searchers who gathered at the edge of the pond were provided a drag by Field, the landlord of the Artichoke. Constable John Beeson of Aldenham Parish threw it into the water and drew it out without bringing up anything. Hunt, who had remained in the carriage, shouted new directions: "It is not there but further that way." The drag was thrown in again with more success; this time the grapple drew out the body of a man enveloped in a sack. The corpse was placed on a ladder and carried to the Artichoke. An onlooker described its appearance: "The head, and as far as the abdomen, were enveloped in the sack, the body having been thrust into it head foremost; the feet were tied together with a piece of cord, to which were appended a pocket-handkerchief, filled with flint stones, about thirty pounds' weight. Another cord was tied over the sack, round the waist of the deceased, to which was affixed a very large flint stone, and in the end of the sack a great number of stones had been placed before the body was put into it."[20]

While most of those present were preoccupied with the recovery of Weare's body, Hunt found a moment to catch Field's ear: "I and Probert were sitting under the tree in front of your house for an hour, on the night of the murder, drinking: you know this!" When Field nodded, Joe continued: "Probert wanted me to sing, but I was so very 'muzzy' (drunk) that I could not." Hoping he had revived the innkeeper's memory, Hunt turned away and went back to the police carriage.[21]

Chapter Five

THE REVELATIONS
AT THE ARTICHOKE

———

The Artichoke, which had received the burden of Hill Slough, now was pressed into service as the place of inquest. Benjamin Rooke, the coroner, arrived at the inn about eleven o'clock on Friday morning, October 31, and a coroner's jury of twelve men was sworn. When the jurors had performed their repellent task of viewing Weare's body, Hunt and Probert were separately brought into the room where the corpse was lying. Neither of the men betrayed any strong emotion, but their eyes constantly fought away from the body. Hunt was silent, but Probert declared solemnly: "I never saw that corpse before in my life. I declare to God I never did. You may rely upon it I never saw that unhappy man before." Then the jury returned to its hearing room where the magistrates and other local worthies were assembled. The inquest began with a reexamination of the witnesses who had already been heard in the preliminary investigation. The billiard room proprietor Rexworthy identified the dead man as Weare, and each witness drew deep from his memory to produce new sensations. Farmer Nicholls had more details about the Sunday visit of Probert and Heward, which had perhaps acquired new significance for him in light of the discovered hiding place of Weare's body. He now recalled Heward's having said to Probert: "As Mr. Barber intends filling in the fishpond, tell him he had better drag it first, he will find some good fish in it." The servants Woodruff and Addis concurred that on Friday evening, October 24, Probert, Thurtell, and Hunt had all gone out for an hour with a candle and lantern; Mrs. Probert had told Woodruff that they were gone to visit Nicholls and instructed her not to cook the pork loin until they returned. Addis remembered having fetched a backgammon board from the parlor on Saturday morning which he gave to Hunt to put into the gig. It was this same board containing two dice boxes and a pair of dice that had since been recovered by Ruthven on Hunt's arrest.[1]

The inquest then turned to the medical evidence. Thomas Abel Ward, a Watford surgeon, testified that he was present when Weare's body was identified on its recovery from the Hill Slough. It was his opinion that the immediate cause of death was a fracture on the left side of the head, with a depression near the anterior inferior angle of the parietal bone, which had apparently been made by forcing in the muzzle of a small pocket pistol; about the edge of the fracture, there were several marks on the skin that corresponded with the pistol's mouth. The perforation in the skull was large enough for the insertion of a finger. The wound extended obliquely upwards and backwards to the left ventricle of the brain, in which there was a considerable quantity of extravasated blood. A bone fragment, about the size of a shilling, had been driven nearly two inches into the brain. The murderer, however, had taken no chances. A wound, sufficient in itself to have caused death, was made by some sharp instrument under the ear on the same side and had divided the external jugular vein. There was another wound under the ear, made by a similar instrument. A gunshot wound had also been inflicted immediately below the prominence of the cheekbone. The teeth of the upper jaw had been forced out and the mouth badly mutilated.

When Weare's body had been removed from the sack, it was found to be completely naked. Although searches for his clothing had been for the most part unavailing, the inquest heard from the next witness that at least one article had been recovered. Thomas Bates, a boy employed by James Wardle who had taken possession of Gill's Hill Cottage on Probert's arrest, testified that when he was cleaning Probert's stable on Thursday afternoon he found under a dung heap a shirt steeped in blood and cut down the middle from top to bottom. It appeared to correspond in size and style with some shirts of Weare's found by Ruthven in Hunt's lodgings. Together with the bloody shirt Bates had discovered a sack and some pieces of cord.

When Bates left the stand, Ruthven, who had been with Probert in another room, informed the magistrates that Probert wished to make some statement to them. But when Clutterbuck and some of the other magistrates went to see Probert, his words were a disappointment. He fell on his knees and swore again that he had never seen Weare before.

When the inquest resumed on Saturday, James Heward, the proprietor of the Gill's Hill property, was given an opportunity to explain his suspicious allusion on Sunday to a well-stocked fishpond. His comment had had no sinister overtones, Heward assured the jury. Someone had brought up the fact that Mr. Barber, who had bought the place of Major Wood, intended to fill up the fishpond. He acknowledged his remark that Barber should drag the pond before filling it as there was "a great quantity of fish" in it, but who should know that fact better than he, for he had stocked the pond three months before. Heward was taken to a side room to see Hunt, but he could not identify him as one of Probert's visitors. One of the guests had been a black-whiskered man, and if Hunt was the man, he had shaved his whiskers.

Hunt was brought in for an encore of the disclosures he had made to the magistrates. Coroner Rooke said that it was his duty to hear any statement Hunt wished to make but cautioned the prisoner that no promise or reward was held out to him. Joe said he was ready to repeat his earlier testimony. Before he could begin, however, the officious John Noel observed that the confession Hunt had made before the magistrates could not in any way interfere with the proceeding before the coroner and that the magistrates would, in good faith and at the proper time, submit the confession already made for the consideration of the court at Hunt's trial. Hunt then dictated his confession to the coroner's clerk, following the lines of his earlier statement with which he had grown comfortable. Like all good raconteurs, he could not resist adding a fresh detail here and there. For example, he now recalled that when they stopped to examine the pistols at the jeweler's shop, Thurtell had observed that he wanted the weapons "to kill cats with." Hunt also reworked his itinerary, mentioning that the first stop on his way to Hertfordshire was at an Oxford Street pork shop, where he bought a loin of pork for dinner. Moreover, he had underestimated his liquor consumption at the Artichoke: "I thought we had three, but from what appears from the landlord, Mr. Field, we had five more glasses." Perhaps his renewal of acquaintance with Field at the Hill Slough had caused him to strike an expansive vein, for he now recalled Probert's having observed to Field that the friend who was with him could sing a very excellent song; Field had said he should be very happy to hear one, but Joe had declined.

All this was mere ornamentation of his earlier statement, and the hearing room was taken by surprise when Joe suddenly, without breaking stride, made a significant change in his story. He had maintained before that Bill Probert and he had been together during the whole journey, but now he swore that when they had proceeded about a quarter of a mile beyond the Artichoke, Probert stopped the gig and ordered him to get out and await his return. The obedient Hunt had complied, and after half an hour or more, Probert had returned and had driven Joe to Gill's Hill Cottage.

Hunt also filled in some details on the events of Sunday, October 26, and their aftermath. At Probert's invitation, he had returned to Gill's Hill that day for dinner, complying with his host's injunction to bring a piece of roast beef along or to go hungry. Along the way to Hertfordshire, Jack Thurtell and he had picked up Probert's brother-in-law Thomas Noyes and Tom Thurtell who was visiting his two daughters who had been staying with the Proberts. The four men had walked across a plowed field into a lane, and when they returned to the cottage they were visited by a gentleman whose name he did not know but who he believed owned the property (Heward). After dinner they sat up with rum and water. On the following morning Tom Thurtell and Hunt returned to London with James Addis. It was later that day that Tom asked Hunt to go back to Gill's Hill to inform Probert he had not succeeded in obtaining bail. As he was starting off on this mission, Jack Thurtell had come up to him at the end of the street and said: "If you are going to Mr. Probert's, I may as well go with you, and get that man away."[2]

The revised "confession" ended, and Joe nervously awaited Rooke's examination. As soon as the coroner began his questions, it became clear that the witness knew much more than he had told. The first question was devastating: "I do not observe that you have stated what became of the property which was divided at Probert's house. Was any property divided between Probert and you?" Though visibly shaken, Joe was still able to grope for an answer: "There were six pounds given to me, which I considered as payment for my professional duties." But the questions poured out unrelentingly and the coroner took no pains to hide his sarcasm and contempt:

Q. What do you mean by professional duties?
A. I was taken to Mr. Probert's to sing, to amuse the company.
Q. Who gave you the £6?
A. Mr. John Thurtell.
Q. What did he give to Mr. Probert?
A. I observed him giving Mr. Probert the same.
Q. Was any agreement made with you, by Probert, before you left town about singing?
A. Certainly.
Q. Where was the agreement entered into?
A. It was talked of where we dined, at the Coach & Horses.
Q. Who was present when you talked of it?
A. I, Mr. John Thurtell, and Mr. Probert; only we three. . . .
Q. When Mr. Probert said he would take you down in his chaise, did you consider that he was taking you down for the purpose of singing?
A. Yes, certainly.
Q. Did you sing?
A. Yes.
Q. Who was present when you sang?
A. Mr. Probert, Mrs. Probert, her sister, Thomas and John Thurtell, and Mr. Noyes.
Q. On what day was this?
A. On Friday night, or more properly speaking, Saturday morning. It was after 12:00, I dare say.
Q. Then of course it was after John Thurtell had come in the room and informed you of the murder?
A. Yes.
Q. In the presence of Mrs. Probert and Miss Noyes?
A. Yes.
Q. Then you state that after John Thurtell had informed you that he had murdered this unfortunate person, you sat down and sang?
A. Yes, I did, for some short time.

Having established to his satisfaction that Hunt was a heartless tenor, the coroner attempted to broaden Joe's admissions of in-

volvement in the concealment of the crime and its preparations.
Joe denied all charges he safely could. The servants were wrong,
he maintained, in testifying that on the murder night he had gone
out of the cottage with a lantern. Although he had been with
Thurtell when the pistol was purchased, he had never been told
afterwards what it was to be used for. Finally, however, one of the
coroner's thrusts drove home: Joe admitted purchasing the sack
and cord that had shrouded Weare's body. Reluctantly he recalled
that the sack was purchased at a shop in Broad Street, St. Giles, but
he had had no guilty knowledge of its intended use, for Thurtell
had told him it was for "putting game into." What then was the
cord for? Joe couldn't say.

The coroner then reverted to the subject of Hunt's concert fee.
On Friday night, after Mrs. Probert had gone to bed, Joe had seen
Thurtell take some money out of a small notecase, which he then
threw into the fire with a purse and a betting book. The coroner
had not yet given up on winning an admission that Hunt had know-
ingly received his six pounds as his split of the murder proceeds:

> Q. Did you not hear John Thurtell say, when he paid you and Probert
> six pounds, "That is your share of the money found?"
> A. He did not say "that is your share" but "that I consider your share,"
> or something to that effect.
> Q. I will take your own word; but of what was the money a share?
> A. I do not know.
> Q. Did not Thurtell say it was of the money found?
> A. Never.

Unexpectedly, the coroner now produced a signed statement by
Hunt which included the assertion that Thurtell had in fact said:
"That is your share of the money found." Joe, shrinking visibly
from his own words, confirmed the accuracy of the quotation.

The coroner, sensing he had gained an advantage, pressed his
attack. Where were the murdered man's clothes? Hunt assumed
that they were cut off from his body near Probert's pond, for the
body was naked when Thurtell carried it. He vehemently denied
ever having had any of the victim's clothes on his own back. The
coroner, however, continued to show great interest in the witness'
apparel:

> Q. Had you any clothes on but your own on Sunday?
> A. I had on a suit of black belonging to Mr. John Thurtell.

Q. Why did you change your dress?

A. It was Sunday, and I wished to appear decent and respectable. . . .

Q. Have you never seen the clothes of the deceased from Friday up to the present time?

A. Yes. I am given to understand that the clothes which Mr. John Thurtell sent to my lodgings were the property of the deceased, and I gave that information to the officers.

A juror joined the questioning, inquiring what direction Probert had taken when he set Hunt down from his gig on the murder night. Joe said evasively that Probert continued on the road and came back in about half an hour. Asked what excuse Probert had made for leaving him so abruptly, Hunt said that he gave no explanation but told him to wait until he returned. Another juror was curious as to why the witness had shaved off the thick mustache and whiskers he had worn when he went to Gill's Hill. Hunt responded: "For nothing particular, my beard is very strong and grows fast."

After Hunt finally made good his escape from the witness stand, the coroner resolved the speculations that had been in the air since the end of the previous day's sessions: he brought Bill Probert into the hearing room. Mr. Rooke stated that since the jury had just heard from Hunt he thought it right to give Probert an opportunity of saying what he wished; he cautioned him, however, not to say anything that might incriminate himself. Probert then proceeded to make a statement that, like Hunt's, threw sole blame for the crime on Thurtell.

Setting the stage early for a laundering of his share of the murder booty, the witness claimed that on Friday evening, October 24, he had lent Jack five pounds that he borrowed from the Coach and Horses proprietor, Tetsall, and also gave Joe one pound at Jack's request. About six o'clock, as Bill was leaving for home, Jack told him he was coming down to spend a day with him and would bring a friend. Probert told him that he would be happy to see him and agreed at his suggestion to drive Hunt. Probert and Hunt drove to the Bald-Faced Stag, an inn on the highway just below Edgware, where they stopped. (Hunt had failed to mention this pub in his statements, while Probert had glossed over their first refreshment at the Red Lion.) Hunt had told Probert that he must not go into

the inn, for he had not returned two horse cloths he had borrowed. Joe had walked on to Clarke's White Lion pub in Edgware,
where Probert took him up again and drove on very close to Phillimore Lodge. There, according to Probert's version, Joe got out of
the gig again, saying, "I must wait here for Mr. Thurtell and you
may go on." Prompted by the coroner, Probert added that they
had also stopped for three or four brandies at the Artichoke and
that it was about nine o'clock (an hour after the murder) that they
had reached Phillimore Lodge.

Probert had driven home alone and met Thurtell within a hundred yards of Gill's Hill Cottage. Jack asked him brusquely, "Where's
Hunt?" and when Probert told him he had left him on the road
waiting for him, added, "You must fetch him, for I have killed my
friend and do not want him." Probert said that he hoped he had
not killed anyone, but Thurtell repeated that he had and was now
happy, "for he has robbed me of several hundreds." Probert then
returned for Hunt and brought him to Gill's Hill. Braving the sight
of Thurtell, Hunt ventured the question: "Where could you pass
me?" but Jack brushed the query aside; "It doesn't matter where I
passed you, I have done the trick."

Probert told the jury that he still didn't know at that point who
the victim was and had asked: "For God's sake, who is the man you
have killed?" Thurtell evaded his question: "It is no matter to you,
you don't know his name, and never saw him." He added a threat
that if Probert ever said a word about the murder he would share
the same fate. He had more to kill, he blustered, and if Probert did
not do what was right, he would be one of the victims. The three
men had then gone into the parlor and had dinner. Afterwards
Jack pulled out a purse, shook it and said: "I believe this is all that I
have got for what I have done." His spoils came into view piecemeal: a gun and a watch and after a time several papers, which he
looked through before throwing them into the fire with Hunt's assistance. Probert slipped away to seek temporary refuge upstairs
with his redoubtable wife, and when he came back down Thurtell
told his two companions that they must go and fetch the body and
throw it into Probert's pond. Overriding his host's protest, Thurtell
said they must do as he said and that he would return to take the
dead man away the next day. According to Probert, Thurtell and

Hunt then dumped the body into his pond. After this operation was concluded, Jack produced three five-pound notes from a small notecase. He told Probert as he handed him one of the notes and a sovereign: "Here are the six pounds which I borrowed of you yesterday." It was the witness' naïve hope that this self-serving "confirmation" of the supposed borrowing would convince the coroner and jury that he had entered no prior agreemeent to share the fruits of the crime.

When Probert finally went to bed, he found his wife in tears. Her greeting must have given him little comfort: "For God's sake, what are you, Mr. Hunt, and Thurtell doing up? If I knew what it was about I would inform against you." The next morning Probert awoke at 9:30 and found both Hunt and Thurtell already standing together in the parlor. The boy Addis after breakfast put one or two bundles, a gun and a carpetbag in the chaise. Probert "suspected" that those things had belonged to Weare. As Jack left for London he gave him the unwelcome news that they would return the next day with Tom Thurtell and Probert's brother-in-law Noyes. The four men arrived for dinner, true to Thurtell's word, only to find that their reluctant host had a rather dull appetite. Thurtell derided Probert's low spirits: "You will never do for a Turpin." This reference to the eighteenth-century highwayman Dick Turpin moved the coroner to warn Probert again against self-incrimination, but the witness pushed on, determined to cast further aspersions upon Joe Hunt. After the Sunday dinner the men had walked in the garden for about ten minutes and Jack had commented on Hunt's unusually spruce appearance: "Do you see how my Joseph is dressed today; does he not cut a good figure?" Hunt was wearing a buff waistcoat and a plaid handkerchief which Jack said were Weare's clothes. He had said to the squeamish Probert: "What is that to you? They are not your clothes." At this point the coroner intervened, saying that if the witness would take his advice he would give no more testimony. But Probert had reserved a moment of melodrama: "If you please, sir. I can only say that I am not a murderer, I never saw the man, and I never knew his name, I declare to God." (Clutterbuck, listening skeptically, probably recalled that Probert and Weare had shared the same solicitor, but of course the admirable Mr. Noel could have deservedly enjoyed a wide clientele.)

Coroner Rooke, before discharging the witness, could not resist a few more questions about Hunt's vocal renditions. Probert stated that he had never employed Joe as a professional singer but believed that he had sung one song after Thurtell had told them of the murder. Then the witness withdrew, and as Rooke prepared to give his instructions to the jury, the foreman ventured his opinion on Hunt's complicity: "It would be a pity if this cold-blooded villain should escape justice, for in my mind he is the most guilty of all; he assisted in planning the murder—he bought the sack in which the victim was to be deposited after his murder—and also the spade to dig his grave, and the cord to tie up the sack, and assisted in buying the pistols. I consider Probert an innocent person in comparison with Hunt." In the first words of his charge, the coroner concurred that Hunt's participation in planning the crime with Thurtell "cannot be doubted by any rational and thinking person." As the foreman had noted, Hunt had purchased the tools of the murder "and why should Hunt have been set down by Probert, from his chaise, near Phillimore Lodge, but for the purpose of joining John Thurtell, to aid him in murdering Mr. Weare?" That this was their purpose was evident from the words exchanged by Hunt and Thurtell when they met at Probert's gate after the murder, and also from Hunt's explanation to Probert when they arrived at Phillimore Lodge "that he had to wait for John Thurtell by appointment."[3]

Probert, Rooke proceeded, was inculpated by a chain of events established by the testimony: he had dined with Thurtell a few hours before he left London with Weare, he had agreed to bring Hunt down to the cottage but instead had put him down from the gig at some distance from Gill's Hill with the avowed purpose of waiting for Thurtell. The witnesses who had seen Thurtell and Hunt in the lane looking around the place where the pistol and knife were later found had stated they had seen a tall man come down the lane after the two men with a large dog; and Probert's own servants had stated that their master was in the habit of taking walks with his dog. Rooke inferred that Probert's object in going down Gill's Hill Lane that morning was the same as that of the other two men, namely, to recover possession of the lost weapons.[4]

Deliberating for only a few minutes, the jury returned a verdict of murder against Thurtell as principal and against Hunt and Probert as accessories before the fact. After the verdict was rendered, the coroner and the magistrates had Tom Thurtell brought into the hearing room. His handcuffs were removed and the coroner congratulated him that he was not inculpated by the verdict. At first Tom, who suffered from a speech impediment, struggled unsuccessfully for a reply. At last neither stammer nor fraternal love barred him from declaring that he would not be his brother's keeper: "It was a horrible transaction; but I thank God I had not the remotest idea of the dreadful intentions of my brother or that the murder was committed, till it was communicated to me after my apprehension."[5]

While this dramatic phase of the murder investigation was going forward, the victim had been all but forgotten. Now, however, with the inquest over, his delayed funeral took place. Shortly before eleven o'clock on Saturday night, an hour chosen to discourage attendance by curiosity seekers, the bell of Elstree Church began to toll. Weare's coffin was borne on the shoulders of six men. His brother and most of the jurors of the inquest attended as mourners, and several persons carried lanterns in advance and on either side of the coffin. Despite the late hour the procession was followed by a large crowd as it proceeded up Elstree Hill towards the church, about a quarter of a mile from the Artichoke. The funeral service was read both in the church and at the graveside by the Reverend Thomas Haydow, curate to the rector of Elstree. Weare's body, which had twice been buried unceremoniously, was to suffer another indignity: as the coffin was being lowered into the grave, the rope placed around its foot broke. That end of the coffin slid to the bottom while the upper end, sustained by the other rope, rested against the side of the grave so that the coffin stood almost upright. A sexton immediately imitated Hamlet by jumping into the grave and at last succeeded in bringing the coffin level at the bottom of the twelve-foot-deep tomb. The *Times* has left an affecting landscape of the burial:

> The scene which now presented itself was one which can never pass from the recollection of those who witnessed it. The unusual hour of interment—the horrible and extraordinary manner in which the man whose corpse had just been consigned to the grave had lost his life—the solemn stillness of the night, for the wind which had been loud and bois-

terous during the day, had now fallen, and did not even shake the
branches of the high trees with which the church-yard is surrounded—
the impressive nature of the beautiful and affecting composition which
was read by the clergyman who stood conspicuous, in his white gown, at
the head of the grave, whilst all around him was darkness, except where
the faint light of a lantern happened to fall on the countenances of some
of the mourners—all these circumstances produced an effect on the be-
holders which we think can hardly be surpassed.[6]

But the poetry of Weare's burial could not distract the press
more than briefly from the mysteries of the inquest that had just
been concluded. Principal speculation centered on the strange testimony of Joe Hunt. Where had Coroner Rooke obtained the
signed statement with which he had successfully confronted Joe on
cross-examination? On November 4 the *Times* published the solution to this riddle: after his confession to the magistrates, Hunt
had given an additional statement to Noel. It was in this supplementary statement that Hunt had acknowledged for the first time
that after sinking Weare's body in Probert's pond Thurtell had produced a "reader" (slang for notecase) out of which he took three
five-pound notes and also a purse from which he removed four
sovereigns and that he had given Probert and Hunt six pounds
each as their shares of the property found. Thurtell had burnt the
notecase and the purse as well as a red betting book. In the same
statement Hunt had added Thurtell's lurid account of his assault:
at one time Weare had nearly mastered him and got on top of him.
Weare's blood rushed onto his face and into his mouth in such profusion that he had nearly choked. It was this bloodbath that had so
nauseated Thurtell that he could not eat any pork at supper. After
Jack had cut Weare's throat he took his own shawl handkerchief
and wrapped it around the neck of the corpse to stanch the blood.[7]

Why had Hunt held these revelations back in his testimony before the magistrates, and stranger still, why, after communicating
them to Noel in writing, had he repeated them to the coroner only
under the pressure of cross-examination? Noel's promise of the
magistrates' support in a future plea of Hunt for immunity had
been conditioned on the prisoner's making a "full and candid confession" of all he knew regarding the case, and it was clear that his
admissions had been neither full nor candid and that he had done

his best to fix the entire guilt on Thurtell and Probert. The *Morning Chronicle* on November 3, 1823, while withholding any prediction as to whether Hunt's lack of candor would cause the magistrates to revoke their pledge of support, argued that Hunt, for all his deceptions, was still deserving of mercy: "Certainly he seems to be quite as horrible a miscreant as John Thurtell. His confessions, however, led to the finding of the body, which from the place in which it lay, might have remained undiscovered for months. The pond is situated close to the side of the road, and would not contain more than three bodies, and is the last place, from its publicity, to which suspicion would have attached. . . . Under all the circumstances, we think the Magistrates were perfectly justified in the course they pursued." Despite its harsh and instantaneous condemnation of Thurtell, the *Chronicle* found space in its columns to publish an expression of sympathy for his family. A Norwich correspondent reported that on the day after news broke of the Thurtells' implication in the crime, their father came to Norwich "ignorant of the heavy charge against his sons." Everyone in Norwich was talking of the murder but felt compassion for the grief-stricken alderman: "Connected as some of the actors in that bloody deed are with the city and county, and associating the names of their relatives, as we have ever done, with all that is respectable and friendly, we do pity them most heartily."[8] Norwich had spoken in tones of civility that were soon overwhelmed by the angry rumblings of the newsmills of London.

Chapter Six

THE WHITE-FACED HORSE

———

As the month of November passed, patient and skillful police work, building upon the fragmentary admissions of Hunt and Probert, put together a powerful evidentiary case against the three men. From witnesses that Ruthven and his fellow officers brought before the magistrates, it was now possible to trace the preparations for the crime and to follow the conspirators along the road to Hertfordshire. The sources of all the implements of the murder were accounted for. Benjamin Cogswell, shopman to a Marylebone pawnbroker, identified the murder weapon as one of the pistols he had sold on Friday afternoon, October 24, to the taller of two genteelly dressed strangers. A rope maker, Edward Buckingham, confirmed that on the same day he had sold a sack and eight yards of cord to a gentleman above middle height, who had left his shop in a gig and driven off down Monmouth Street. For good measure, the police also produced Richard Slack, who testified that on Thursday morning, October 23, he had sold to a person he would recognize again (presumably Hunt) a shovel with a wooden handle bearing his trademark. For a while, the police entertained the theory that the defendants had originally intended to bury Weare's body on Probert's grounds but they ultimately did not press this hypothesis, so that Mr. Slack and his proprietary shovel proved to be of no importance to the prosecution.[1]

Hunt had the misfortune of hiring his horse from men with vivid memories. Stephen Probett, of White Lion Inn, Golden Cross Yard, Charing Cross, and his ostler Stephen March, deposed that between two and three in the afternoon of Friday, October 24,

they let a dark iron gray horse with a white blaze in his face to
Joseph Hunt who pretended to be going to Dartford. Hunt showed
promise of becoming a regular customer, for after returning the
horse about noon on Saturday he turned up again at eight o'clock
in the evening and told Probett he wanted a horse and gig on the
next day to take his wife to Dartford and to return on Monday.
The liveryman's pretentious customer said that he must have "something decent" and turned down Probett's suggestion of the gig he
had used the day before. Probett countered with the offer of a yellow stanhope and a bay horse, but Hunt said that the gray horse he
had had before would do. Probett declined, "for that horse had
been driven so fast as to be much distressed." Settling on the
stanhope and the bay, Hunt then pulled out a five-pound Bank of
England note and asked the stable owner to change it, but Probett
preferred to be paid in sovereigns. He noted that his customer
looked "very wild" and his talk was even wilder. Inquiring as to the
name of a gentleman who was leaving the coffee room of the inn,
he ranted, "I will go and knock him on the head, and take his
money from him, it will do him good." Putting his hand into the
side pocket of his coat and drawing out a pistol, he added, "This is
the boy to do business for them." Probett said that the pistol found
in Gill's Hill Lane, which was shown to him, resembled the gun
brandished by Hunt.

On Monday, October 27, shortly after noon, Hunt returned the
horse and gig, praising himself for returning it "safe" and on
schedule: "I always like to bring a horse and gig home according to
appointment; for, if I stayed beyond time, people might fancy
something." He asked to have another horse available for Monday,
and it was agreed that he could have Friday's gray horse and the
yellow stanhope. He set off at 3:30 P.M. on Monday and returned
to the stable about 2:00 on Tuesday morning. Probett and his ostler
observed that the horse was "very much distressed," the thong of
the whip was unraveled nearly to the top, and the bottom of the
gig was covered with blood and dirt.

The police had meticulously reconstructed the movements of
the victim on the fatal Friday. Weare's laundress, Mary Maloney,
had been working that day in his chambers in Lyon's Inn. About
three in the afternoon Weare sent her for a hackney coach, and

she brought one from the Strand, ordering the coachman, as she had been instructed, "to place the horse's head towards Charing Cross." Weare entered the carriage with a double-barreled gun and a carpetbag containing apparel that she had seen him pack; he had previously told her that he was going to spend a few days in the country and would be back on Tuesday. She remembered how her employer had dressed for his journey; he wore a drab great-coat and an olive-colored coat, a buff waistcoat, brown trousers, boots, and a black hat. Many of the articles Ruthven had recovered she positively identified as belonging to Weare, including the carpetbag, the backgammon board, and many pieces of clothing. The police were particularly interested in having her describe her employer's watch. This she did with ease, for she had seen it almost every day and would know it again were it to be shown to her; it was like a lady's watch with a gold face and gold hands, and attached to it was a long chain with a plain red carnelian seal set in gold, a gold key and a diamond ring. She was sure that he had this watch in his pocket when he drove away.

Thomas Kay (or Cave), whom the laundress identified as the driver she had obtained for Weare, recalled his passenger, a short-ish gentleman who had told him to drive to Maddox Street, Hano-ver Square, where he had gotten out near the church. The gentle-man had walked off towards Regent Street and returned after half an hour; he descended again at the top of Cumberland Street and walked towards York Street. In about five or ten minutes the pas-senger returned with a tall gentleman, who was wearing a light rough coat buttoned up. When they came to the coach walking side by side, Kay handed them Weare's gun, carpetbag and box coat and they turned back to York Street.

From this point on Weare was lost from view. His brother Rich-ard, a tailor, deposed that, being concerned about William's disap-pearance, he agreed to meet John Noel at Lyon's Inn on the morn-ing of Friday, October 31. In William's chambers they found some clean linen that appeared to have come from the wash, and every-thing else seemed to have been left undisturbed. After identifying his brother's body at the coroner's inquest, he returned the next morning to Lyon's Inn. A smith he had engaged picked the locks of William's drawers, but no great hoard was found to have been hidden by the renowned hater of banks—only about twenty pounds in gold and silver. Richard also identified many articles of his brother's property that were in Ruthven's custody. He was particularly confident about his identification of the waistcoat, for he had made it himself.

The diligent Ruthven and his men looked in vain for a witness who could place Weare in Thurtell's company after Thomas Kay saw his passenger walk off with the "tall gentleman." They were not optimistic about the results of this quest, for was it not Thurtell's plan to hurry off his victim unseen to the remote place he had chosen for the murder? A stroke of luck, however, enabled the investigators to close what might have otherwise been a significant gap in the tightening net of circumstantial evidence. On Friday night, October 24, Thomas Wilson, a mounted Bow Street patrolman, had been on duty on the road from the village of Edgware to London. About 6:40 P.M. he had met on the top of Harp Hill between the fifth and sixth milestones two gentlemen with drab greatcoats, in a dark-colored gig, drawn by a roan gray horse with a white face, driving at a furious rate on the wrong side of the road. When they came near him he challenged them with the words "Bow Street patrol" and asked why they were driving so fast. One of them replied contemptuously, "Goodnight, patrol!" and they drove on. Once again, the ghostly blaze in a horse's face seemed to loom large in the accumulating evidence against Jack Thurtell and his comrades. Another eyewitness seemed to place the two men at Edgware shortly after their encounter with Wilson. Richard Bingham, ostler to William Clarke, the host of the White Lion, in Edgware, deposed that a little before seven o'clock a gig had driven up from the direction of London carrying two gentlemen. The taller man, who was driving, wore a light greatcoat, and his shorter companion was of darkish complexion, "rather Jewish," and had high cheekbones and whiskers that pointed towards his mouth. They had a glass of rum and water or brandy and water. Their horse had, as always, made a clear impression: it had a "bald face" and seemed to have sweated very much.

The testimony of Wilson and Bingham was lent substantial confirmation by the only witness who positively identified Thurtell on the Hertfordshire road. This was Bingham's employer, William

Clarke, who, returning home to Edgware from the north, met a gig a little before seven o'clock near the ninth milestone on the London–St. Albans road. The gig carried two gentlemen both dressed in dark clothes. The driver was about to pass a lighted stagecoach and was calling out to the coachman; the gig passed on the wrong side of the coach, which was nearly in the middle of the road. When the reckless driver called out, Clarke recognized his voice as that of John Thurtell, whom he had known for two or three years. In the light of the coach he had also seen that a bag or parcel lay in the front of the gig, which was low and drawn by a gray horse.

Because of the confessions (however incomplete) of Hunt and Probert, it was far easier for the police to produce witnesses whose testimony would pinpoint their movements on the day of the murder. John Fleet, assistant messenger to the commissioners of bankrupts, recalled that on Friday afternoon Hunt had driven up in a gig drawn by a horse with four white legs to the door of the Cock Public House in the Haymarket, of which Fleet had taken possession under the bankruptcy order issued against Tom Thurtell. Hunt gave Fleet a note addressed by John Thurtell: "Have the goodness to give Mr. Hunt my blue greatcoat and red shawl, which you will find in the closet in my room, No. 10." Fleet had complied with the request; he believed that the red shawl, which had since been found around the neck of Weare's body, was twilled. Elizabeth Strange, a former servant of Probert at Radlett, deposed that she had often seen Thurtell wearing a red cotton shawl and that the shawl produced by the police was very much like it. The first stop that Hunt and Probert made to wet their whistles was confirmed by William Harding, who kept the Red Lion Public House at the Hyde, in the north London suburban parish of Kingsbury. Harding testified that Probert and another, shorter man called at his pub for about five minutes between 5:30 and 6:30; they each had a glass of brandy and water. Bill Probert seemed intent on fixing his identity in Harding's mind; when his host admitted that he did not recollect him, the taller man had reminded him that his name was Probert.

Their second stop, at the Bald-Faced Stag on the Edgware Road south of Edgware village, was recalled by John Butler, ostler at the

inn. Probert had driven up to the Stag in a gig coming from the
direction of London. He had asked Butler to make haste and give
his horse a bit of hay and a drop of water, for he was in a hurry. He
then repeated: "I am in a hurry, for I have got a lady to take up on
the road." The "lady," of course, was Joe Hunt, who had left the
gig before it arrived at the Stag, being unwilling to face the proprietors to whom he had failed to return horse cloths borrowed
two months before. Butler confirmed the loan of the horse cloths
and that Hunt had not brought them back.

The third pub at which they called was the White Lion. It appeared from the testimony of Clarke and Bingham that Thurtell
had passed through Edgware before them, for they arrived at the
White Lion a few minutes after Clarke returned home from his
encounter with Thurtell's gig farther north; moreover, Bingham
testified that Probert and Hunt arrived about a quarter of an hour
after the departure of the two customers who drove the gig with
the bald-faced horse. Clarke knew both Hunt and Probert. The
gig in which they traveled looked new to him and was drawn by a
bay horse that Probert had sometime before told him was his. The
pub keeper speculated that the horse and carriage had cost a good
deal of money. While his customers drank their ritual brandy and
water, Clarke, who knew they were friendly with the Thurtells, observed that their controversy with the County Fire Office would
"turn out a bad business." Joe Hunt said that it was all nonsense
and took a newspaper out of his pocket folded up with a letter that
he handed to Clarke to read. The letter was from Tom Thurtell
and contained his version of the fire loss. Hunt and Probert had
another glass and departed. Clarke noticed that Joe was then wearing large whiskers but on the following Wednesday when he saw
him again in the custody of the Bow Street officers, he was cleanly
shaven.

The final drinking bout of Hunt and Probert was at the Artichoke in Elstree. Its proprietor, Robert Field, testified that they
arrived in a gig from Elstree about ten minutes after eight o'clock.
Probert ordered brandy and water and after some casual conversation announced: "My friend here is an excellent singer." Field
said that he would be glad to hear him but Hunt could not be
coaxed into performing. At about ten minutes before nine they
had driven away towards Radlett.

Field had a curious conversation with Joe Hunt on the following Tuesday afternoon, when he returned in a gig drawn by a black horse. While Hunt was smoking a pipe, William King, a farmer, had ridden up to the door and said that a woman had been found in the gravel pits murdered. Field remarked, "This is a very odd thing, I think there is no truth in it." Supposing that the rumor was a distortion of the mystery of Gill's Hill, Field had related in the presence of Hunt that he had heard a pistol and knife had been found in the lane and that some person was supposed to have been murdered there. Hunt took no part in the conversation and did not appear surprised. However, about a quarter of an hour later Joe went out into the yard and said to Mrs. Field: "What has all this talk been about?" She replied that King had said that a woman had been found in the gravel pits but that she believed it was "all stuff." Hunt made no comment and drove away.

The star witnesses of the continuing investigations, however, were two family members of the accused—Tom Thurtell and Probert's wife, Elizabeth. Tom, imprisoned in Newgate on the Fire Office charges, had no reluctance to give damning testimony against his brother but could not quite bring himself to disclose any explicit murder confession on Jack's part. He stated that on Thursday afternoon, October 23, while Tom, Jack, Probert, Noyes, and possibly Hunt were at the Coach and Horses, Jack had asked Probert to repay some money lent him a day or two before. When Probert made some excuse for not paying, Jack had hinted darkly: "You know what I want it for: I shall lose three hundred pounds if I don't have it." In recalling these words, Tom may have added the weight of his recollections to rumors beginning to circulate that Jack had been offered a substantial sum to murder Weare.

On Friday, October 24, Tom had witnessed Jack's departure from the Coach and Horses followed in a quarter of an hour by Hunt and Probert. Before dinner that day he had seen two pistols in the dining room and asked his brother what he was going to do with them. Jack told him to mind his own business, but the foul-mouthed Joe Hunt used a very vulgar expression and asked Probert: "Bill, will you be in it?" Tom, never losing an opportunity to implicate any of the accused, could not recollect whether Probert answered but thought he had smiled. He also recalled that Hunt earlier in the afternoon had bandied threats against a broader circle of enemies. He had said that "our friends had better be civil, or they will be served out." Since Tom had heard them talk so often of putting a knife into one and shooting another in the course of common conversation, he did not pay much attention to their words.

On the following afternoon Jack had come into the Coach and Horses when Tom and Noyes were at dinner; he joined them at the table and seemed in very good spirits. Tom observed that his brother's hands were badly cut, and Jack explained: "Oh, Hunt, Probert and I, were out netting partridges last night, and the bushes tore my hands." Jack had also pulled out a gold watch but would not answer any questions about it. A little later Hunt came in and laid on the sofa a bundle containing a blue coat, buff waist-coat, and leather breeches, which he said he had taken out of pawn for Jack. Joe then took out of his pocket two or three sovereigns, some silver and a five-pound note and bragged to Noyes that if he wanted change for a fifty-pound note Joe could provide it, add-ing, "We Turpin-like lads can do the trick." After Noyes left, Tom asked Jack and Joe what they had been doing. Hunt said, "Why, committing bloody murder to be sure." He then added cryptically that they had been shooting game, and Probert had been holding the bag.

On Sunday morning Tom was walking to Probert's to visit his little girls when Jack and Joe Hunt overtook him in a gig. The three men rode together until about a mile from Edgware, where they came upon Thomas Noyes; here Jack got out and walked along the road with Noyes. After he and Joe Hunt drove on, Tom noticed at the bottom of the gig a spade that was quite new and half covered with a coat. Joe told him that Probert wanted it for his garden; then, while they were passing Probert's garden hedge, Hunt unexpectedly threw the spade over the hedge explaining: "Don't you think I know what I am after—Probert don't want his wife to know that he is extravagant."

Earlier that day the vanishing spade had not escaped the keen eye of Charles Tetsall of the Coach and Horses. When they set off with the spade in their chaise, Tetsall testified, he had observed to a Mr. Price, who was at the inn when they drove away, "What the devil can they want with a shovel on a Sunday, when they are going out in a chaise on pleasure?" Tetsall told the magistrates that he was also struck by changes in Jack Thurtell's appearance over the murder weekend. On Sunday morning, Jack was dressed in a new pair of leather smallclothes, new gaiters, and a waistcoat with a double row of buttons on it. His shirt was open at the front and thrust under his waistcoat collar, baring his neck; he looked extremely wild and his landlord thought "he appeared like a madman." Jack had crossed the street for a shave, and on his return there was no more sign of his negligent dressing; he had put on a new blue coat and a new hat, and Tom had remarked to Tetsall "how fine my brother is today."[2]

Certain of the details of Tom's story were confirmed by other witnesses, including Thomas Winter, who had seen the Thurtells at the Coach and Horses on Tuesday, October 28. He had also noticed Jack Thurtell's scratched hands and had been told that Jack had been catching birds and had caught seventeen brace of partridges. Jack invited him to the parlor window to admire his "handsome gold watch." It was a double-cased gold watch with a gold dial plate and an ornamental wreath around its outer edge. Jack supposed it must be worth fifty or sixty guineas but told Winter he would sell it for thirty. When Winter told him he didn't want it and knew nothing of its value, Jack was angry: "You fool, I could lumber [pawn] it for twenty."

Tom Thurtell's disclosures paled before the sensations that Elizabeth Probert had in store. She was the only person apart from Probert and Hunt who could shed any light on the events in Gill's Hill Cottage on the murder night. Her brother and sister, Thomas and Anne Noyes, had been arrested briefly only to be released when it was discovered they knew nothing significant that they had not heard from Mrs. Probert. Elizabeth told the magistrates that when she entered her parlor on Friday evening the three accused men were already there. Probert was standing by the sofa and a stranger hung back a little in the dark. Her husband had introduced "Mr. Hunt," whom she had never seen before, and then they had had some brandy, having complained of being very cold. About half an hour later Probert said that they were going out "a little way" and when she asked him where, replied, "We have a little business with Mr. Nicholls, of Battlers Green." She was surprised, for Nicholls was an "early man" and would have gone to bed; it was then about 10:30, but they told her their business could not wait until morning. More than half an hour had passed before they returned telling her to her amazement that the sleepyheaded farmer was out.

After supper John Thurtell took a watch out of his pocket and asked Hunt if he thought it handsome. When he elicited her opinion next, she looked at it across the table and noted it had a great deal of work about it; she said sententiously that "the plainer they were the neater." The gallant Hunt rushed into the conversational breach, observing that the chain was not fit for a gentleman but more of a lady's chain; he suggested that Thurtell make a present of it to Mrs. Probert. Thurtell had replied grandly: "She shall have it; what is there I would not give Mrs. Probert?" She thanked him, but declined at first. However, she ultimately could not resist the touch of romance he supplied by telling her it had been given by a favorite young lady whom he was to have married but who had died in 1811. Thurtell took the chain from the watch, but Probert declined Hunt's suggestion that he "jump up and put it around his wife's neck." Thurtell then performed that courtly office himself and when Mrs. Probert said she did not mean to keep it, he scolded her gaily: "If you return it I shall throw it on the fire."

The polite skirmishes over the chain were a prelude to a horrifying night. Elizabeth and her sister Anne had retired at midnight, leaving the three men in the parlor. Later Elizabeth was aroused from sleep by the sound of the parlor door opening. Going to her dressing room window, she saw two men walk to the stable, bring out a horse and take it into Gill's Hill Lane. When the horse was brought into the lane she thought it went towards Radlett. (At this early point in her testimony, she was already in error, for the murder site was in fact in the opposite direction, towards Battlers Green.) In a short time the men brought the horse back to the stable and stayed there for a while. Soon afterwards she heard "something dragged along very heavy under the shrubs, by a man who looked like John Thurtell, and another carrying a candle in a candlestick, who looked like Hunt. What they were dragging looked like something tied in a sack; it was dragged along the walk adjoining the barley field, soon after which she heard a noise like that of stones thrown on the ground." She thought the men had been out about two hours.

Her curiosity overcoming her fear, Elizabeth ventured down into the parlor but did not see anyone. The fire was still going well and there was a light on the table. Warming to her role as spy she nearly closed the shutters and put a chair against them, so that she might hear when anyone came in. After she went back upstairs she heard the men entering the parlor from the porch. They closed the doors and then there was a short span of silence, broken by activity that was at first more puzzling than sinister—they seemed to be trying on clothes. She heard Thurtell say, "That fits very well." A rustling noise followed as if made by papers thrown on a table. She heard them say something about "a five-pound note each" and then the noise of gold and the crackling of papers thrown into the fire. Her sharp ears next picked up snatches of a conversation that seemed wrenched from a blood-curdling melodrama:

Thurtell: Hunt, we have laid a nice plan for them, we shall have them all nicely; that bloody Holding shall be next, and another or two.
Hunt: Does Holding have any money?
Thurtell: No, it is revenge, not money; he has ruined my friend here, he has destroyed his piece of mind forever.
Probert: No, no.
Hunt: Nonsense about revenge; it is money we want, we must have money.

Elizabeth remembered the name of Holding as that of one of her husband's adversaries in his bankruptcy. But her mind had little more than time to register that fact, when the men's conversation raced off to new horrors. Hunt had said that they must dispose of the bloody things in the bag in the morning; they had better be off by four or five o'clock. Thurtell, however, thought they had better not go until the usual time after breakfast and had twitted Probert: "What is the matter, Probert? You seem down in the mouth, your wife is a-bed and asleep hours ago; there is no one who has heard or seen anything this night."

When Probert came to bed he found his wife crying. He said, "I thought you were in bed" and was shocked when she cried out,

"Good God, what have you been about, what have I seen tonight?" He tried to calm her down. "Betsy, do not make yourself uneasy, you have only seen the netting; we have been trying to get some game."

On Monday morning she had seen a five-pound Bank of England note in a pair of trousers belonging to her husband. When she mentioned this to Probert, he asked her with an aggrieved air whether it was strange for him to have a five-pound note in his pocket. Later that day when the magistrates were at Gill's Hill, Elizabeth took the five-pound note out of his trousers pocket and put it in the fire, because she supposed that this was one of the notes the men were speaking of.

Mrs. Probert's testimony, while convincing for the most part, left some doubts. It was apparent that she was determined to minimize the role of her husband. Could she actually have identified the two men in the stableyard as Thurtell and Hunt? Contemporary sketches of the cottage indicate that Mrs. Probert could have had a clear view of the garden and the pond, but would she have been able to see over the fence and thick foliage that separated the cottage from the stableyard? Moreover, the words that floated up to her from the parlor incriminated Thurtell and Hunt only, and the only comment she explicitly attributed to her husband was an objection to a further act of revenge. The magistrates surely must have noted, too, that Elizabeth's shock and moral outrage had their limits, for as far as they knew, she had risen from her bed on Saturday morning after a night of horrors and bid Thurtell a cordial farewell—and she had kept the watch chain.

Despite the cumulative evidence that placed Thurtell on the road to Gill's Hill on the murder night, the authorities were still dissatisfied that no witness had identified the victim as his traveling companion. They therefore sought an exhumation order so that Bingham, the ostler at the White Lion, would have an opportunity to identify the corpse as that of one of the two persons who had called there on the Friday evening. Weare's family doubted whether it would be of any use to inspect the body at this late date, but a physician confidently declared that the corpse would be found almost in the same condition as when buried, and this view prevailed. In order to avoid unnecessary publicity, and with greater success on this score than on the occasion of the burial, the disinterment was performed at midnight on December 3. "The night was dark, and the weather most inclement. Storms of rain and hail assailed the individuals who had taken upon themselves the unpleasant task. . . . The grave was nine feet deep, and for the purpose now in view it was necessary to dig a much larger pit than had originally been prepared. From this circumstance, though every practicable exertion was made, the work proceeded but slowly."

The observers included Clutterbuck, Dr. Ward, Field of the Artichoke, and Bingham, the witness on whom the police pinned their hopes. When the gravedigger and his laborers had almost reached the coffin, they found that the grave contained a great deal of water and that the surrounding earth could not easily be removed. When a very spacious hole had at last been formed, a rope was passed under the head of the coffin. However, the coffin was so deeply imbedded in the soil and so heavy from the water it contained, that it required the efforts of about ten men to raise it. The results were a dreadful disappointment and a cautionary reminder of how soon human flesh returns to dust. "When the contents of the coffin were looked upon, it was instantly obvious to everyone that recognition was impossible. The ostler approached the much wasted remnant of mortality, but to no purpose. Unusually rapid decomposition, occasioned, it was supposed, by the water in which the body was found immersed, rendered all the toil which had been undergone utterly useless."[3]

During the long investigation Thurtell, Hunt, and Probert were kept apart from each other in three airy apartments in Hertford Gaol, for cells were not proper housing for prisoners of such distinction. Jack Thurtell grew accustomed to the close surveillance that the nervous prison authorities imposed on him and to his confinement in irons, which, the newspapers assured their readers, were not the heavy shackles ordinarily reserved for felons and weighed a mere fifteen pounds. Jack calmly smoked his pipe and announced magnanimously that he would be pleased to have John Noel conduct the prosecution. When chaplain Franklin suggested some religious reading, Thurtell remarked that he would rather have a copy of the orations of barrister Charles Phillips to enable him to prepare his defense speech. This was not mere bravado, for until the passage of the Prisoners' Counsel Bill of 1836, counsel for murder defendants could not address the jury in their clients' behalf. If anyone mentioned the Weare murder to him, Thurtell dropped into sullen silence but if any other subject was broached, he burst into "hurried pursuit of the question, as most anxious of obtaining a momentary relief from the thoughts of the murder."[4]

Chapter Seven

THE RUMORMONGERS

William Weare's body had already been recovered from the Elstree pond when the *Times* on October 31, 1823, published its first article on the case under the headline "Most Horrible Murder":

> On Friday night last, a murder was committed at a place about six miles from the town of Watford, Herts, which for cold-blooded villainy in the mode of bringing it about, and the ferocity which accompanied its perpetration, has seldom been equalled. Half the county of Hertford has been for the last three days in a state of agitation upon the subject, and nothing can exceed the anxiety evinced by all classes for the discovery of the perpetrators. This, we are happy to say, is now in a fair way of being brought about, and the circumstances which have led to it afford another striking proof that
>
> > murder, though it hath no tongue,
> > Doth speak with most miraculous organ.[1]

This was the opening salvo in a press campaign that helped make the Thurtell-Hunt case one of the obsessions of the decade. Writers have speculated to this day about what it was that gave the case its unique hold on the public mind. No doubt there were certain extrinsic factors, such as an explosion of readership in the early nineteenth century, the growth of the newspaper industry, and the discovery by shrewd publishers of newspapers, chapbooks, and street literature that nothing boosted circulation like a good murder. England's newspapers were involved in an era of rapid expansion, increasing from 50 in 1782 to 135 in 1821. During that same time the number of London's dailies had almost doubled from 9 to 16, and more significantly, the London weeklies that specialized

in crime and other sensations, not yet born in 1782, numbered 32
by 1821. Despite this rapid development, the great metropolitan
dailies were still searching for ways to multiply their relatively
modest circulation, which totaled only six thousand for the *Times*
and half that number for its rival the *Morning Chronicle*.[2]

Another factor in the surprising popularity of the Thurtell-
Hunt case was the relative rarity of murder in England at the time.
In the seven years from 1817 through 1823, according to the *Annual Register,* there were only thirty-five capital convictions for
murder and attempted murder in England and Wales. In the metropolitan area, murder was even less common than in the provinces. For example, in London's Middlesex County, which contained a population of one million (of the total of twelve million in
England and Wales) and knew the extremes of poverty as well as of
wealth, there was only one person committed for murder in the
course of 1823.

These circumstances, however, were only stimulants to the enormous natural appeal of an extraordinary crime. The murder,
committed on the very fringe of the metropolis, involved as principal suspect John Thurtell, a man well known not only to sporting
circles but to many of the journalists who would later write his
story. Moreover, his downward path from a respectable provincial
home to London's lower depths pointed a moral that was eagerly
seized upon by those who were repelled by the *Life in London* furor
of 1821. Was not John Thurtell a real-life equivalent of Jerry
Hawthorn who, instead of pleasure, had found crime and degradation behind the allure of London's fast set? More specifically, the
reports of Thurtell's activity in boxing and gambling stirred fresh
debates between the devotees and foes of those two unlawful amusements. The passions of these controversies were to be heightened
by the suggestion of some that Weare's murder was in fact a gangland slaying, rooted in the gambling hells and connected with
other crimes yet undiscovered.

These social claims of the case on the country's attention were
joined to details whose attraction was more theatrical. According
to Bow Street historian Percy Fitzgerald, the case "is so extraordinary in its melodramatic incidents, so lurid in its details, that it
holds the reader with a sort of fascination, akin to the attraction of

some repulsive but absorbing melodrama." There was, of course, the unique feature of the double water burial, but even more gripping were the gig that carried Weare to his doom and the phantom-faced horse by which it was drawn. The horse, then as now one of England's favorite creatures, played an ambiguous symbolic role in the case. Viewed by itself, the horse implied a link with the romantic past of highwaymen. However, the conventional vehicle to which it was hitched summoned up an antiromantic image of domesticated modern life in which the highwaymen would feel ill at ease, and the cold-blooded murder also seemed strangely out of place. Fitzgerald focuses on the gig as the lodestar of the case:

> But through the lurid light which played upon the tragedy, the public eye seemed to settle, as if fascinated on one object—the mysterious gig in which the victim and its murderer had driven down. Whether it was that the use of such a vehicle in such a tragedy was without precedent, or that its homely, sociable character added a new horror to the murder, or that there was something piquant or *bizarre* in the idea, there would be no doubt that *the gig,* jogging along its course, appeared all through the tragedy in almost a spectral way.[3]

From the very beginning, the newspapers, which reported the details of the investigation, the inquest, and Hunt's confessions, left no doubt of their confidence that Thurtell and his confederates were guilty. As early as November 5, the *Times* had already accepted Hunt's statement "that a desperate struggle took place between John Thurtell and Weare before the latter was completely overpowered." The newspaper described Weare as a pallid, puny man under middle stature and of delicate constitution and therefore not capable of offering serious resistance to Thurtell's assault. On November 11 the *Times* published "Outline of the London Life of John Thurtell," which connected the crime with Thurtell's gambling losses to Weare and other sharpers. Two days later the *Times* praised the rigorous surveillance over Thurtell, Hunt, and Probert in Hertford Gaol as due to the "laudable desire of the magistrates to secure the guilty culprits." The *Morning Chronicle* showed equal certainty about the guilt of the accused men. On November 6 it reported erroneously that on the very day when Thurtell and Hunt committed the murder Thurtell's father had been reelected mayor of Norwich. Two days later it published plates supposedly illustrating the murder and showing figures representing Thurtell, Hunt, and Probert at Gill's Hill, two of them in the act of dragging Weare's body to the pond.[4]

The press was unanimous in finding a link between the murder and organized gambling interests. Beginning on November 14, three days after its publication of the sketch of Thurtell's gambling career, the *Times* began to caption its articles on the case, "The Gambling-House Murderers." Early in its coverage of the case, the newspaper signaled its intention to use the murder as a bludgeon against the twin vices of gambling and boxing. In its issue of November 7, 1823, it noted ironically that "the prosecution of the murderers of Weare seems to have fallen into pretty hands." As soon as John Noel had been mentioned as counsel to the magistrates' investigation, the *Times* thought it had heard his name before. After inquiry it was discovered that he was one of the persons who in the summer of 1822 was apprehended in a raid on a minor gambling house in Pall Mall. Weare, a close friend, had been present at Noel's examination at Bow Street and had procured legal assistance for him. The *Times* editorialized:

> While we hope that the late murder will tend to ruin all those haunts of vice and villainy called gaming-houses, from whence murders issue, we cannot help extending the remark also to prize-fights. . . . Prize-fights being more matters of publicity than gaming-houses, may be more easily abolished. The frequenters of the one will be, we believe, with little exception, the frequenters of the other. . . . We believe that if in one moment all the prize-fighters, their abettors, connexions, and the frequenters of their exhibitions, were swept from the earth, the nation would soon discover, from the comparative peace and security consequent upon such a judgment, that it had lost all its quack-doctors, moneylenders, pickpockets, housebreakers, circulators of base coin and false notes, chargers with unnatural crimes, brothel-keepers, incendiaries, and bullies.

On November 11, the *Times* reported that the "loose gamblers of the metropolis" had been thrown into a great state of consternation by warrants issued against some of them by the magistrates investigating Weare's murder. It stated: "Like all desperate and marauding confederacies, the moment a link in the chain of fellowship is broken, suspicion awakes, and the want of any moral tie of principle renders the whole party a prey to their several guilty recollections." It was high time, argued the newspaper, that the magistrates sum up their evidence for there was enough as the case stood "to bring down the vengeance of the law upon those who are guilty of the murder, as well as to expose the machinations of the gamblers who infest the metropolis." The *Times* demanded that there be regularly published a list of the gambling houses and the blacklegs who supported them, as well as of the persons who fitted out swindlers to make their periodic excursions for fraud and plunder at country fairs and races.[5]

On the following day, the *Times* reported that its campaign had already achieved results: an "offer of a general disclosure of the gambling system was made to a person high in office, by means of an anonymous letter, in the early part of last week." The informant, having obtained assurance that his name would not be linked with any investigation, reportedly delivered a scroll on which more than two hundred gambling houses were described "with a minuteness and accuracy that none but the most intimate of their visitors could have accomplished." The *Times*'s readers responded with enthusiasm to the newspaper's crusade. One reader, commenting that "it is impossible duly to appreciate the good you have done to society in your remarks on gambling and prizefighting," stated that a prizefight, and a fight arising from accidental causes, were as different as light and darkness:

> Supposing two men quarrel in a public-house, and turn out to box; be it so—and God forbid that we should ever see them use their knives, and not their fists, but a prize fight is a far different thing; it is an assemblage of the worst characters. At these boxing matches, perhaps, there are ten thousand persons; of which number, one hundred (to their disgrace be it said) are men of fortune; but the remainder (with the exception of the thieves) are working men, depriving their families of their support, and in the high road (as recent circumstances have proved) to ruin.

On November 15, another reader calling himself Castigator leveled a similar attack on gambling. He placed the blame for the spread of the vice squarely on the aristocracy: "To the higher orders of society . . . we are indebted for the introduction and promotion of this pernicious vice. Many of those who have since kept common gaming houses were the creatures of these noble *black legs,* and were by them initiated into all the art and mystery of deep-laid confederacy and fraudful avarice."[6] The press and its readers, then, agreed in finding a double link between gambling and the Radlett murder: not only had the dissipation of gambling-house life prepared Thurtell's soul for the worst of crimes, but his grievance at having been tricked at play had given him a revenge motive against Weare.

There was also, however, an even more alarming possibility, and speculation focused on it early. Suppose Thurtell had in fact carried out a gangland execution at the bidding of the mysterious gambling overlord Lemon. In its issue of November 23, 1823, *Bell's Life in London,* which as a sporting journal much prefered that the blame for the murder be thrown on gambling than on Thurtell's boxing associations, referred to Lemon as "the monied employer of Thurtell and others in their diabolical practices." Lemon was a master of roguery and the boss of a gang of blacklegs and sharpers who visited spas and watering places to fleece the unwary. In 1823, *Bell's Life* stated, some of the gang had been operating in Kent, making Margate their headquarters.[7] Lemon had supposedly formed a partnership with Weare, Thurtell, and Hunt in the spring. Thurtell and Hunt would appear in the gambling hells in the guise of casual spectators. If the stakes were high, and the gang could not make off with their winnings without revealing their crooked tricks, they would start a row that would end the play and provide a cover for them to scoop up their profit and decamp. In the resulting melee, Thurtell and Hunt would act as "champions" or "bullies." Joe Hunt, who had not studied the manly arts of pugilism, had been quoted as saying that "he never minded a few kicks or cuffs so long as he made money."[8]

On November 4 the *Times* quoted a statement attributed to Tom Thurtell that Jack had informed him on the Saturday after the murder that Lemon had promised him three hundred pounds to dispatch Weare and that he expected to collect in full since he had performed his assignment. The report cited by the *Times* offered the following explanation for the Lemon-Thurtell "contract": A few months before, a gentleman named G. had been swindled out of several thousand pounds at play with Weare, Lemon, and three confederates. Shortly thereafter G. was put in prison for a small debt and Lemon and Weare called upon him there, expressing sorrow and leaving him the princely gift of six shillings. Subsequently, the report went on, Weare betrayed his fellow blacklegs by revealing the swindle to a lawyer, who freed G. and instituted proceedings against Lemon and his three henchmen for criminal conspiracy. Learning these circumstances, the source quoted by the *Times* found little difficulty in believing it possible that Lemon had made an offer to Thurtell to get rid of Weare.[9]

It was a week later, in its sketch of Thurtell's gambling past, that the *Times* also accused Lemon of having cheated Thurtell. On November 13 the *Times* quoted an item from the *British Traveller* asserting that Lemon was the only additional witness sought by the magistrates and that he "is lurking either in or about the metropolis." The article added that "there was scarcely any transaction of consequence in which the Thurtells were engaged for the last two years, in which this man did not take an active part." On the same day the *Morning Chronicle* reported (erroneously) that Lemon had surrendered himself to the police at Paris and was to be returned home.[10]

How could the public be led to believe that the son of a Norwich alderman had become an assassin in the pay of an archcriminal? Strange as the allegation seemed at first reading, it gradually won credence as the papers reported earlier murders and acts of violence on the part of Thurtell. In searching out and disseminating these rumors, the press spared no corner of Thurtell's life, not even his naval career. On November 6, for example, the *Times* reported falsely that Thurtell had been with the English forces at the storming of San Sebastián and that he had wantonly murdered a weary Polish officer who was in the French service. Thurtell was quoted as offering a heartless explanation for the killing: "I thought by the look of him that he was a nob, and must have some blunt [money] about him; so I just tucked my sword in his ribs, and settled him; and I found a hundred and forty doubloons in the pocket!" This story failed to convince at least two veterans, who wrote to the *Times*, one asserting that he had served in the German Legion at the seige of San Sebastián and that Thurtell was not there. The other, a born detective, noted the improbability that the fatigued victim would carry so much heavy coin on his person, claiming that 140 Spanish doubloons weighed ten pounds. However, another correspondent to the *Times,* on November 8, was responsible for the dissemination of another libel against Thurtell's naval service. He claimed that Thurtell, while serving on board the *Aboukir* with a sailor named Young, had willfully violated the eight o'clock curfew and had received a severe cutlass wound in a resulting scuffle with Young.[11]

When the newspapers searched Thurtell's London life for more recent disorders, they began on solid ground with the arson conspiracy. On November 10 Barber Beaumont, managing director of the County Fire Office, presented a motion to set aside the verdict in Tom Thurtell's damage case and to grant a new trial. In addition to reviewing the suspicious circumstances of the fire, Serjeant Taddy, in behalf of the defendant, cited three affidavits as new grounds for a retrial. In the first, a warehouseman of Margraves & Company swore that the Thurtells had shortly before the fire sold Margraves at a substantial discount merchandise that corresponded to the description of goods later claimed to have burned. The second affidavit was a surprise: it was a statement that Beaumont had obtained from Hunt in Hertford Gaol in which Joe quoted Jack Thurtell as having told him that he knew the exact time when the fire would break out since a certain light had been so placed as to cause the house to burst into flames at a predetermined moment. Beaumont had added his own affidavit that the grand jury had recently returned indictments against the Thurtells and their associates for conspiracy to defraud the County Fire Office. Mr. Justice Park, who participated in the hearing of the arguments, defended the earlier judgment, warning that it would be a dangerous precedent to grant a new trial on the basis of a perjury indictment since such a ruling would open the door for constant claims of perjury. Lord Chief Justice Robert Dallas agreed that the Beaumont affidavit should be disregarded and Mr. Justice James Burrough added that there was little, if any, reliance to be placed on Hunt's statement. Nevertheless, a majority of the court decided that the plaintiff's evidence was so questionable that a new trial should be granted.[12]

Considerable interest was attracted by the hearing, an interest that was magnified manyfold by the report of the *Weekly Dispatch* on November 16 that the Hertfordshire magistrates were in possession of evidence regarding "the Thurtells' gang, which disclosed acts of even more dreadful atrocity then the horrid deed which has lately so much occupied the public mind." The new outrage was nothing less than the intended assassination by Thurtell of Barber Beaumont:

> That gentleman has been in the habit of frequently sitting in his office, or study, on the ground-floor, of an evening, and close to the window . . . without having the shutters closed. It was planned that something should be thrown against the window, which would cause him to remove the blind, and look out, when J. Thurtell was prepared with his air-gun to effect the murder. It fortunately happened that Mr. Beaumont did not sit in this room on that evening, or the following; and on the third the murderers were occupied in dispatching their victim, Weare.[13]

Whatever doubt there might have been as to the reality of the alleged murder plot, there was none at all that Thurtell had indeed possessed a deadly and insidious airgun. From prison he had written to Mrs. Walker, a recently married former barmaid at the Cock (who had apparently been Tom Thurtell's sweetheart), asking her to take care of the gun, and the Bow Street police had seized the weapon after intercepting the letter. The gun was in the shape of a common walking stick; composed of metal cased with tin, it was colored to look like wood and had knobs resembling the knots of a wooden stick. The top of the gun-stick was removable, and a separate air pump could be attached in a moment. Police tests showed that the lethal device could send a small-caliber bullet through an inch-thick deal board at a moderate distance.[14]

Another more exotic murder attempt had reportedly been made by Thurtell on James Woods, a rival suitor of the pretty twenty-two year old Caroline Noyes. Woods had been courting her for three years, and while he was in France about six months before, she had lived with her sister Elizabeth Probert at Gill's Hill. While she was there Thurtell, according to the newspapers, used to persecute her with unwanted attentions. When Woods returned from France in August, 1823, Caroline had told him of Thurtell's conduct, and Woods had helped her move from the cottage. On November 10 the *Times* published Woods's account of his narrow escape from Thurtell's revenge. Woods claimed that he had been decoyed to a rendezvous at 10 Manchester Buildings by a man dressed as a journeyman carpenter, about five feet, nine inches, tall, of dark complexion, and with large black whiskers. On his arriving at the house his suspicions were awakened when he noticed that the door was ajar and he asked the carpenter to enter first. When the man entered and had proceeded along the hallway as far as the back parlor door, Woods saw Jack Thurtell spring out from the parlor and strike the man a heavy blow with a pair of dumbbells that knocked him violently against the opposite wall. Woods calmly retreated from the scene, neither running nor pursued by Thurtell. The *Times* added its own note of confirmation to Woods's account, reporting that in the course of their search of the Thurtells' premises at 10 Manchester Buildings, the bankruptcy commissioners had found a pair of dumbbells, which they had delivered to the police at Bow Street. The story of the dumbbells carried added credibility, since sporting circles were aware that they were commonly used in the training of boxers.[15]

Probert himself was cited as an authority on Thurtell's serial murder plans; he was said to have told the Hertfordshire magistrates of Thurtell's boast that he had "picked out 17 persons of substance that he intended to rob and murder, and that [Weare] was one of them." Taking their cue from Probert, the newspapers, after exploiting the close encounters of Beaumont and Woods with Thurtell's rage, reported a large number of other "escapes from the late horrid conspiracy."[16] One lucky survivor was supposedly an importer of coral beads named Sparks, who had decided to pass up a business appointment with the Thurtells after he had made proper inquiries into their reputation, "to which circumstance his family and friends attribute his escape from the horrible doom, which otherwise, in all probability, awaited him." The public paranoia that was being created and fueled by the ever more sweeping charges against the Thurtell conspirators did not spare even the young. Perhaps the most astounding juvenile record of Thurtellmania is found in the correspondence of the thirteen-year-old boarding school student James Milnes Gaskell. Writing home to his mother on November 18, 1823, he reported that the boys at Dr. Roberts' school were quite full of "the 'Thurtell'" and that they "are continuously sending for papers to throw some light on this mysterious affair." Rumor at the school had turned the murder into an Anglican equivalent of the popish plot: "The son of a worthy Mayor of Norwich murders Mr. Weare, a man of some fortune, and positively forms a plot to put to death a long catalogue of rich persons. Mr. R. told us that the bodies of 6 persons have been found in the Thames, 2 of them are women. Two clergymen are engaged in this scandalous affair. Two clergymen of the Established Church!" [17]

It was not only the newspapers that fed the limitless public appetite for the Thurtell-Hunt case in the mad autumn of 1823. As soon as the news of the crime broke, curiosity seekers breathlessly hurried up from London to inspect the Gill's Hill property. By November 11 the daily visitors numbered two hundred. The enterprising proprietor, James Heward, charged one shilling for admission at the stable gate, and "the usual pains are taken to keep alive the interest of the scene." The parlor armchairs in which Hunt and Thurtell were thought to have sat on the night of the murder were placed cozily next to the fire, and the sofa on which Joe had slept was also there to be gawked at (though stripped of its cover which the magistrates were holding because of suspicious spots that looked like blood). The crowds soon more than doubled in size and included such notables as the marchioness of Salisbury and Mr. Phillimore, whose lodge had been immortalized as Hunt's hiding place. By November 13 the part of the hedge through which Weare's body had been dragged was no more, "having been cut away piecemeal by the persons who have visited the spot." On the same day a sale of the cottage furniture was held and perhaps the most valuable lot was Thurtell's double-barreled shotgun. [18]

The publishers of overnight books, pamphlets, broadsides, and other street literature also cashed in on the case with remarkable speed. On November 7, J. Edgerley of Fleet Street advertised a comprehensive *Narrative of the Murder of Mr. Weare*, including the coroner's inquest, the lives of the accused, unpublished letters, the dumbbell plot against Woods, and a copperplate engraving of the murder scene. James Catnach, the famous catchpenny publisher of Seven Dials rushed into the streets 250,000 copies of his first broadside of the case, which had been churned out by four presses working full time for a week. One of the earliest childhood recollections of publisher Henry Vizetelly harked back "to a tranquil autumn evening in 1823, when our quiet neighbourhood was suddenly disturbed by the sonorous shouting of several of Mr. Catnach's gruff-voiced hawkers, but the only words one could distinctly catch were, "orrible murder of Mr. William Weare!'" Catnach would eventually gross over five hundred pounds from the Weare murder case.[19]

Two of the most curious of the pretrial publications sounded the gambling theme. A pamphlet issued by W. Chubb, of the Strand, under the title, *The Hoax Discovered; or, Mr. Weare Alive,* declared the murder to be the bogus fabrication of a gambling-house wager. According to confidential information supposedly received from a gamester friend of Weare, Thurtell had bet that he and two friends could simulate a murder and cause themselves to be arrested and tried "when, at the very crisis of their fate, the supposed murdered man should appear, stagger the belief of the world, and make John Bull confess his being hoaxed."[20] When the stakes were put up, Thurtell, Probert, and Hunt had procured a corpse from grave robbers and mutilated the dead man's face to prevent recognition; Weare had gone into hiding, perhaps on the Continent. To the writer's mind, the hoax theory explained many strange features about the case: the mangling of the body and its transportation from place to place without fear of detection, the voracious appetites of Probert and Hunt on the murder night, and Thurtell's unembarrassed observation of the body at the inquest.

Another, unnamed London author produced a pamphlet titled *The Gamblers: A Moral Poem.* In rhyming couplets the clumsy poet sings the crimes of Thurtell after a long prelude attacking gambling hells and particularly their aristocratic habitués. Oddly, though the piece is "respectfully dedicated to the Army and Navy," Thurtell's first fall from virtue is attributed to shipboard vices: "Religion's principles flew far away, / 'Ere he had been 'a little month at sea.'" The author seemed to be somewhat of a gambling man himself, for he had no reluctance to predict the outcome of the trial:

> Hark! now the solemn verdict *Guilty* hear
> And sentence pass'd upon the wretched pair,
> While Thurtell, still denying the offence,
> Calls God to witness for his innocence.[21]

Llewellyn "Boiled Beef" Williams, manager of the Surrey, one of London's melodrama theaters, conceived a much more dazzling promotion: he would stage the murder complete with the original horse and gig. He first approached the young writer Edward Fitzball, who was under contract to the Surrey. Fitzball, however, despite his ill health and poverty, indignantly threw up his engagement and quit the theater in disgust, his blood "absolutely chilled at the proposition."[22] Some less squeamish hack was soon found, for on November 17 *The Gamblers* opened at the Surrey.

In the play the figures in the Weare murder case are but thinly veiled. The curtain rises in the cottage of William Mordaunt (Probert) whose wife, Amelia, laments her absent husband's "boundless dicings and voluptuous riots." The scene then shifts to a London street where Thomas Woodville (Thurtell) and Joseph Bradshaw (Hunt) plot the murder of William Frankly (Weare) and hope to persuade Mordaunt to assist them. In the third scene a gambling house is shown in which Frankly, enjoying a winning streak at dice, wipes out the last remnants of Mordaunt's money. As the act ends, Frankly accepts Woodville's invitation to drive a few miles out of town to a gambling party, but Mordaunt spurns Woodville as the man who "spread all those snares about [him], which first entangled, then overthrew [his] virtue." At the opening of the second act Mordaunt returns home in despair over his losses. The action moves next to the Bald-Faced Stag, where the horse and gig make their long-awaited entrance at the door; to remind the audience of what lies ahead Woodville cocks his pistol and conceals it in his clothing. On the roadside Bradshaw is shown in hiding but he later climbs over the hedge into Gill's Hill Lane where he comes upon Woodville and is told of the murder. They then make an unexpected appearance at Gill's Hill Cottage and try to bribe Mordaunt into helping them by offering to return a bond that Frankly had won from him in crooked play, but Mordaunt in horror notices that there is blood upon the bond and will promise the murderers only his silence. In the lane two workmen are then seen discovering blood, a pistol and a knife and they rush off for the police. Now the way has been prepared for the denouement: as the police officers arrive at the cottage to confront Mordaunt with the evidence of the bloody bond, the body of Frankly is brought in by countrymen who call on the murderers to look on the victim. Frankly is discovered to be still alive, identifies Woodville as his murderer and expires as the curtain falls.[23]

In its review of *The Gamblers*, the *Times* quoted the playbill as stating that the piece was written and about to be produced before the dreadful murder of Weare took place, but that when that tragedy occurred, "motives of peculiar delicacy" induced the proprietors to keep it back until the present. The *Times* regretted "that these motives did not continue to exist, at least until after the approaching assizes at Hertford." The critic opined that it was impossible for spectators not to identify incidents that so closely resembled circumstances connected with Weare's death; as if to remove all doubt as to the writer's intention, the scenery was composed of views of the various locales associated with the crime. In a related article the *Times* noted the theater management's claim that the horse and gig were the same that conveyed Thurtell and Weare out of town and observed that "the identity of the vehicle and the horse formed the strongest feature of interest in the eyes of the audience, if we could safely collect that expression from the applause that followed their appearance." The first-night critic, however, took some comfort from the audience reaction: "There was hissing at the scene of the murder, and at the end of the piece the disapprobation was considerable. We were pleased to find that the audience eagerly applauded those parts of the dialogue in which the vice of gaming was condemned."[24]

In the same issue the *Times* also reviewed a melodrama at the Royal Coburg Theatre called *The Gamblers; or, The Murderers at the Desolate Cottage*. This was a "ridiculously improbable" piece in which a murder is solved by an appearance of a ghost, following the more respectable precedent of Hamlet's father. The story had nothing to do with the Weare murder but had been tricked out with a new title intended to catch the unwary. The *Times* commented on the deception:

> Much expectation was on the wing, that when "Gamblers, and a Desolate Cottage" formed the title of the piece, the allusions in the dialogue would have borne upon the recent murder; but no such thing, except we could fancy the cabriolet in which the ghost travels to be Probert's gig, one or two trite remarks to the spirit of gaming having whetted the as-

sassin's knife, and a French hut being Gill's-hill-cottage, and a pool of fire to be his pond,—unless all these can be fancied, the piece has no recent application.

The newspaper critic wrote that the piece was well received, but the enthusiasm had its limits. When announced for repetition, "there was partial hissing from a party of gentlemen in one of the dress boxes."[25]

On November 19, after a second performance of *The Gamblers* at the Surrey, Thurtell's counsel Joseph Chitty, renowned legal writer and special pleader who had become a barrister at age forty in 1816, moved the Court of King's Bench for a criminal information against the management of the theater "for an indecent and unlawful excitation of the public mind, by representing, in a dramatic form upon the stage, a tragedy, founded on the supposed incidents of the late dreadful murder." He presented the affidavit of a gentleman who had attended the theater on the night before and seen the play displayed to a crowded house. The gentleman stated that "it produced extraordinary excitation, and such applause as was disgraceful to a British public, professing the feelings of humanity, and boasting of its justice." Chitty told the court that he need not suggest the atrocious and monstrous indecency of such an exhibition, calculated as it was to destroy all hope of a fair trial of a human being innocent until declared guilty and whose life was placed in jeopardy by this and other extraordinary proceedings that had been taken for the excitement and gratification of public curiosity. After a long hearing, the proprietor and manager of the Surrey were enjoined from further performances until the trial was over.[26]

Chapter Eight

THE SECOND SOLICITOR

———

Another front of the pretrial battles had opened in the very precincts of Hertford Gaol. The local magistrates, knowing that they
had a major criminal case in their inexperienced hands and were
responsible for prisoners whose rescue or silence might be precious to the London underworld, were determined to guard their
captives closely. The three men were kept under a rigorous watch
with two inmates placed in the apartment of each as additional
guards. Attributing the special precautions to "some improbable
notion that a rescue was intended," the *Times* reported that special
watchmen were provided within and outside the prison walls, and
the prisoners were kept absolutely segregated from each other. In
mid-November, the magistrates tightened security further by making an abrupt change in the places of confinement of the prisoners.
On his committal, Hunt had been placed in the female ward,
which adjoined the debtors' wing of the prison, and the yard in
which he was permitted occasional exercise was separated only by
a wall of middle height from the part of the jail where Thurtell
was kept. But suddenly, without explanation, the two men were required to switch rooms.[1] There were new rumors of an escape
plot, but the explanation, when it was forthcoming, turned out to
be even stranger: the switch had been motivated by an unprecedented effort to restrict contact between Thurtell and his legal
advisers.

This ill-advised campaign began at a meeting of the Hertfordshire magistrates on November 8, where it was resolved that none
but magistrates and professional advisers of the prisoners would

be admitted to visit them and "that no professional adviser shall be admitted to see any prisoner until he had satisfied a visiting magistrate that he is employed as a professional adviser of such prisoner, and that he claims to see such prisoner with the sole view of supplying his professional assistance."[2] The resolution received its first test later that morning when London solicitor Charles Pearson called at Clutterbuck's house and requested admission to the prison to see Thurtell, who he understood had appointed him his legal representative. Asked what proof he could produce of his engagement, Pearson was caught in a vicious circle: he replied that unless he was given access to the prisoner, it would be impossible for him to have his appointment confirmed, although it was well known that Thurtell had expressed his desire that Pearson act for him. Clutterbuck unmoved, insisted that Pearson write to Thurtell to request confirmation of his appointment.[3] On November 12, George Jay, a Norwich solicitor and his London colleague, Francis Tarrant Fenton, in the company of Pearson, made a second run at the magistrates. Receiving them politely, the magistrates expressed their readiness to admit a solicitor appointed either by Thurtell or his family but throwing up a new obstacle, they now interpreted the resolution of November 8 as barring admission to any second representative, and indeed as forbidding the first gentleman who applied as solicitor to have even a preliminary conversation with Thurtell before he decided to undertake the case. This gloss on the magistrates' regulation was apparently the brainchild of the Reverend Thomas Lloyd, one of the visiting magistrates at Hertford Gaol, who intruded himself more and more into the governance of the famous prisoners. A personal visit by the three solicitors to Lloyd at his home on the evening of November 12 left him adamant. The magistrates' grudging terms left Jay in a dilemma, for he had intended to share responsibility for preparation of the defense with Fenton who could more conveniently travel to Hertford. However, for the moment, he yielded to the magistrates' stubbornness and visited Thurtell alone.[4]

The harassing tactics of the Hertfordshire authorities, it soon appeared, were not exhausted by the exclusion of Fenton. Shortly after the arrival of Jay and Fenton, Charles Pearson was arrested by an officer of Undersheriff Nicholson, on a charge of debt for a bill of exchange. The reporters who hovered around Hertford Gaol learned that it was Pearson's arrest and jailing that had led the magistrates to order immediate exchange of the cells occupied by Thurtell and Hunt. Acting "upon an opinion that it was possible the arrest of Mr. Pearson might be connected with some plan for secret communication with the prisoners," the magistrates had moved Thurtell to preclude any possible access between him and Pearson.[5]

About one o'clock on Saturday afternoon, November 15, Fenton appeared at the magistrates' session at the Hertford Town Hall to make formal application for permission to visit Thurtell. He was received by the Reverend Mr. Lloyd, who coolly informed him that the order limiting access to a single solicitor would not be rescinded. He also referred to "some circumstances of a serious nature" that had come to light since Fenton was last in Hertford, making it necessary that Fenton's character be strictly investigated. Lloyd then went upstairs to confer with the magistrates and kept Fenton cooling his heels for half an hour in the lobby. When he was at last summoned by the magistrates, Fenton was told that they would enforce the rule that only one adviser could be admitted. Upon his insisting that he also be informed of the question that had arisen concerning his character, Lloyd replied for his colleagues: was it not a fact that since 1821 he was indebted to Mr. Nicholson, in the amount of eleven shillings and sixpence, for fees as undersheriff? Fenton, swallowing his outrage over this trivial charge, explained that in that year he had sent down a writ to Nicholson to be executed not as undersheriff but as solicitor of Hertford; Nicholson had only recently sent him a bill for the trifling amount which would have been regularly paid by one of his clerks if presented in person. He added that, on the first day he had come to Hertford he had called on Nicholson to offer bail for Charles Pearson and had taken the occasion to remind him of his paltry debt; Nicholson professed to have no recollection of it but Fenton had immediately paid it.[6]

Most of the magistrates seemed perfectly satisfied with this explanation, but not the Reverend Mr. Lloyd, who was now off on a new trail. How was it that Fenton had offered to put in bail for Pearson, he asked. Fenton said he had done so for the best of all reasons, that he thought Pearson if at liberty could be of service to him in Thurtell's defense. Wondering at the magistrates' proclivities to find conspiracies wherever they looked, he alluded "to the inconsistency of altering the rooms of the prisoners upon any supposition of his being concerned in a collusive arrest to place Mr. Pearson in the gaol, when he had instantly offered this undertaking for his release, and could only want his assistance while at large." One of the magistrates mustered the defensive remark that "they could not be too cautious."[7]

On November 19 the *Times* reported that the rigorous confinement of the prisoners and most particularly the refusal to admit Fenton had created controversy among the county magistrates and that the storm center was the Reverend Mr. Lloyd, who was the most zealous in enforcing restrictive regulations. Yet despite his ardor for isolating the prisoners from the outside world, Lloyd himself spent several hours each day in the jail in constant communication with the three men. (Moreover, Lloyd's quarantine failed to prevent the indefatigable Barber Beaumont from meeting with the prisoners and obtaining a statement from Hunt in support of the motion for a new trial in the fire insurance case.) The *Times* noted a possibility that a change of policy was in the wind, reporting that on two occasions when the treatment of the prisoners was recently discussed at meetings of the magistrates, Lloyd had carried his position by a majority of one. The greatest danger posed by the exclusion of advisers was, in the *Times*'s view, the "excitement of a sympathy which does not belong to the case."[8]

In an accompanying editorial the *Times* subjected the Reverend Mr. Lloyd's conduct to even closer scrutiny. Citing information that the magistrates who had visiting power at Hertford Gaol had relinquished their rights with regard to Weare's accused murderers, the *Times* complained that not only was this a neglect of their duty but that Lloyd had taken upon himself "ten times more of those attributes than could have been, or ought to have been, exercised at all." Although the public could be expected to be little moved by feelings of humanity for the wretched men charged with the murder of Weare, "yet if they are to suffer, they should suffer by the same rules as other malefactors." The *Times* urged that Lloyd should be examined as to the conversations he had had with the prisoners and particularly Thurtell, and it should be determined whether these conferences were secret or before witnesses. The magistrate should be called upon to explain by what law he required Thurtell to choose once and forever his solicitor for defense of his life. "This much is certain," the editorial concluded, "that in the whole history of the English criminal law, there never were men placed in such a situation as these men, Thurtell and his associates."[9]

On the same day Thurtell's lawyers obtained a writ of mandamus from the Court of King's Bench ordering the Hertford magistrates to grant Fenton access to his client Thurtell. The *Times* was jubilant, commenting that the proceedings "on Lloyd, a clergyman's impeding Thurtell's course of defense, will be read with extreme interest, as well as the affidavit on the subject," and noting that the other magistrates were apparently not concerned in "this absurd act," and that Lloyd, "though actually a Justice of the Peace, violates all decorum and feeling, not by visiting the prison only, as the law would enjoin, but by almost living in it." The *Times* pointed out that no similar application for admission of legal advisers had ever been found necessary, not even for such traitors as Arthur Thistlewood, the Cato Street conspirator, or Colonel Edward Marcus Despard. Instead, "it was reserved for the present day to exhibit this new prodigy, of an accused man being obliged to demand the interference of the Court of King's Bench, in order that he may obtain the ear of his solicitor before trial on his life or death." The *Weekly Dispatch* drew a more partisan conclusion—that, as it had endeavored to point out on former occasions, it was an absurdity to allow clergymen to hold commissions as justices of the peace. "They are a set of men wholly unfit for the exercise of civil power: they are in general not only ignorant of the law of the land; but certain habits of Spiritual domination lead them to think that a sort of passive obedience must be yielded to whatever mandates their caprice, their conceit and self-importance may dictate."[10]

On November 25 the *Times* published a narrative that the embattled Lloyd had composed to justify his conduct in the case. On Friday morning, October 31, the day after Thurtell was brought to Hertford Gaol, Lloyd had immediately offered his services to him and he paid similar visits to Probert and Hunt on Sunday after

they had been committed as accessories. He gave each of the prisoners religious books with instructive passages marked. It was on
November 5 that Lloyd's concerns left the spiritual domain. On
that day, while he was visiting the prison with High Sheriff Robert
Sutton, a letter "of considerable importance" arrived addressed to
Hunt; the letter was delivered by Prison Governor Wilson to Lloyd,
who felt he must detain it. Although he would not reveal its contents in the narrative, Lloyd regarded it as so significant that on
November 6 he went to London and showed the letter to Home
Secretary Sir Robert Peel and other officials.[11] The mysterious
letter was presumably one of the origins of Lloyd's advocacy of
tight surveillance of the prisoners.

The clergyman asserted that as early as November 7 he advised
the prisoners to procure professional advice. Thurtell strongly
preferred Charles Pearson but did not think that he would be
available for the trial; he also mentioned George Jay of Norwich
whom he knew as a friend of his family and believed would come if
asked. Lloyd recommended that he write to Jay and understood
that he in fact had already written once before. On November 8
Lloyd attended the meeting of the county magistrates, explained
the nature of the letter to Hunt and all the steps that he had taken.
It was after hearing his report that the magistrates unanimously
adopted the order restricting access. He had been faithful and
evenhanded in carrying out this order, Lloyd claimed; Barber
Beaumont had obtained admission to the prison from another
magistrate without his knowledge.[12]

Lloyd maintained that he continued to assume that Thurtell had
engaged Jay. On November 10, during a visit to Thurtell, he expressed regret over the fact that the prisoner's money had run out
and that he and Probert were reduced to the minimum prison al-
lowance; he even offered to pay for their further support out of
his own pocket. Thurtell thanked him and subsequently told him
that he expected Jay to arrive at any hour. Then, on the evening of
November 12, Jay, Fenton, and Pearson had called on him at dinner and sought admission to Thurtell; he told them that he had no
power to alter the magistrates' order but agreed to meet them at
the prison on the following morning. He proceeded to the jail as
arranged and told Thurtell that the three gentlemen were in town

but that he must select one as his solicitor. Thurtell responded that he greatly desired to see Pearson because his knowledge of London would be valuable to the defense and his cleverness would be helpful in arranging what he had to say at trial. However, the prisoner again expressed his belief that Pearson could not attend the trial and said that, under the circumstances, he would select Jay. Lloyd maintained that on that occasion Thurtell declined seeing Fenton since he did not know him. The clergyman had accordingly refused Fenton admission but brought Jay to Thurtell, affording them every facility of privacy and writing materials. It was during their three-hour conference that Lloyd first heard that Pearson either had been or was about to be arrested, and it was this information that led him to make arrangements to change the cells of Hunt and Thurtell. When Jay left, Lloyd told him that he would have the same access to Thurtell when he returned. The minister insisted that Jay was subsequently informed that Thurtell absolutely declined to see Fenton, and that he himself had reason to know that up to the hour of the mandamus Thurtell was adamant in his objection to the second solicitor.[13]

Unpublished correspondence in the archives of the Public Record Office confirms that the Reverend Mr. Lloyd's conduct, however misguided, was in good faith. In a letter written on the occasion of Pearson's arrest, Lloyd suggested "the propriety of having one or two trustworthy Bow Street officers (if they can be found) down here for the present, for I am informed that at this moment there are some extremely suspicious looking persons in the town."[14] The genuineness of his fear of the prisoners' outside allies is also demonstrated by his delivery to higher authorities, presumably at the Home Office, of a true copy of a rather innocuous letter sent by Thurtell to his former barmaid Mrs. Walker. For what it reveals not only of Lloyd's terrors but of Thurtell's prison mood (and his abominable spelling), the letter merits reproduction in full:

> I wish you to go as far as Mr. Cozens of Kensington & ask him for Mr. Phillips speach which belonged to me—and wil be oblidged if you will pack it up with all the things you have of mine & send them to me. You will hear in Pickadilly were there is a Coach start for his Place. I wish you to write me by return of Post & let me know were my Brother Tom is—if you should see him tell him I am quite whell & expect my attorney from

Norwich tomorrow. I had a letter from him this morning—I have seen
no one but Mr. Beaumont since I have been here. Mr. Probert has not
even heard from any of his family since his confinement here. We are
both without money. I have wrote twice to Mr. Cozens & Mr. Probert has
also wrote but we have not even received an answer. We shall get over all
our enemies. Our tryal comes on in the beginning of next month when I
have no doubt truth & justice will obtain for us a complete triumph over
our enemies. Will you go to the Cock & see if you can get one of our
printed books against Mr. Beaumont as I wish particular to have one. I
understand my air gun is at Bow Street. Let me know who took it. If you
should see Annison remember me to him likewise to your husband and
all enquiring friends. God bless you Mrs. Walker.

    I am yours faithfully
        John Thurtell

N.B. you have no occasion to say much in your letter as it will be read
before I have it. I hope Annison is at home with his whife. You will not
mention to anyone but my friends that you have heard from me. Mr.
Noyes has behaved very ill to poor Mr. Probert he is very low spirited. If
you can manage to send me a little snuff No. 37 your husband know
were I get it & I will send you the money for it by Mr. Jay.

In his note forwarding Thurtell's letter to an unnamed official, the
Reverend Mr. Lloyd noted that, while it "otherwise perhaps would
have been immaterial," he felt it his duty to bring the communication to the official's attention since he was "not aware that Annison
who is mentioned in it has ever been named in the inquiry."[15] It
turned out that poor Annison was only the Thurtells' porter.

    The Public Record Office files show that, as in the instance just
cited, Lloyd regularly reported to higher government officials the
steps he took to restrict access to the prisoners by their advisers or
other outsiders. Therefore, though the newspapers were quick to
blame him for excess of zeal, it seems that some of the responsibility for Fenton's exclusion must, in fairness, likely be attributed to
Home Secretary Sir Robert Peel or his administrative circle.

    There was, however, at least one additional motive for the strict
isolation of the prisoners that escaped the prying eyes of the journalists: the Reverend Mr. Lloyd was playing detective as well as
jailer. One of his letters to the higher-placed official quoted Jay as
indicating his intention, at the suggestion of Thurtell's father, to
persuade Jack to acknowledge his guilt and to throw such light on

the gambling transactions in which he was involved "as may tend, if not to extirpate, at least to crush for the present those dens of vice which abound in the metropolis." Jay had further hinted that Thurtell could incriminate "other persons than those who are known to be implicated in the murder."[16] Lloyd also relayed Thurtell's comment to a jailer that a gambling house was about to be established in Spring Gardens (Rexworthy's neighborhood) "& that it is owing to the large sums of hush money which is paid to the officers that more discoveries respecting the gaming houses & gambling transactions are not made." With respect to the latter revelation Lloyd commented, "By using a proper precaution I think it is not improbable that I shall be able to get pretty correct information upon these points."[17] It would seem clear from this correspondence that the Reverend Mr. Lloyd, through his incessant visits to the prisoners and his restriction of outside influence, hoped to obtain valuable admissions with respect to underworld involvement in the Weare murder or corruption of police by London gambling interests. In the enthusiasm of his quest, however, he came close to forgetting that his prisoners were on trial for their lives.

Chapter Nine

THE FAIRNESS OF
MR. JUSTICE PARK

The court order ending the Hertfordshire magistrates' restriction of Thurtell's consultation with his solicitors by no means spelled the end of his troubles with the local authorities. When High Sheriff Sutton paid a visit to Hertford Gaol on November 29, Thurtell was glad to see him; he told the sheriff that his solicitor Fenton on the previous Saturday had successfully resisted an attempt to exhibit him to possible witnesses, and he was surprised that he had in fact been compelled to submit to such an examination yesterday. Sutton apologized, telling Thurtell that he would immediately present his complaint to the magistrates and would personally recommend that nothing further be done that would distract the prisoner's attention from preparation of his defense during the week remaining before the assizes. At their town hall meeting that day the magistrates concurred in Sutton's opinion. According to the *Times,* the witness confronted with Thurtell had been the coachman Kay who had picked up Weare on the night of the murder. The authorities explained to reporters rather lamely that their object was not to have the coachman identify Thurtell as the person who assisted Weare from the coach "but to see, if circumstances might not render it necessary to take fresh depositions, of which the prisoner ought to apprised." Unimpressed, the *Times* pointed out that the magistrates were ignorant of the fact that the dress Thurtell was wearing in the prison had been frequently described in the newspapers and the coachman might thereby have been induced to a recollection that otherwise might not have been aroused. In fact, Kay had not read the newspaper description but the very distinction in attire between Thurtell and the magistrates who accompanied him into the yard for the confrontation caught his attention at once. Still, the honest Kay could not say that he recognized Thurtell.[1]

On Thursday, December 4, 1823, the Hertford Assizes opened with age-old ceremony. At nine o'clock that morning High Sheriff Robert Sutton, attended by the Reverend Thomas Lloyd, twenty liveried javelin men on horseback, and two trumpeters, set out from the town to meet the two assize judges, Mr. Justice Park and Mr. Justice George Holroyd, on their way from the home of the earl of Verulam, the lord lieutenant of the county, where they had dined and slept.[2] Sir James Alan Park, who had already formed a low opinion of John Thurtell as a witness in the County Fire Office trial over which he had presided, was to play the key judicial role in the murder case. Serjeant Ballantine has written of him: "He is not unworthy of being remembered as a lawyer of the old school, with prejudices of the oldest. I am not sure whether he wore a pig-tail; he ought to have if he did not. He was singularly like his Majesty George the Third, a fact of which he was proud. He was called 'St. James's Park,' to distinguish him from the judge of the same name, who was called 'Green Park.'"[3] Some of his superficial courtroom traits appear to have been unattractive: his truckling to the nobility, unctuous false modesty, and irritability in exchanges with counsel. Eric Watson gives an amusing instance of the ludicrous positions into which the judge was apt to fall because of a lack of worldliness and his implacable pursuit of the trivial:

> Once, examining a little girl on the *voir dire* to see if she had the capacity to give evidence, he sought to test her knowledge of right and wrong in the customary manner with reference to the awful truths of Christian eschatology and the duty of every good child to offer up its nightly orisons. "What do you do, my little maid," he kindly asked, beaming at her with all the animation of his lively countenance, "just before you get into bed?" Confusion reigned in the maiden's cheeks. A more worldly-wise man would here have put a "leading question." Sir Alan merely repeated his, and got the answer that everyone but himself was expecting [that she took off her clothes and put on her nightcap].[4]

But even those contemporaries who treasured Park's *faux pas* recognized that the judge possessed qualities that outweighed the quirks of his personality—an abiding sense of fairness and a respect for his judicial duties.

At ten o'clock the judges and their retinue entered the Hertford Town Hall. After Mr. Knapp, the clerk of the arraigns, opened the assizes, Mr. Justice Park adjourned the court for an hour and a half so that the judges could attend services at the Church of All Saints. The judges then returned to the town hall and Park took his seat in the Crown Court. Spaces on each side of the judge and opposite the petit jury box were filled by the lord lieutenant and other nobility, the magistrates, and several of the most distinguished county residents. To the left of the bar of the court a large box had been arranged for the reporters while the center was kept free for the peace officers and the witnesses. The space between the courtroom and the staircase leading to the grand jury room had been fitted with seats and warmed with stoves so that the witnesses could wait there until needed. Mr. Justice Park turned to address the grand jury panel whose foreman was William Lamb, the future Lord Melbourne. In his opening words he appeared to be playing to his noble audience. "The present appearance of the gentlemen whom I am now addressing," he said, "satisfies me that his Majesty's wisdom in issuing these commissions will never be frustrated, as frustrated it would undoubtedly be, if ever the time should come when the administration of justice was not attended by gentlemen of the first dignity, rank, and respectability, because such an event could not but lessen the administration of justice in the eyes of the common people of England."[5]

The judge regretted the great number of crimes of various description that were set down for trial. For the most part they were offenses of weekly or daily occurrence, but there was one case among them that required comment, for as Mr. Justice Park explained with his customary emphatic understatement, "I understand it has made considerable noise in the world." He self-righteously assured the courtroom that he had "most cautiously abstained from reading one single word which has appeared in any of the public prints" and that, "as far as any previous opinion of the case is concerned, a more impartial person than myself never entered a Court of Justice." He told the grand jury that the language of reproach was never pleasant to him, was in fact hostile to his feelings, and he

begged not to be understood as throwing any personal reflection
on the conduct of any gentlemen; yet he was bound to say that the
fault for the pretrial publications "certainly originated in the magistrates' allowing any person whatever to enter their private room
during the investigation of the matter, and to take notes of the
case." Park drew a strong distinction between the investigative and
judicial powers of the magistrate. When a magistrate was acting in
a trial, he was liable like all other judges to be judged by the public.
When, however, a magistrate was inquiring into a crime, Mr. Justice Park maintained, the proposition that all depositions should
be published "cannot be listened to for a single moment." He explained that the statute of Philip and Mary, which had been passed
more than 250 years before, required all examinations in felony
cases to be taken before magistrates in writing and transmitted by
them to the judges; the depositions were subject to inspection by
the prosecution and the judges but not by the accused parties and
their advisers. The result of such pretrial publication of the evidence as had occurred in the present case is that "the accused
party knows all that will be produced against him at his trial, and
the object of sending the depositions to the judges is in this manner entirely defeated." To confirm the seriousness with which he
viewed such publication, Park ventured the opinion that pretrial
publication of deposition testimony was a high crime and misdemeanor, punishable by fine and imprisonment. Having lashed the
newsmen, Park could not withhold a flick of the whip at the reading public: "There seems to be a pruriency, and an appetite for
news among the people of this country, such as characterised the
Athenians of old, who, as the Grecian historians inform us, were
always desirous of reading something new."[6]

By beginning his attack on the press along these lines, the judge
no doubt intended to express his firm belief that the primary victim of the newspapers' disclosures was the Crown, which had been
deprived of its right under the antique statute to have the magistrates gather evidence in secret in their intended roles as inquisi-
tors. This ground of Park's attack on pretrial publicity became ob-
solete fifteen years later, when Parliament adopted a new law that
abolished the secrecy of preliminary hearings, gave the defense a
right of cross-examination in those proceedings and changed the

magistrates' role from investigative to judicial.[7] However, the second basis of Park's criticism has not weakened with time: he also told the grand jury that he regretted the publication as possibly harmful to the defendants. In particular, he deplored the printing of the confession of "one of the prisoners," observing that "a confession is, of all things, that of which it is impossible to say, until the period of trial, whether it be or be not admissible in evidence; and nothing, therefore, could be more unadvised, independently of its illegality, than its premature publication." Turning then to the Weare murder, he described it as "a most awful crime, under whatever circumstances it may have been committed, but which appears to have been committed in this case under circumstances of peculiar atrocity." He extolled the virtues of circumstantial evidence and also said that Mrs. Probert would give evidence before the grand jury; he advised the panel that if all three defendants were indicted, Mrs. Probert could not be called as a witness either to convict her husband or to exculpate him.[8]

The grand jury retired and first considered some minor bills of indictment. At about ten minutes before three o'clock Mr. Broderick, one of the counsel for the prosecution in the Weare murder case, appeared before Mr. Justice Park. Broderick gave promise of becoming one of the future leaders of the bar, a promise that was to be cheated by ill health; he was described by Serjeant Ballantine's father as "a most acute and learned lawyer."[9] The barrister asked Mr. Justice Park for an order authorizing him to bring Probert, presently in the custody of the Hertford prison governor, before the grand jury to give evidence concerning Weare's murder; in short he was requesting that Probert be granted immunity from prosecution in return for his appearance as a Crown witness. Park responded to Broderick's application in his characteristic fawning manner: he did not mean to say anything that could be interpreted as flattery, but he was sure that if Mr. Broderick did not think the application essential to the purposes of justice, he would not have made it. When Broderick confirmed the importance of the motion, the judge granted the order of immunity.[10]

The news that Probert was testifying before the grand jury caused great excitement in Hertford. Edward Herbert, a journalist covering the trial for *London Magazine,* vividly evokes the scene:

I hastened to the Town Hall (a poor pinched-up building, scarcely big enough to try a well-grown petty-larceny in) and found there the usual assize scene; a huddled cold crowd on a dim stone staircase,—a few men of authority, with their staves and longcoats, thence called javelin men; patient oglers of hard-hearted doors, red cloaks, plush breeches and velveteen jackets—and with all these the low hum of country curiosity!

My friend [a lawyer] exclaimed—"There—there goes Probert!" . . . And I saw an unwieldy bulk of a man sauntering fearlessly along (he was now safe!) and sullenly proceeding to descend the stairs. I rushed to the balustrade—and saw this man, who had seen all! go step by step quietly down,—having just sealed the fate of his vicious associates (but his associates still). . . . He was dressed in black, and had gloves on:—But through all these, I saw the creature of Gill's Hill Lane—I saw the miscreant that had held the lantern to the rifled pocket, and the gashed throat,—and I shuddered as I turned away from the staircase vision![11]

When the grand jurors finished their deliberations at nine o'clock that evening, they were brought back to the judge's lodging, where their foreman reported that they had returned a true bill against both the prisoners. In expectation of the trial that was scheduled to begin the next day, Hertford did not sleep that night. Herbert has described the passing of the tense hours until dawn: "The buzz of conversation, amidst all and in all places, was a low murmur, but of 'Thurtell'—'Miss Noyes'—'Probert'—'Mrs. Probert'—and 'Hunt'. You heard one of these names from a window—or it came from under a gateway, or over a wall,—or from a post,—or it met you at a corner! these vice-creatures were on all lips—and in no hour betwixt the evening and the morning was their infamy neglected to be tolled upon the night!"[12]

Long before daybreak, all the approaches to Hertford were thronged with horses and carriages all converging on the town hall, which was filled shortly after the doors opened at 7:30. A half hour later a trumpet announced the entry of Mr. Justice Park. Immediately asserting mastery over the crowd, he gave directions that no one would be permitted to stand in the galleries and that the prisoners would not be called until the courtroom was perfectly quiet. The silence won by the judge's words was soon broken by the clanking of chains as the prisoners were led into the courtroom. Hunt was placed on the right of the dock, Thurtell on the left, and their common adversary Probert between them. All were respectably dressed, Hunt and Probert in rather worn black, and Thurtell in a blue coat, with fawn colored trousers and waistcoat. The *Times* found Hunt's general appearance unpromising, his face of little expression with a nearly straight profile, and stature of middling height with slender proportions. Probert, plump cheeked and corpulent, had clear but expressionless eyes, surrounded by features that seemed sensual. Thurtell's appearance seemed the most genteel; his frame was well-knit, his countenance bold and his auburn hair combed backwards. His projecting brows, receding forehead and air of martial firmness made a rather agreeable impression on the reporter who noted, however, that "the worst part of his face is his mouth, which has a very obstinate and rather stupid expression." [13]

The case had attracted a constellation of legal talent. For the prosecution appeared John (later Baron) Gurney and William (later Baron) Bolland, assisted by Mr. Broderick. Gurney, the son and brother of two famous shorthand reporters, for many years prior to his elevation to the Court of Exchequer had a very successful practice as king's counsel in the Court of King's Bench. Acute and well versed in law, he was known for his bitter sarcasm and a rapid delivery, so accurate that he "seldom had to recall a word for the purpose of substituting a better." The good-natured and humorous Bolland had served as city pleader for the City of London and had developed an extensive practice at the Old Bailey. Thurtell was defended by three distinguished barristers, Thomas (later Serjeant) Andrews, Thomas Joshua (later Baron) Platt, and Joseph Chitty. Andrews, a prominent practitioner at the Old Bailey, in one respect resembled his client: his hot temper sometimes got the better of him. On one occasion, he actually came to blows with his archrival Mr. Adolphus, and it is recorded by James Grant in his *The Bench and the Bar* (1838) that "in that instance a pugilistic demonstration on one side was resented by the application of an umbrella on the other." Andrews was a man of athletic proportions, with a full face and "a good deal of that expression which will be understood by the term John Bull-ish." He had a fine sonorous voice, whose effect was increased by great fluency and readiness of expression. His colleague Platt was a plain speaker, whose addresses gained much from telling facial expressions; he was not a great legal scholar and appeared at his best when he could take "a common sense view of a case." Chitty, who had already won the King's Bench orders prohibiting performances of *The Gamblers* and terminating the restrictions on Thurtell's consultation with his solicitors, was expected to argue points of law that arose in the course of the trial. In behalf of Hunt appeared Frederick Thesiger (later Lord Chelmsford), who concealed his legal shortcomings by a showy manner, an animated and distinct delivery, and extreme ardor for his client's interests. Not only his hands and arms but his whole body participated in his arguments; he seemed on occasion to stretch himself "at least three or four inches beyond his usual altitude, by way of giving greater effect to particular parts of his speeches." Probert's counsel were the famous Irish lawyer and orator Charles Phillips, who had been admitted to the English bar in 1821, and Charles Frederick Williams. Phillips, in light of the grant of immunity to his client, was to have only a brief role in the case, but the spectators singled him out with special interest, having read of Thurtell's plan to base his defense on Phillips' published speeches.[14]

The day's proceedings began with the reading of a two-count indictment. The first count charged that Thurtell with a certain pistol of the value of ten shillings, struck and penetrated the left side of Weare's head and gave him a mortal fracture of the depth of two inches and of the width of one inch, and that Hunt before the murder was committed by Thurtell "did stir up and move, abet, procure, command, hire, counsel and direct" him to kill Weare. The second count differed only in charging that the murder was committed by the use of a knife of the value of sixpence to strike, cut, and penetrate the left side of Weare's neck, inflicting a mortal wound of the depth and width of one inch and the length of two inches. Thurtell and Hunt pleaded not guilty to the indictment; then they and Probert were charged under the coroner's inquisition, Thurtell with murder and the others as accessories before the fact. All three men pleaded not guilty.

Now the audience, bursting with impatience for the trial to begin, received a bitter disappointment: Andrews moved the court for permission to present an affidavit, sworn by Thurtell's solicitors and Fenton's clerk, in support of an application for the postponement of the trial. Mr. Justice Park ruled that the affidavit, with bulky exhibits attached, would be received. As the clerk Knapp proceeded to read the affidavit, it soon became clear to listeners that two grounds were put forward for the delay: interference by the Hertfordshire magistrates with Thurtell's access to his professional advisers, and prejudicial pretrial publicity. Some additional insight into the state of mind that had justified the barring of Fenton from Hertford Gaol was provided by his assertion in the affidavit that Undersheriff Nicholson had told him that in his view any professional man should decline to accept the responsibility to defend "John Thurtell the murderer" and that he was so satisfied of the guilt of the three prisoners "that he should not complain if they were hanged without trial."[15]

When Knapp began to read the portion on the affidavit that dealt with prejudicial publications, Mr. Justice Park stopped him. He was ignorant, he said, of the contents of the remaining part of the affidavit, but it appeared that quotations from the offending newspaper publications were about to be read. He raised the question whether or not the very course Thurtell's counsel were about to pursue "was not likely to aggravate the very evil of which they complained." He observed sanctimoniously: "I know not what others may have done, but I can most satisfactorily assure you that there is at least one individual in this Court who had not read those statements." He speculated that among the respectable persons impaneled on the jury array there were many who had not seen the articles and who were free of any prejudice. When Andrews assured the judge that he had given careful consideration to this matter with his colleagues and that, with deference to his lordship's recommendation, they felt it their duty to press the reading of the affidavit, Park said testily: "Very well. Proceed with the affidavits, and let the responsibility fall where it ought."

Knapp proceeded to read Fenton's carefully catalogued list of the worst excesses of the *Times* and the *Morning Chronicle*. The affidavit also described his attendance at a performance of *The Gamblers* at the Surrey Theatre on November 17. "The incidents in the said spectacle or entertainment," he stated, "are very similar to, and indeed parallel with, the occurrences in the evidence given before the Coroner on the inquest on the body of the said William

Weare, except that the scenic representation appears to exculpate one of the supposed murderers at the expense of the other two." There was a crowded audience at the performance "who appeared to be much excited, and expressed great and peculiar applause when the officers seized the person who . . . was intended to represent the said John Thurtell." In another section of the affidavit Fenton's clerk, John Helme, identified copies of the books on the murder that had been published by Joseph Edgerly and by Sherwood and Jones. Helme estimated that upwards of ten thousand copies of the Edgerly book had been sold, five thousand of them in Hertfordshire, and that three thousand copies of the Sherwood and Jones book had been printed and distributed. In each of the books and related advertisements were statements "not upon oath, the plain deduction from which is, that the said John Thurtell . . . was guilty of the murder of which he . . . stands charged" and that he intended to murder Woods and Beaumont and was in other respects a man of infamous character. The affidavits informed the court that orders against further performance of *The Gamblers* and continued distribution of the books had been obtained from the Court of King's Bench. Finally, Thurtell's solicitors identified a copy of an additional book about the crime that they had purchased at Gill's Hill Cottage itself; an advertisement for the publication had been pasted against Probert's stable.

When the affidavit and exhibits were before the court, Andrews addressed Mr. Justice Park:

> In a country . . . where . . . pure administration [of justice] was its glory and its boast; and where it was the admission of every man, that those enlightened Judges who presided in our Courts were wholly free from the suspicion of bias or prejudgment, it was still strange to say, that efforts of the most determined and unceasing character were made to contravene the maxims of the law, and to defeat that calm and dispassionate investigation which that law in its wisdom and its mercy extended to the accused. The effect of such a steadfast and unceasing influence upon public opinion must inevitably be, to create impressions and preconceptions which go to defeat that dispassionate inquiry.

Bowing to Park's complacent view of his own impartiality, Andrews conceded that the mind of a man of the rank and reputation of his lordship could not be subjected to outside influence, yet common experience must satisfy everyone that "from the infirmity of our nature and the inherent curiosity of mankind on questions arising out of such calamities as that for which we are this day convened in this Court, impressions must have been created, through such means, on the minds of the great body of the people." Conceding that it was an acknowledged maxim of British law that justice should be quickly administered, yet "a more paramount claim upon those who administer that justice, is to take care that those who are brought to the bar of criminal justice shall have a fair and dispassionate trial." Andrews reminded the judge of Edmund Burke's observation on the impact of the repetition of lies: "Let a man be told the same story every day of his life for a year, and though he might at first regard it as totally false, he would come at length to believe it."

Thurtell's advocate then referred to a ruling that M. Justice Holroyd, Park's colleague in the present assizes, had made in *King v. Mead* at York, where the judge had recently found it necessary to postpone a trial under similar circumstances. Not so, said Mr. Justice Park, interrupting Andrews; he had discussed the case with his learned brother and had been informed that the facts were quite different. At York, papers had been distributed among the jury at the very moment they were about to go to trial and contained evidence that related to the atrocious crime they were to consider. The populace at the courthouse had also called out: "Make way for the witnesses against William Mead." Unruffled, Andrews argued that he had never been acquainted with a case as strong as the present one, and never recollected a case in which the press had done so much mischief as in this. It could not be expected from the jurors "that when all the society, and all the people around them are in a state of excitement, they should remain free from all bias, and be in a state of calm neutrality."

Andrews was followed by his colleagues Platt and Chitty. Platt argued that it was not enough for the administration of justice that a criminal be punished or an innocent man acquitted, but it was also "of essential importance that the public should be satisfied as to the propriety of the condemnation or acquittal." He noted that on application for the injunctions against publication of the prejudicial book and continuation of the theatrical performances, the

King's Bench had granted the requested orders immediately, ob-viously recognizing that there was cause for serious apprehension by defense counsel. When Chitty rose to present other considera-tions supporting a postponement, he found himself often at swords' points with the judge. He noted at the outset that in view of the great excitement of the public mind, it was difficult to say "not when the effects of the poison would cease to operate, but to what limits it had now extended." He proceeded to point out that En-glish law provided that juries should be taken from a venue near the place of the crime. Mr. Justice Park interrupted him imme-diately, saying that this point told against his own argument. Chitty responded that this no doubt would be so if he were contending that there should be no trial at all, but instead he was only asking a postponement. He cited the case of *King* v. *Fleet* where an injunc-tion had been granted against a printer for publishing the report of a coroner's inquest; in that case it had not even been objected that the report was unfair, for indeed it had been accompanied with a comment that juries should not allow their minds to be bi-ased by evidence that was wholly ex parte; still, the publication had been declared illegal. When Park impatiently interrupted him to note that he had already instructed the grand jury that publishing pretrial evidence was punishable by fine and imprisonment, Chitty observed that this remedy would not remove the influence to which the minds of the jury had been exposed. In fact, in *King* v. *Jolliffe*, defense counsel had himself applied for postponement when it was proved that the defendant had circulated three printed papers in which he had endeavored to prejudice the case.

But what good would a postponement do here? the judge in-quired. If the trial were now postponed, would he not hear the same objections again and be obliged to choose a jury from the same neighborhood who would still be under an improper bias? Chitty said that he would leave the issue to the justice of the jurors themselves; he was sure that they would desire a postponement of a month or longer so that they would not hear so important a case with prejudiced minds. He suggested that "the very thought might endanger the course of justice in another way; and the jury might, under the influence of fearing to do wrong, pronounce an acquit-tal." He noted that he himself had been counsel in the trial of

Mead at York; he quoted the decision of Mr. Justice Holroyd in that case and the arguments with which he had supported it to show that the prejudicial statements made on the eve of trial were sufficient grounds for a change of venue. He concluded by asking Park to postpone the trial until the excitement died down. In the meantime the proceedings in the King's Bench would teach the public press to stay within the due limits of public order.

Replying for the Crown, Gurney staked out lofty ground: he was not interested in the success or failure of the defense motion but appeared as counsel for none of the parties but for his country. After rejecting the contention that the actions of the Hertford-shire magistrates had hampered preparation of the defense, he turned quickly to the matter of pretrial publicity. He agreed with defense counsel as to the nature of the publications, for he had read them with the greatest pain, knowing that it was impossible that such productions "could issue from the public press without creating an effervescence in the public mind which might possibly defeat justice, but which, beyond all doubt, must render its admin-istration less satisfactory than it would have otherwise been. There was no doubt that publication of the depositions before coroners and especially before magistrates was a high misdemeanor, and he blushed for his country that an English audience had witnessed a dramatic entertainment founded on the murder and "wondered that the audience had not risen from their seats with one accord, and driven the actors indignantly from the stage." However, as he came to the end of his argument, he left room for the judge to deny the postponement, noting that the last publication cited in the affidavit was November 16 and that the judge could not offi-cially know whether any subsequent publications had occurred.

Andrews, in reply, expressed gratification that Gurney had sup-ported his arguments. If any man doubted that the prejudice ex-cited by the publications survived to that moment, "let him look at the crowds which surrounded the doors, and overflowed the Court, obstructing those whose duty it was to assist in the administration of public justice." He asked for a trial delay of three or four months.

As Mr. Justice Park began to announce his opinion on the appli-cation, the defense cannot have taken heart from his first words. He stated flatly that the contention that sufficient time had not been afforded to the prisoners for preparation of their defense could not be sustained; much more time had elapsed than was generally granted to prisoners. In approaching the subject of publicity, the court bowled down all the cases cited by the defense like tenpins. *Fleet* was an application against a printer for having violated the law by his publication; *Jolliffe* was a case in which the trial had been postponed on the motion of the prosecutor, Park said, as a result of attempts made to influence the minds of the jury against the prosecutor. In *King* v. *Mead*, the prosecution, which was brought against an excise officer and defended by the government, was put off as a result of the prosecutor's publication of statements charging the government with nefarious conduct and declaring that the attorney general was in league with the defendant and that the judges had no disposition to do justice. After sweeping aside these precedents cited by Thurtell's counsel, Park indicated that he thought just as little of their tactics. He felt compelled to say "without meaning offense to any particular individual" that it did not seem a very wise measure, if the trial were to proceed, to have brought all the affidavit exhibits "under the review of the jury." He added the astounding appraisal that the affidavit had given him a much greater insight into the case than the pretrial depositions that it had been his duty to read. His mind was unhappily divided on the issue of postponement. He feared that the "Palladium of English Liberty" would be endangered if such a licentious pruriency existed in the public to run after something new and if publications of enormous circulation were to poison the sources of justice whenever their editors thought fit. On the other hand, the prosecution, which had summoned fifty-five witnesses, would incur enormous expense in the event of postponement. Mr. Justice Park's sense of justice resolved the issue. "Still," he said, "God forbid, that any consideration of expense, or any additional difficulty and labour which may be imposed on those who administer the justice of the country, should induce me to refuse an application the denial of which might operate with undue severity in so important an issue as that which affects the lives of the men who sit there before me." What he lamented most was the necessity of doing today what his brother Holroyd had lately been obliged to do in

York. Justice had been impeded and retarded, and he earnestly hoped that the gentlemen of the press who had erred on this occasion, though without any bad intention, "will bethink them of the cruelty committed by such conduct, and of the deep injury they may inflict on society by doing that which has a tendency to pollute and corrupt the fountains of public justice." Park said that though he had no appetite to try the case, he did not want to throw the burden on others by deferring it to the Lent assizes when, in any event, the same prejudices might exist; therefore, he adjourned the trial to Tuesday, January 6, 1824.

As might have been expected, Mr. Justice Park's postponement of the trial, and his sharp attack on pretrial publicity, was not greeted with universal warmth in the press. The *Weekly Dispatch* published a harsh commentary: "When the Judges of the country, in the most solemn manner promulgate doctrines which not only are inconsistent with our notions of common sense and public utility, but which convey an indirect attack upon the liberty of the press, it becomes the imperative duty of the press to defend itself, and at the same time to maintain the right of giving publicity to all transactions, during all their stages, in which the people of the country feel themselves interested." Mr. Justice Park had not convinced the *Weekly Dispatch* that either the common law or any statute prohibited the publication of pretrial evidence; to the contrary, the newspaper opined that the public was more likely to be misled by misshapen reports when the depositions were not published than when they were. The editorial concluded with an unqualified tribute to the justice of English juries: "We defy any man to produce an instance of an English Jury having ever given an unjust verdict, in consequence of *ex parte* statements previously published respecting the prisoner whom it tried."[16] Another newspaper noted the paradox that juries, although deemed "capable of forming a most correct judgment in cases in which a great body of intricate and conflicting evidence is adduced," had been pronounced by Mr. Justice Park to lack "sufficient understanding to distinguish between any statements they may have read out of Court, and what they hear in Court," and the anomaly that statements unfavorable to defendants might be in universal circulation in a neighborhood without being regarded as prejudicial, while the same statements if published in a newspaper "are injurious to them in the highest degree."[17] Another newspaper, the *Courier,* pointed out the further irony that Fenton, on the night before he presented his affidavit, had given it to the *Times,* which published it on the very morning of the court arguments for trial postponement. The *Courier* expressed the view that if Mr. Justice Park had known of this publication, he would have decided the matter differently.[18]

The *Times,* however, regretted the disposition to blame Mr. Justice Park, when the slightest investigation would prove that the blame lay elsewhere. At an early moment of Andrews' pleading, it noted, the judge had asked defense counsel how long a delay they claimed. On their replying "until the Lent Assizes," he shook his head disapprovingly, but it was clear that he had come into court prepared to grant some postponement. Subsequently, but before Gurney had indicated he would not oppose a delay, a disturbance had arisen in the right-hand gallery, and his lordship had said to one of the disorderly persons, "Should I be obliged to commit you, sir, and then adjourn this Court for a month, you will lie in prison during the whole of that time." The *Times* speculated that a judge of assizes would not take it upon himself to order a special convening of the court for a trial of an individual case "without a previous consultation with the higher powers—that is, with the officers of the Crown, by whom special commissions are directed, and from whom they must emanate." In the opinion of the newspaper, the pretense assigned for the delay was not the real cause; the actual ground of the suspension decided on before the affidavits of prejudicial publicity had been produced "was the novel and lamentable occurrence that gave occasion to the Mandamus," that is, the interference by the Hertfordshire magistrates with Thurtell's access to his solicitors:

> There is not the least doubt in any man's mind, but that had Thurtell and the other two been kept in gaol in the ordinary way, they would in the ordinary way have proceeded to take their trial. . . . But Government very properly considered, that as they had sustained a wrong, more than a strict reparation was due to men in their unhappy circumstances. They had lost, we will say, only three or four days in the prepa-

ration of their defence: Government, therefore, throws them in a whole month in the time allowed before their trial.[19]

Perhaps the most unreserved defense of Mr. Justice Park's postponement of the trial came in the form of an anonymous pamphlet entitled *A Vindication of the Right Honorable Sir James Allan* [*sic*] *Park.* The author began with the proposition that the liberty of the press, though deservedly considered one of the most valuable privileges that the English enjoyed, was, like all liberty, not without bounds. He lamented that mankind in general but John Bull in particular "is an animal of so strange a disposition, that he is ever more ready to lend an ear to those who seek to make him dissatisfied with himself than to those who would do the reverse." Just as there was no lack of "factious democrats, whose sole delight seems to be in kindling the torch of sedition . . . so there have ever been found knaves and fools ready to fan the flame and flock round any standard that bore but the name of 'liberty' of any sort." The most infamous instances of such conduct, the writer urged, had arisen in connection with the Hertfordshire murder, in attacks on the magistrates' proper but vain attempt to suppress the pretrial publication of Hunt's confession and, more recently, on the decision to postpone the trial. No man could have been found more fit for the trial of the case than Mr. Justice Park who was "eminent for benevolence, Christian charity, and compassion" and "anxious to give the unhappy men every possible chance."[20]

The pamphleteer praised Park for having condemned the publication of Hunt's confession in his address to the grand jury and expressed disgust that from that moment to the present the radical press "has teemed with the most virulent abuse, the most insulting irony, and the most indecent ridicule of him, and of the mode in which justice is administered." If anything was wanting to exhibit the conduct of these radicals in its true colors, the author concluded, it was that Hunt's statement had turned out to be far less than a full confession, with the result that "the unhappy man must take his trial as a principal felon, with all the disadvantages of a previously published statement furnished by himself." Far from meriting the abuse that had been heaped upon him, Mr. Justice

Park deserved "the apprehension and gratitude of every well wisher to our matchless Constitution."[21]

In a letter of December 12 John Jekyll, master in chancery, expressed a view of Mr. Justice Park's action that neatly cut through the legal complexities that had been debated in court and in the press: "The postponement of the Hertford trial was not necessary, but perhaps it was politic to sacrifice a little month to popular clamour."[22]

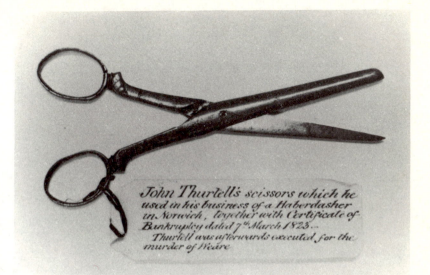

Memorabilia of John Thurtell were sought after and carefully preserved in several English museums. That Norwich considered an artifact as minor as his scissors worth preserving and displaying for over 150 years reveals both the importance of the case and the characteristic British fascination with murder.

Courtesy of the Norwich Public Record Office

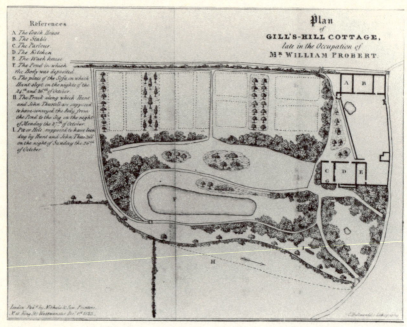

Shortly after the murder, this schematic drawing was published in London.
From George Henry Jones, *Account of the Murder of the Late Mr. William Weare* (London, 1824).

J. D. Harding produced a lithograph of Probert's cottage. The building, which appears to have been ramshackle even then, has long since been torn down.
From George Henry Jones, *Account of the Murder of the Late Mr. William Weare* (London, 1824).

This depiction of the recovery of Weare's body from Hill Slough was published in London in 1824.
From *The Fatal Effects of Gambling Exemplified in the Murder of Wm. Weare . . .* (London, 1824).

In this 1824 lithograph, J. D. Harding depicts the temporary hiding place of Weare's body.
From George Henry Jones, *Account of the Murder of the Late Mr. William Weare* (London, 1824).

A contemporary illustration reconstructs the scene after supper, when Thurtell paid his accomplices.
From the collection of the Aldenham School

This illustration of Weare's burial appeared in London, 1824.
From *The Fatal Effects of Gambling Exemplified in the Murder of Wm. Weare . . .* (London, 1824).

The gig in the narrow, overgrown lane would become a powerful symbol of the murder.
From Pierce Egan, *Trial of John Thurtell and Joseph Hunt* (London, 1824).

Focusing on the head, William Mulready captured John Thurtell's intense watchfulness at the trial.

Mulready's sketch of Joseph Hunt contrasts sharply with the portrait of Thurtell. Here, Mulready takes care to render the clothes of a dandy.

Mulready, like all the illustrators of the day, emphasized William Probert's five o'clock shadow.

The illustration of Thurtell's last moment appeared in London in 1824.

From *The Fatal Effects of Gambling Exemplified in the Murder of Wm. Weare* . . . (London, 1824).

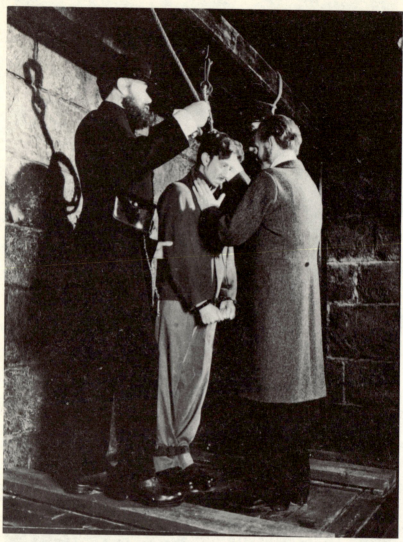

The gallows and drop on which Thurtell died is exhibited to this day in the Chamber of Horrors at Madame Tussaud's, but the prisoner about to be executed on it is Percy Lefroy, a criminal of a later date.

NEW SURREY THEATRE.

RE-PRODUCTION OF THE GAMBLERS!

st 3 Nights of FOX and GEESE!!---Second Week of FOUR INSIDE!!!

THURSDAY, Jan. 15th, 1824, AND DURING THE WEEK, at Half-past Six o'Clock precisely,

The peculiar and interesting Piece of The

GAMBLERS!

OR,

"——Murder, though it have no tongue, will speak
"With most Miraculous Organ."——

WILL CERTAINLY BE PERFORMED.

New Music by Mr. ERSKINE.   The Dresses by Mr. HEAD and Miss LUCAS.   The Properties by Mr. KELLY.

Mordaunt,.................. ⎱   ⎰ ....Mr. H. KEMBLE.
Woodville,................. ⎱ .....THE GAMBLERS..... ⎰ ....Mr. ROWBOTHAM.
Bradshaw,................. ⎱   ⎰ ....Mr. GALLOT.
Frankly,.................. ⎱   ⎰ ....Mr. JULIAN.
rueman, Mr. HENDERSON,   Giles Copsely, Mr. BUCKINGHAM.   Thomas Ruthby, Mr. AULD.   Groom Porter, Mr. SMYTH.
Porter, Mr. BARTLETT.   Hazard Players, Mess. MORGAN, JEFFERSON, PARR.   First Officer, Mr. LLOYD.   Second Officer, Mr. GREGORY.
Alfred and Agnes, Miss VINCENT and Miss M'DONALD.

Amelia,.................. Wife to Mordaunt,..................Mrs. W. CLIFFORD,

In the course of the Piece,

The Identical Horse and Gig,

Alluded to by the Daily Press in the Accounts of

THE LATE MURDER,

TOGETHER WITH THE

ABLE AT WHICH THE PARTY SUPPED,

The SOFA as DESCRIBED to having been SLEPT on,

WITH

ther Household Furniture,

AS PURCHASED AT THE LATE AUCTION.

AMBLERS is Published, and may be had of *Mr. Rowswer*, at the Theatre, and of *John Lowndes*, 36, Bow-st. Covent Garden.

fter which, an entirely New Comic Operetta, in Two Acts, with New and Selected Music, New Scenery, Dresses and Decorations, Called,

Once Thurtell was dead, the theaters rushed to capitalize on the murder.

Not to be outdone by the Surrey, the Royal Coburg put its own production on the boards.

This broadside, which appeared in 1824, resembles the many that were published before and after Thurtell's trial and execution.

Wonderful Discovery!

THE

CONFESSION

OF

W. PROBERT,

Respecting the murder of

Mr. WEARE,

MADE THE NIGHT BEFORE HIS

EXECUTION.

With further particulars, never before known.

This catchpenny pamphlet was published to capitalize on the renewed interest in Probert at the time of his execution. The confession is undoubtedly fictitious.

Hunt's
Farewell to England, Written by Himself.

While on Board the Hulks, at Woolwich.—— Also an account of his Treatment there; with the Particulars of his failing on Saturday Last, on board the Countess of Harcourt Convict ship; for New South Wales.

JOSEPH Hunt [the unfortunate man who was concerned in the celebrated Gill's Hill Lane Murder,] has this day bid adieu to his native shores for life. On his arrival at Woolwich he was placed on board the Justatia, here he underwent what was to him a most unpleasant operation.—His fine curling locks and large whiskers were shorn off, and he was stripped and put into a tub of water, where he was thoroughly scrubbed, He was amazed during the operation but he was still further to be assured of the privations of a Convict. for instead of being permitted to resume his own clothes. he was attired in the costume of the other prisoners—coarse grey jacket waistcoat and trowsers, yellow stockings & worsted night cap He appeared to feel this treatment acutely. he has conversed little ever since On Friday Feb, 18th 1824 he was removed onboard the Countess of Harcourt, Convict Ship, bound to New South Wales, he expressed some surprise that he was not treated with greater tenderness than the rest of the convicts, and even expressed a desire to suffer the fate of his associate Thurtell, rather than the indignities he now suffered. On Saturday last, every preparation being completed, the ship weighed anchor, and sailed for the final destination of the unfortunate man & his wretched companions,

Lines Written by HUNT;

FAREWELL to the land of my birth,
  Old England I bid thee farewell,
I sigh, as from thee I go forth,
  As these tears my heart can best tell,

The sails of the vessel unfurl'd
  Seem impatient to bear me away
As a stain and disgrace to the world
  That my sorrows can ne'er wash away

Farewell to the scenes of my youth,
  Where the days of my infancy past,
But now the sad lessons of truth,
  Rush into my mind at the last

I once was the pride of my sire,
  I once was my poor mother's joy
As they sat by their own cottage fire
  And smiled at the tricks of their boy

I once cheered the board with a song
  With companions so jovial and gay,
Till to Gambling they drew me along,
  I then grew as wicked as they,

The precepts I heard in my youth,
  No longer the trial withstood
I slighted religion and truth
  And was ready to wallow in blood,

How the dark flag of death is unfurl'd
  Too oft has been heard with a tear,
And the deed shall be known to the world,
  When I shall have pressed the cold bier,

So farewell to the land of my birth
  Tho' banish'd I love thee the while
In some far distant part of the earth,
  I shall think of my own native soil

Pitt, printer Wholesale Toy & marble warehouse 6 Great st Andrew street 7 dials

No doubt it was the publisher of the broadside and not Hunt who composed these farewell lines.

Michael Hardwick photographed Gill's Hill Lane in 1960, when it was still a shady, over-grown byway.
Courtesy Michael Hardwick

Chapter Ten

EGAN'S INTERVIEWS

———

It was hardly a surprise that the sports reporter Pierce Egan decided to write an account of the murder trial of Jack Thurtell, a familiar figure from boxing circles, where Egan's journalism reigned supreme. Facing intense competition in press coverage of the case, the enterprising Egan could be counted upon to embellish his edition of the trial with personal touches, and he had already planned to include as a supplement to the customary narrative of the courtroom proceedings his personal reminiscences of Thurtell as a boxing devotee and promoter. Then, on the very day the grand jury was scheduled to receive the Crown's presentation, December 4, Egan revealed his masterstroke: as a promotion for his book, he had arranged for exclusive prison interviews with Thurtell.

At ten o'clock that morning he sent his card in to Thurtell, who immediately returned the answer that he was dressing but would see the reporter in a few minutes. Egan was ushered into the prison office and shortly afterwards Thurtell entered, accompanied by prison governor Wilson, and advanced towards Egan with "a cheerful step and a smiling countenance." The journalist had never seen Jack look better: "In fact, his personal appearance was altogether considerably improved. He was fashionably attired in a blue coat with gilt buttons; a yellow waistcoat, and dark trowsers. His irons, which are rather heavy, were tied up with a silk handkerchief. His shirt and handkerchief white as snow; his pin tastefully displayed; and his collar and wristbands corresponding with the style of the present period."[1]

Thurtell said he was glad to see Egan, and the scribe entered into a conversation that was remarkably airy considering the charge of brutal murder that was to be presented that very day against the prisoner:

E.: You look well, Thurtell; nay, you look as if you had been in training.

T.: . . . I have often read many of your sporting accounts with great pleasure; but I suppose you, like the rest of the press, have lashed me severely.

E.: No, upon my word, I have not written a single line at present about you to the public.

T.: Well, I feel obliged to you. . . . What a parcel of lies the papers have inserted against me; and in addition to which, they say I am sullen and dejected. Do I appear dejected? (laughing)

E.: You have seen the newspapers, then?

T.: Yes, I am now reading the whole of them. It is too bad; the paragraphs are all false. I never committed any serious crime in my life. My friends know it full well. You may believe me, Mr. Wilson, I never was before a magistrate on any charge in my life till the present. I do the crime for which I am charged, indeed! (indignantly).

When Egan interjected that he had seen Weare at the Doncaster horse races, the name of the dead man appeared to make no impression on Thurtell, although his eyes met Egan's for a moment. Seizing on the allusion to Doncaster, Jack launched into another diatribe against the press. That was another direct falsehood, among a hundred others. He had never been at Doncaster in the whole course of his life and had not been in a gambling house for upwards of two years; it was nearly three years ago that he was last at a prizefight, when Sanders fought against Israel Belasco. "I, indeed, kill Weare, and take his money!" he exclaimed. "It is well known that I have been more duped than engaged in duping others."

When Egan said that he supposed Thurtell meant to read a defense speech prepared by his lawyers, Jack cried: "No, no! I shall speak for myself, and I will give some of the papers *pepper* for what they have said falsely against me." He added that he should not be tried at the present time, for he needed three witnesses to complete his defense, but so much had been published to his prejudice that they were afraid to testify. The trial must be postponed, he said, "unless they mean to murder me. But I do not like Judge Park."

The prisoner confirmed Egan's understanding that he wished to have their mutual friend Charles Pearson conduct his defense. He asked the reporter where he had seen Pearson last, and Egan responded that it was, about a month before at Brighton. Thurtell laughed, "At Brighton; aye, he wished me to appear some time since on the stage, as Richard the Third, there." Thurtell's obvious pride in Pearson's offer impressed Egan as quite in character, for Jack had once been regarded as stagestruck. The reporter commented on Jack's histrionic flair: "Thurtell, at one period of his life, was attached to theatricals; and his imitations of Mr. Kean, were considered very far above mediocrity. Thurtell was likewise very fond of reciting sentences that operated upon his mind as fine writing or specimens of eloquence. He would frequently burst forth, in familiar company, like some stagestruck hero, and at the conclusion of his heroics ask his companions, if that speech was not delightful!" But at the present moment, Thurtell had a serious quarrel with the world of the theater, and his own bantering remarks about Pearson's project reminded him suddenly of his grievance. Rising from his seat with great indignation, Thurtell thought of another dramatic presentation that had touched him to the quick: "Could anything be more cruel, unmanly or diabolical, than to publish in a play-bill, at the Surrey Theatre, that the chaise and horse should be exhibited in which it is said I committed the murder? It is a most infamous falsehood; and the press has dealt with me most unfairly."

At this point, Wilson interrupted their conversation to call Thurtell's attention to a letter he had received from the persistent Barber Beaumont, who wanted Thurtell to answer whether he had set his warehouse on fire. Thurtell was indignant that his adversary would send such a letter to him at this moment and, in a display of the verbal violence that he had generally suppressed during his prison days, he said that before he would acknowledge the arson he would "like to break his head into a thousand pieces."

Before he ended the interview Egan asked Thurtell whether he could do anything for him in connection with the trial, and after hesitating briefly, Thurtell replied, "If you should see Mr. Chitty this morning, tell him I wish to consult him respecting my defense."

The publication of the interview in the *Weekly Dispatch* drew a hot denial from Barber Beaumont that he had "obtruded" the alleged letter on a man on the eve of trial for murder, and he declared that Egan's report was "grossly false." In a response on December 13, however, Egan confirmed his story and added the circumstantial details that Wilson during the interview was sitting at the desk near the window about three yards distant from him, that when he called Beaumont's letter to Thurtell's attention the governor took it off the desk and opened it, and that after advising the prisoner of its contents he had folded it up and laid it down again. Despite these supposedly convincing stage directions, Egan offered a partial retraction when the interview was subsequently published in the appendix to his edition of the trial: "'Fair Play' is my motto, and I am anxious upon all occasions to do justice to every individual. Truth demands it. The letter read to Thurtell, by Mr. Wilson, from Barber Beaumont, Esq., was done *prematurely*. On Sunday, December 9th [*sic*], I ascertained, at Hertford gaol, that the intent of Mr. Barber Beaumont's letter was, that it should be read to Thurtell *after* his conviction, and not *before* that circumstance."[2]

On Friday, December 5, about an hour after Mr. Justice Park ordered an adjournment of the trial, Egan returned to Hertford Gaol for a second interview. Thurtell, who saw him crossing the prison yard, left the fireside where he was smoking a pipe and came out of the office to meet him, offering him a pinch of snuff. Egan asked Thurtell how he evaluated his counsel's exertions. Jack thought that Chitty was excellent, but Andrews was fine and his language so good that he carried his point with the judge. Then Thurtell unexpectedly treated Egan to what later generations of journalists would call a scoop. Taking a long roll of manuscript out of his pocket he said: "Here is my defence; I will read a few sentences to you, for your approval." When Egan said he would like to hear it, Thurtell read several separate passages with strong emphasis, observing with an author's pride that certain lines were "beautiful," "fine," or "very good." Encouraged by Egan's show of appreciation, he decided to read the whole speech to him and said that if the reporter could assist him to improve it he would feel greatly obliged as he had "more nerve than ability." Jack proceeded to read the complete defense with great animation, "but when he came to the passages which spoke of the piety of his mother, and the universal good character of his father, his tongue faltered, and he put up his hand to wipe his eyes." Egan "partook of his sorrow, knowing him under circumstances of a very different description."

Thurtell took pains to convince Egan that the fine family sentiments expressed in his speech were sincere. It was not true, as the papers had asserted, that he had not seen his parents for two or three years; seven weeks ago he had dined with them at Norwich at his father's house in the company of Mr. Jay (not knowing then that he would soon call upon his professional services). Although his father had not visited him at Hertford Gaol, his absence was due to their attachment, not estrangement: "I could not see my father," said Thurtell. "My feelings would not permit me: and if he was to come to that gate, I would not see him." He added that he had seen his brother Tom the day before and that that was quite enough for his feelings to undergo. Parenthetically, he wondered what his brother had been saying, for "he has no *nerve*, poor fellow! He has no strength of mind."

Egan asked how Thurtell was bearing up under the strict prison regimen. Jack assured him that his irons did not trouble him and that the only thing he found disagreeable was being locked up as early as five o'clock in the afternoon. Egan was glad to hear he was so well treated and hoped that Thurtell would be able to make it appear "all right" at his trial. Of this, the prisoner had no doubt. If but two of his witnesses would come forward and if they had any nerve at all, he would get through the trial safely. After all, once he had heard that a murder had been committed in the neighborhood, was he such a fool, if he had been guilty, to have had a ball in his pocket and a pistol about? He had been shooting some birds, and the blood on his waistcoat pocket was due to that circumstance only. When Egan expressed again the hope that Thurtell would be able to substantiate his innocence, Jack swore by the Great God Almighty, before whom perhaps he would soon appear, that he did not commit the crime. Then he slipped into a more pessimistic mood: "But ultimately, I suppose, I shall be convicted; and if so, it shall all come out! It is like my *right* and my *left* hand trying to hang me; two such contemptible, cowardly rascals! wretches! Probert and Hunt; a disgrace to mankind." He looked forward to putting questions to Probert at the trial that would "hit him to death."

Why, the man had been tried for sheep stealing, and he could prove it. Worse still, he was utterly devoid of gratitude; Thurtell had lent him money to prevent him from starving in prison, but when he had asked the other day for a little repayment, knowing that Probert had just received five sovereigns, all Probert had sent him was two shillings in a snuff box.

For Mr. Justice Park, Thurtell had only harsh words: "He sticks to the legal thing so much; he will have points for his decision. If the judge attacks me for my attachment to sporting, and hits me too hard, I shall repeat to him, that if I have erred in these things, half of the nobility in the land have been my examples, and some of the most enlightened statesmen in the country have been my companions in them." Egan urged moderation on Thurtell and asked whether he had any message for him to take to Charles Pearson in London. Yes, Jack said, Egan should tell Pearson he would wish to see him but was afraid it was impossible: "Poor Charley Pearson! I should have liked much to have had him for my solicitor, he writes so finely and speaks so well. His language is beautiful; he is a wonderful clever fellow." The interview wound to its conclusion and Egan said goodbye, retiring with his great prize—the premiere of a defense speech that would enthrall England.

With the publication of Egan's second interview, the press, bowing to Mr. Justice Park's stern decision, downplayed the Weare murder case as they waited for the trial at Hertford to begin on January 6. On December 11 the *Times* even found space for another murder case, an "instance of barbarous assassination, which is accompanied by points of aggravation, if possible, still more appalling than those of the unfortunate Mr. Weare's death." The murder victim was James Mumford, the son of a respectable farmer in Essex, who had last been seen walking home one afternoon after being left off by a coach at a public house. About 8:45 P.M. he was found about a mile from his father's house in the middle of the road most inhumanly murdered, his head dreadfully bruised as if by a club or hedge stake so that his features were not recognizable, and his throat was partially cut. The suspect was a man named Parrot, who attended the elder Mumford's horses and had been punished by the murdered man for lopping his father's trees and other trespasses.[3] Brutal as the new crime was, it did not nudge the Thurtell-Hunt case from the public mind.

In fact, the slightest tidbits about the life of the prisoners in Hertford gaol were greedily seized upon. It was related that at Christmas prison governor Wilson had some friends spending the evening with him and that Joe Hunt, to entertain the company, "voluntarily sang a plaintive song." Thurtell, who was in the room beneath Hunt, reportedly joined in the applause for the singer and called out "Joseph" in a friendly tone. When Hunt asked what he wanted, Jack replied, "I will thank you, Joe, to give me my old favourite—you know what I mean." Hunt immediately obliged with the song "The Look Out," or "Old Conwell, the Pilot"; at its conclusion Jack expressed thanks and clapped vigorously. It was a wonderfully sentimental Christmas story but Wilson denied the report indignantly.[4]

Chapter Eleven

A TROUT IN THE MILK

Hertford spent a sleepless night before the trial, and its inns—the Plough, the Half Moon, the Seven Stars, and the Horse and Magpie—"abounded with tippling witnesses, all dressed in their Sunday clothes, and contriving to cut a holiday out of the remnant of the murder." At half past seven on the next morning, January 6, 1824, the London journalist Edward Herbert made his way into court with great difficulty, for order was kept by "great country-constable-bumpkins with long staves, which they handsomely exercised upon those excrescences in which they themselves were deficient, the heads of the curious!" The court was packed, and even at this early hour the windowpanes were steaming from the great heat.[1]

Herbert had heard that Thurtell threatened violence against Hunt and that the humane jailer Wilson had protested in vain about the danger of removing the fetters from the prisoners. At eight o'clock the trumpets of the javelin men "brayed the arrival" of Mr. Justice Park, and shortly after his entry the prisoners were led in. On the bench by the judge's side sat the earl of Verulam, lord lieutenant of the county, and several noblemen and magistrates; other officials filled the jury box. At a table below the judge and to the right of Knapp, the clerk of the arraigns, the lawyers for the parties were in attendance: for the prosecution, barristers Gurney, Bolland, and Broderick; for Thurtell, barristers Andrews, Platt, and Chitty and his two solicitors Jay and Fenton; for Probert, barristers C. F. Williams and Charles Phillips; and for Hunt, barrister Thesiger and solicitor Harmer.

Hunt entered the dock first with Thurtell right behind him. Joe was dressed in black with a white cravat and white handkerchief carefully arranged to give the appearance of a white underwaistcoat. "There was," wrote Herbert,

> a foppery in the adjustment of this part of his dress, which was well seconded by the affected carriage of his head and shoulders, and by the carefully disposed disorder of his hair. It was combed forward over his ears from the back part of his head, and divided nicely on his forehead, so as to allow one lock to lie half-curled upon it. His forehead itself was white, feminine, and unmeaning; indeed his complexion was extremely delicate, and looked more so from the raven blackness of his hair. Nothing could be weaker than his features which were small and regular, but destitute of the least manly expression.

In striking contrast, Thurtell stood by his side, revealed as "the murderer—complete in frame, face, eye, and daring!" He was dressed in a plum-colored frock coat, with a drab waistcoat and gilt buttons and white corded breeches. He wore a black stock fitted stiffly up to the bottom of the cheek and the end of the chin, which pushed forward the flesh of the lower part of his face and gave it "additionally sullen weight." Jack's jaw, Herbert noted,

> was unusually large, muscular, and heavy, and appeared to hang like a load to the head, and to make it drop like the mastiff's jowl. The upper lip was long and large, and the mouth had a severe and dogged appearance. His nose was rather small for such a face, but it was not badly shaped: his eyes too were small and very deep under his protruding forehead, so indeed as to defy you to detect their colour. The forehead was extremely strong, bony, and knotted;—and the eyebrows were forcibly marked though irregular;—that over the right eye being nearly straight, and that on the left turning up to a point so as to give a very painful expression to the whole face. His hair was of a good lightish brown, and not worn after any fashion. . . . His frame was exceedingly well knit and athletic—and if you have ever seen Shelton the prizefighter, you will have a perfect idea of John Thurtell,—even to the power and the stoop of the shoulders.[2]

The oddly paired faces of the two defendants were also captured in the pencil sketches by the Irish-born genre painter William Mulready. Mulready's delicate line does not soften the simian character of Thurtell's lower face or the deadliness of his stare, while the dandified Hunt, eyes cast down, looks capable of venturing a modest opinion on the Romantic poets in a polite salon.

As he waited for the proceedings to begin, Thurtell unwrapped and neatly arranged a bundle of books and papers that he had brought into the dock, tied in a handkerchief. The prison governor asked whether Probert was also to come to the bar and was instructed by Knapp that he must be there. Probert was then brought in and bowed to the court; Wilson and an assistant kept him separated about a half yard from the other prisoners.

Before the swearing of the jury, Thesiger rose to advise the court that he had a motion to present for a postponement of the trial of Hunt. Mr. Justice Park reminded him that he had previously ruled that no further applications for postponement would be entertained. However, he ordered a brief recess to permit Hunt's solicitor Harmer to complete two affidavits that were to be submitted in support of the motion.

While the statements were being prepared, Gurney for the Crown called upon Thesiger to state the nature of the intended motion and was told that the purpose of the delay was to enable Hunt "to apply in another quarter, upon the promises of favour which have been held out to him by the magistrates." Gurney promptly told the court that he would not accede to such a request, and the judge stated his view that it was impossible to entertain such an application after arraignment; the trial must go forward and afterwards it might still be possible for the prisoner to apply to the Crown for mercy. Nevertheless, Park said he would consider the facts presented by Thesiger though he took exception to his comment that the trial was being "hastened on."[3]

When the affidavits were completed and read to the court, it turned out that they were statements of Joe Hunt and John Noel about the representations that were made in behalf of the magistrates that Joe would be granted immunity and admitted as a witness for the Crown if he made full disclosure of his knowledge of the crime. In rebuttal, Gurney offered the affidavits of magistrates Clutterbuck and Mason, which set forth their version of the circumstance of Hunt's confessions and asserted their belief that he had not made a full and true disclosure of everything he knew about the murder. The battle of affidavits, once joined, seemed likely to continue indefinitely. Hunt's counsel countered with an affidavit of the coroner on which Harmer had been working feverishly; in the paper Rooke confirmed that while the inquest was proceeding Clutterbuck had assured Hunt that there would be no breach of faith in the promise made to him. Gurney, in response, sought to introduce affidavits of billiard room keeper Rexworthy and Officer Upson. Gurney told Mr. Justice Park that Hunt's statements to the magistrates and the coroner had not admitted any advance knowledge of the murder but that the two affidavits that he now handed up to the judge included many things not found in either of his pretrial confessions that were very important and tended to prove a crime of a different description.

Finally, the paper storm settled down, and Thesiger spoke in behalf of his motion. The issue before the court was not whether the magistrates had acted inconsiderately but whether the prisoner Hunt relied on their pledge. It was not surprising that Hunt had not detailed all the facts in his first confession considering his agitated state of mind (and in any event he had supplied the omitted facts in subsequent communications with Noel and the magistrates). Finally, the public interest in inducing accomplices to give evidence required the keeping of faith and that magistrates should be permitted to act promptly in emergencies without fear that their actions would be questioned in a calmer moment. When Gurney rose to reply Park waved him off and announced his rejection of the motion: "The argument addressed to me is more applicable in another quarter than to this Court. A great deal of what has been said might be properly the ground for an application to his Majesty for his royal mercy, but I see no reason for putting off the trial." He added that the magistrates "have no right to exercise those powers which belong to a judge of assizes, and therefore their authority in this respect was exceeded."

After the jury was selected (following twenty-four challenges including two by the Crown), Knapp read them the indictment. Gurney then rose and announced what was an open secret, that Probert had won the race for immunity. Gurney said that as it was not intended on the part of the prosecution to offer evidence against the prisoner Probert, who stood charged in the indictment on the coroner's inquisition as being an accessory before the fact, he was willing that the jury should record a verdict of not guilty on the charge against him. The judge accordingly instructed the jury

to find a verdict of acquittal for Probert. Bill made a respectful
bow to the court and jury and was ordered removed from the bar
into an adjoining room. Wilson was instructed to detain him there
until his time came to testify against his less fortunate comrades.

All the delays and all the preliminaries were over at last, and
Gurney rose to make his opening statement for the Crown. He
spoke in a "slow, distinct, and concise manner," and the jury listened with "an almost breathless attention—and in several of the
most appalling parts of his statement,—there was a cold drawing
in of the breath and an involuntary murmur throughout the whole
court."[4] Gurney referred first to the fact that the trial had been
delayed on the basis of an affidavit swearing that there had been a
great excitement of public opinion. He had no doubt that the time
since elapsed had had a beneficial effect and that the jury was now
assembled in that calm and temperate state of mind that would enable it to administer justice with perfect satisfaction to itself and to
the country. The crime before the jury he proceeded, was "attended by circumstances of no common atrocity," which would call
for stronger evidence than usual, because it would require very
strong proof to convince any man that such a crime could be committed. If the prisoners were guilty of the crime with which they
were charged, they were guilty of murdering a man with whom
they were in the habit of living on terms of intimacy, if not of
friendship.

Gurney was quick to turn aside any possible thought that Thurtell's grievance against Weare would attenuate his guilt. He referred to the allegation by "one of the prisoners" that the deceased
had done him some injury. God only knew if this was so, but the
other prisoner had never sustained any injury "and it will appear that their unsuspecting victim was inveigled into the place
where the crime was perpetrated, under the specious pretence of
friendship."

Crown counsel then took pains to defuse two other claims that
the defense might have to the jury's sympathy—the prosecution's
reliance on accomplice testimony and the bad character of the victim. He noted that the Crown was compelled in most murder cases
to resort to circumstantial evidence and that criminals are frequently condemned through the testimony of an accomplice. It

was desirable that all parties in an atrocious crime be reached by the arm of public justice, but that was not always possible and the Crown was frequently obliged to receive the testimony of the less guilty in order to convict the most guilty. Gurney confided that the prosecution was determined to submit to the court the propriety of admitting Probert, who had just been acquitted, as evidence for the Crown; he also assured the jury that no breach of faith whatever had been committed by the Crown in refusing to grant Hunt similar immunity. Regarding the character of Weare, Gurney observed, "It appears that the deceased was a person addicted to play, and connected with persons who were also in the habit of gambling. Whether the deceased was the most or the least estimable member of society will form no part of your consideration."

The jury then heard a summary of the evidence as to the preparation for the crime and the invitation extended to Weare for a weekend in the country. He asked the jury to recall that Gill's Hill Cottage was hardly adequate as a guesthouse: "It is material to bear in mind that there was very little accommodation in Probert's cottage, and none in fact for the reception of company." It appeared that neither Thurtell nor Hunt was expected by the family, and indeed, Gurney noted, Probert had to introduce Hunt to his wife.

Gurney also surveyed the evidence that would be offered to identify the progress of the three conspirators along the road to Gill's Hill, stressing the fact that the hired horse with white face and legs, if once seen, could be recognized with ease. Apparently Gurney had not convinced himself as to whether and where Thurtell had passed his accomplices, for he merely said it was "supposed" that while Probert and Hunt were stopping at one of their drinking places, Thurtell and Weare had passed by without their knowledge. The Crown, he emphasized, would ask the jury to accept the theory that the murderers intended to commit their crime at Phillimore Lodge and that Hunt had got out of the gig at that place for the purpose of assisting Thurtell.

As Gurney outlined the Crown's theory on the time and place of the crime, it was clear that the prosecution speculated that Thurtell must have taken his horse and gig on a wide detour, either before or after the murder. It would be shown, he said, that about

eight o'clock that Friday night a gig had driven by Probert's cottage
at great speed. A few minutes later two men answering the description of Thurtell and Weare had been seen in a gig in the lane,
and five minutes after that, at a distance of three or four hundred
yards, other persons had heard the report of a gun or pistol and
subsequently "two contending voices followed by groans that grew
fainter." When Thurtell arrived at Probert's cottage about nine
o'clock and gave his horse to the boy Addis, the horse looked as if
it had been overheated and cooled afterwards "which answers exactly to the fact of Thurtell having stopped a considerable time on
the road, instead of proceeding directly on his journey from London to the cottage."

In describing the events at the cottage on the night of the murder, Gurney did his best to advertise the detective skills of his key
witness, Elizabeth Probert. Something had excited suspicions in
her mind, he said, "for it is scarcely possible for persons engaged
in a criminal transaction not to be guilty of some disorderly conduct, and accordingly she determined not to undress herself or to
go to bed." He summarized her evidence and then told the jury
what they all knew well—the events that led to the initiation of the
investigation and the discovery of Weare's body in the Hill Slough.
He put them on notice, though, that he would not place in evidence any part of any supposed confession of Hunt, except that he
had disclosed where the body was and that it had been discovered
in the place to which he brought the police party.

The prosecution's lead counsel ended with comments on the involvement of the three conspirators. Some facts, he said, would be
based on the evidence of an accomplice "for an accomplice Probert
undoubtedly is, though not previously privy to the commission of
the murder." Gurney conceded, however, that Probert subsequently took part in the concealment of the body and admitted
that he was a man of disreputable character and conduct and a bad
man, but then, he added, "what good man would be connected
with such foul deeds?" The jury, however, should weigh Probert's
statements with considerable caution and consider corroborating
evidence offered by other witnesses.

He then recited the litany of circumstantial evidence against the
other two men. (Of this type of proof, Henry David Thoreau would

three decades later write: "Some circumstantial evidence is very strong, as when you find a trout in the milk.") It would be established against Thurtell that he had set off from London with Weare to go to Probert's; that Weare did not arrive; that on the same night the report of a pistol or gunshot was heard in Gill's Hill Lane; that Thurtell appeared with bloodstains on his clothes that had not been effaced even at the time of his arrest; that a penknife belonging to Weare was found in his pocket; that one of the two pistols bought by him at the pawnbrokers was found in Gill's Hill Lane and its mate was taken in his possession; that on Mrs. Probert's person was found a gold chain, Weare's property, which had come to her from Thurtell; and most grisly evidence of all, that there was found around the neck of the corpse a red shawl that belonged to Thurtell. Against Hunt it would be proved that he was an accessory before the fact and privy to its commission; that he came unexpectedly to the cottage on the murder night and was a stranger to Mrs. Probert and the family; that he had hired a gig for Thurtell under the pretext of proceeding in an opposite direction; that he had procured the sack that became Weare's shroud; and that after the murder the victim's carpetbag and backgammon board were found at Hunt's lodgings.

Gurney's last words were reserved for one small chink in the evidence: the gold watch that Thurtell had taken from Weare's body had not been found. However, Gurney would show that the watch had suffered the same fate as the spade, for the prisoner Thurtell "declared to one of the police officers, in whose custody he was, and who asked him respecting the watch, that in the course of their traveling in the gig, he had put his hand behind him and chucked the watch over a hedge."

The statement of its lead counsel having concluded, the prosecution opened its case with the testimony of the police, who, as Herbert observed, "gave their accounts plainly, firmly and ungrammatically as gentlemen in their line generally do."[5] First, Constable Beeson testified as to the finding of the body in the Hill Slough. On cross-examination, Thurtell's counsel Andrews lost no time in making his defense strategy plain: he would hammer home the conclusion that the crime and its concealment could not have been the work of one man, hoping to persuade the jury that, with

Probert acquitted and Hunt half promised clemency, it was wrong for Thurtell to suffer alone. Andrews brought out the fact that the body had been found in the deepest part of the pond, near the hedge. Beeson conceded that it was not possible for any person to place the body in the pond without walking in; two men might have swung the body in, but one man could not have done it alone.

Next, the billiard room keeper Rexworthy identified the corpse. He had known Weare for sixteen years and had "never expressed any doubt about the body being that of Mr. Weare."

The testimony of the Watford surgeon Thomas Abel Ward, describing the injuries Weare had suffered, impressed Herbert as having been delivered "in a very intelligent manner, in spite of Platt, whose questions might have pozed the clearest heads."[6] To the extent we can determine from the paraphrase of his words left to us by the contemporary accounts, Ward's comments were so straightforward and authoritative that cross-examination seemed to serve little purpose. He told the jury that there were many marks of violence about the left temple that had been occasioned by some round, blunt instrument; they might have been occasiond by the muzzle of a pistol driven with force against it. The bruises on the scalp corresponded with the mouth of the pistol that had been produced before the coroner, and the wounds had penetrated the scalp. "Near these wounds was a fracture of the skull," the doctor added, "with several portions of the bone broken off and driven into the substance of the brain, which injury might have been done without the pistol having been fired, but driven into the skull by force. It did appear to me that the injury had been produced by the pistol exhibited in court, and the injury to the brain would have caused almost instant death." There was also a mark on the right cheek that appeared to be a gunshot wound. Ward could not trace this wound deep, for it only penetrated through the skin to the cheekbone; it could not have occasioned either instant death or death at all. There were two incised wounds on the left side of the neck and another on the right side, apparently produced by a knife. One of the wounds on the left side had divided the jugular vein.

When Thomas Platt rose to cross-examine for Thurtell, he had apparently two definable purposes in mind, hopeless though they might seem; to raise doubts as to whether the wounds were caused by the pistol that had been traced to Thurtell and to question the identification of the corpse. Unaccountably, however, he began with a long and needless quest for further clarification of the description of the wounds that could only have demonstrated to the jury with greater force the extreme violence of the attack. Where precisely was the skull fracture? he began. It was "just about the anterior angle of the parietal bone of the skull." Could not an instrument with a larger end than the pistol produced in court have been introduced into the fracture? Yes, Ward admitted, but the marks above the fracture could not have been caused except by an instrument resembling the pistol. The orifice of the fracture was an inch and an eighth or a quarter in length and seven-eighths of an inch in width. Volunteering to draw the wound, he was invited to do so by Mr. Justice Park. He then "drew on a sheet of paper a representation of the wound, and produced from a small box pieces of the skull which had been forced in the wound, and which he had extracted and preserved." The drawing and bone pieces were handed up to the bench and then to the jury. Dissatisfied with this ghastly representation of Weare's sufferings, Platt pressed on. Was it not the fact that the fleshy orifice made by the wound remained intact? The external skin was broken, said Ward, but not detached: "The integuments which covered the skull . . . had been bruised, when forced upon that solid substance which had been broken beneath it by the violence of the blow." Platt attempted to question the accuracy of the witness' sketch: "Would that drawing you have made denote the size of the aperture if it had been drawn out?" Ward, unflustered, responded: "It would have been of considerable size. I could have put my finger into it."

Platt finally obtained the witness's admission that the break of the skin could have been made by a larger instrument, and then turned his attention to the severed jugular vein:

Q. The jugular vein was divided, which, if not stopped, would produce death, was it not?
A. Yes. . . .
Q. Could you say, on your oath, that that wound could have been inflicted after death?
A. I think it possible.

Q. Have you not the means of judging whether a wound that appears
on a dead body has been inflicted during life or after death?

A. Not after a body has been deposited in the water three or four
days. . . .

Q. Are not the features more altered in persons dying of hemorrhage,
so as to make it more difficult to recognize them?

A. Yes, when the hemorrhage is protracted.

Q. Is the hemorrhage from the jugular vein protracted?

A. The bleeding, in the case of the wound of the jugular vein, is uncertain; sometimes it is protracted, sometimes not. In this case the
jugular vein was not entirely divided, but the wound was very
considerable.

After all this rambling, Platt considered himself ready for a final
assault on the identification of the body. He posed his crucial question in hypothetical form: "Suppose an individual had been bled
to death, and laid for a week in a pond, would it not in such a case
have been more difficult for persons to ascertain who that individual was?" The witness conceded that it would, but then demolished
Platt's point by stating with assurance that "from the appearance of
the body I saw at Elstree, if I had known the person in his lifetime,
I should have recognized him then."

On reexamination by Mr. Broderick, Dr. Ward dispersed any
confusion Platt might have created as to the cause of death: Weare
had died from the injury to his brain due to the intrusion of the
pistol. Ward was followed to the stand by Ruthven and Constable
Simmonds, who had no new revelations to add to their pretrial testimony. During Simmonds' testimony, Mr. Justice Park showed
great anxiety that the hair and blood on the fatal pistol not be disturbed before it was shown to the jury.

These early witnesses laid the ground for the appearance of the
mainstay of the prosecution's case, Bill Probert. All eyes turned towards him as he entered the witness box. Each of the prisoners, in
his own way, showed the influence of the air of heightened tension
and anticipation that had swept the entire courtroom: Hunt "stood
up, and looked much agitated," and Thurtell "eyed the witness
sternly and composedly." Probert was very well dressed and wore
a pair of new gloves. It seemed to journalist Herbert that Bill was
not the least ashamed of his situation as he impassively heard Gurney's introductory injunction to tell the whole truth, but Herbert, at

least, doubted that the prosecutor's words had come through to him: "The face of Probert is marked with deceit in every lineament. The eyes are like those of a vicious horse, and the lips are thick and sensual. His forehead recedes villanously [*sic*] in amongst a bush of grizzly black hair—and his ears project out of the like cover. His head and legs are too small for his body, and altogether he is an awkward, dastardly, and a wretched-looking animal." (In the pen and ink sketch by Mulready, Probert seems to come off somewhat better; his rather coarse features are compensated for by a sad vacant gaze.) He gave his self-damning story with a "face of brass," and capping his villainy in the elegant ears of Herbert, "his grammar was very nearly as bad as his heart."[7]

In many respects, Probert's testimony admitted a much greater involvement in the crime than he had been willing to disclose at the inquest. He now admitted that he had foreknowledge of Thurtell's murder plan and even of the place where the attack was to occur. Thurtell had told him of his intentions after dinner at the Coach and Horses on Friday, October 24. When he asked Probert to drive Hunt down to Gill's Hill, Jack had explained: "I expect a friend to meet me this evening a little after five, and if he comes I shall go down. If I have an opportunity I mean to do him, for he is a man that has robbed me of several hundreds." It cannot have escaped the jury's notice that Probert took care to emphasize that Thurtell had equivocated as to whether his intention to murder was fully formed. If Probert was telling the truth and his memory was accurate, the purpose of Thurtell's words was hard to divine. Was his mind at this point still not finally resolved on the killing, or was he simulating uncertainty in order to win some degree of cooperation from Probert? Of course, there was another possibility less flattering to the unappealing witness: that Probert had invented Thurtell's uncertain state of mind to lessen his own responsibility. In any event, the firmness of Thurtell's choice of murder site belied any supposed vacillation about the crime. According to Probert, Thurtell informed him in the same conversation of his planned rendezvous with Joe Hunt near Phillimore Lodge. He had said: "I have told Hunt where to stop. I shall want him about a mile and a half beyond Elstree."

Concerning the details of his ride to Gill's Hill on the murder night, Probert's story had also changed considerably since the inquest. In his earlier statement, he had made it appear that he had never caught up with Thurtell on the road. Now he told the jury that on their way down he and Hunt had overtaken Thurtell about four miles from London. As Thurtell's gig came into view, Hunt said, "There they are, drive by and take no notice," and he had added, "It's all right, Jack has got him." Probert asked who was with Jack but Hunt brushed his question aside. "You are not to know his name, you never saw him and know nothing of him." Probert told of his stop at the Bald-Faced Stag and confirmed that Hunt had walked on, being unwilling to enter the inn because he had not returned the borrowed horse cloths. Probert testified that he had stayed at the Stag for about twenty minutes and then had driven on and overtaken Hunt on the road about a quarter of a mile south of Edgware. By the time they reached Edgware, they began to feel that they had lost track of Thurtell. After stopping for a brandy and water at the White Lion, they made another stop a little farther on in Edgware to buy half a bushel of corn. It was at this point on their journey that Hunt said to Probert: "I wonder where Thurtell is; he can't have passed us."

Probert placed the time of their arrival at the Artichoke with strange precision at eight minutes before eight o'clock. Neither he nor Hunt had got out of the gig, but they had four or five glasses of brandy and water while they waited about three-quarters of an hour for Thurtell to arrive. Probert then drove a mile and a half to Phillimore Lodge, where Hunt left the gig, saying he would wait for Thurtell; Probert drove on through Radlett towards Gill's Hill Cottage and met Thurtell on foot a hundred yards away from his home. As Probert elaborated his recollections of Thurtell's words on their meeting, all the new details he now recalled reinforced his own innocence; Jack told him (echoing his earlier words at the Coach and Horses) that the murder was of no consequence to Probert who did not know and had never seen the victim. But other words Probert attributed to Thurtell at the Gill's Hill encounter seemed to contradict the Coach and Horses conversation. Probert told the jury that Jack had instructed him to "go back and fetch Hunt, you know best where you left him." Yet how could Bill know better, when he had left Hunt off precisely at the ambush Thurtell had appointed at Tetsall's?

Probert also recounted in detail Hunt's reactions when he returned to pick him up at Phillimore Lodge. Joe had protested: "Thank God, I am out of it; I am glad he has done it without me. I can't think where the devil he could pass us, I never saw him pass anywhere, but I'm glad I'm out of it." Joe had confirmed that the murder was to have been committed near Phillimore Lodge. When he brought Hunt back to Gill's Hill Cottage, Probert testified, the following exchange took place between the two conspirators:

Hunt: Thurtell, where could you pass me?
Thurtell: It don't matter where I passed you, I've done the trick—I
           have done it. What the devil did you let Probert stop drinking
           at his damned public houses for when you knew what was to
           be done?
Hunt: I made sure you were behind, or else we should not have
           stopped.

Before supper Thurtell had taken Probert and Hunt along Gill's Hill Lane to a plowed field where Weare's body was lying, its head bound up in a shawl. Probert thought it was red but could not identify the shawl that had been recovered from the Elstree pond. They placed the body in a sack head foremost up to the knees, tied it with cord and left it in the field. As they returned home, Thurtell began to tell his companions the details of the murder assault. When he first shot Weare, the gambler jumped out of the gig and "ran like the devil, singing out that he would pay me back all he had won of me, if I'd only spare his life."

At this point in the testimony, Mr. Justice Park intervened to ask whether Probert knew if Thurtell had been in naval service. When Bill responded, puzzled by the interruption, that he had heard him say so, the judge explained triumphantly, "We know that 'singing out', in naval jargon, means 'crying out.'"

Taking up the narrative thread that had been broken by Park's interruption, Probert completed his recollections of Thurtell's description of the murder. Jack had continued: "I jumped out of the gig, and ran after him; I got him down, and began to cut his throat, as I thought, close to the jugular vein, but I could not stop his singing out; I then jammed the pistol into his head, I gave it a turn round, and then I knew I had done him. . . . Joe, you ought to have been with me, for I thought at once he would have got the better of me. These damned pistols are like squibs, they are of no use." Probert was quite deliberate in his insistence that the vicinity of Phillimore Lodge was the intended murder locale, quoting the disgusted comment of Thurtell that had it not been for Hunt's mistake, he would have killed Weare "in the other lane" and returned to town and inquired of his friends why Weare had not met him, pursuant to appointment.

If any of the testimony of the reptilian Probert was worthy of belief, it was his new version of his role in the concealment of Weare's body. He still maintained that he had initially objected to the body's being dumped into his pond and had refused to help. Thurtell and Hunt had gone out without him but returned after a quarter of an hour to report failure. Hunt told him that the body was too heavy for them to carry, and they had only brought him a little way. Thurtell now suggested that the hired horse be bridled and used to fetch the corpse. Assenting at last, Probert went to the stable with Thurtell and brought the horse out into the lane where the body had been left. Putting the body across its back, they led the horse to the garden gate at the rear of Probert's grounds. Here Hunt had been waiting for them; Joe took the horse back to the stable and then met them in the garden. The three men dragged the body down the garden to the pond, weighted the sack with stones and threw it into the water. To their horror the feet of the corpse, rebounding from the plunge, projected half a foot above the surface, so Thurtell got a cord and threw it around the feet; he gave the other end of the cord to Probert who dragged the body toward the deeper end of the pond where it sank from view.

On Monday morning Thurtell and Hunt told Probert that they had tried to dig a grave for the body the night before, but the dogs had been barking all night and they thought someone was about the grounds. Jack said that they would return on Monday night and "take him quite away, and that will be better for you altogether." After supper on Monday, Thurtell and Probert went to the stable, leaving Hunt talking to Mrs. Probert. They raised the body from the waters of the pond, took it out of the sack and cut all the clothing off. From the stable Thurtell provided a new sack and some cord from his gig. The three men then returned to the green margin of the pond where the naked body lay and placed it head first in the sack. Hunt was left waiting with the body at the garden gate while Thurtell and Probert went around the pond. Probert carried the bundle of clothes and threw it into the gig but after the horse was harnessed, Thurtell decided that the clothes should be left behind since there was no room in the carriage. Thurtell and Hunt then drove away to the Hill Slough. The next morning Probert burned some of Weare's clothes and tucked the rest into the hedges in different places.

In this testimony about the removal and concealment of the clothes, at least, Probert's account matched the results of the magistrates' investigations on the scene. When Clutterbuck and his clerk Jones had searched for the clothes on November 30 they had found near a spring called Scrubbits, about three hundred yards east of the cottage, "curiously folded up, and concealed under the roots of four separate hazel stems, distant about five yards from each other, four pieces of a coat evidently cut asunder hastily by a knife, or some such instrument," which together formed the left half of a dark olive-colored coat corresponding to that described by Weare's laundress as the one he wore when he left his lodgings on the afternoon of October 24.

The principal cross-examiner was Andrews, who immediately pounced on Probert's tardy decision to reveal all; Bill could not tell him when he had initially expressed the desire to become a witness or whether he was first asked to give testimony before or after Hunt's confession. He was also "sorry to say" that John Noel, who had assumed the role of counsel for the investigation, had acted as his solicitor for a few months in 1819. Andrews then moved on to expose a glaring flaw in the witness' credibility:

Q. You say you heard that some injury was intended to certain persons, and yet you gave no alarm?
A. I did hear that at my cottage, but I did not believe it.
Q. You must have believed it when you heard of the murder; and, when you saw the dead body brought to your house, did not you give any alarm then?
A. I did not.

In fact, as Andrews underscored, Probert had received the murderers into his house after the murder and had supped and breakfasted with them in the company of his wife.

The witness' own criminal record was explored. He admitted that he had been accused of taking some silver from the till of the man who kept the coffeehouse in the King's Bench prison but insisted that he had engaged only in self-help, since the proprietor owed him one hundred pounds at the time. As a consequence of the offense he had been sent for six months to the House of Corrections, but this was the only charge of felony against him. He firmly denied having been charged with sheep stealing or lamb stealing in Herefordshire where he was born. But when Andrews pressed him, it was soon evident that Probert was equivocating:

Q. Were you never in Herefordshire?
A. Yes, I was born there.
Q. Were you never charged with sheep stealing there?
A. Never.
Q. Well, perhaps it was lamb stealing?
A. No, I was never charged with either.
Q. Come, sir, you know what I mean by "charged"; were you never accused of such a crime there?
A. Never.
Q. Then the accusation is quite new to you?
A. It is.
Q. Then what was the charge against you?
A. I had bought some skins, which were afterwards [claimed to be] owned.
Q. Oh, then you were accused as a receiver of stolen goods?
A. I was not.

Cross-examining for Hunt, Thesiger established that Hunt had never been previously to Gill's Hill Cottage and thus presumably did not know the neighborhood. The witness confirmed that Thurtell had asked him to drive Hunt to the cottage, that he had not told Hunt there was no spare bed at his house and had not expressed surprise at Hunt's going down "uninvited" and without previous introduction to Mrs. Probert. Thesiger scored his major point at the end of his questioning: Probert admitted that, up to the day he went before the grand jury, he had maintained in conversations with the prison chaplain T. W. Franklin that Hunt and he were both innocent of the murder.

Bill Probert was followed to the stand by his wife, Elizabeth, who struck Edward Herbert as no more prepossessing than her husband. He wrote that her face, by no means well favored, "has a good and a constant colour, which in moments of great grief and hysteric passion, is a great comfort,—but her forehead is ill-shaped and large—and her sly grey eyes have a wildness which I should be loth to confide in." It seemed to him that she was giving her evidence "drop by drop, and not then without great *squeezing*. Every dangerous question overcame her agitated nerves,—and she very properly took time to recover before she answered."[8]

At the beginning of her testimony Elizabeth appeared to lend support to Gurney's theory that the crime had been committed about 8:00. It was around that hour that she had heard the sound of a gig passing the cottage. Nearly an hour later there was a ringing at the cottage bell, but no one came in. It was not until 9:30 or close to 10:00 that she came downstairs to find her husband and Thurtell in the parlor with a stranger who was introduced to her as Joseph Hunt.

As Gurney took her through her story of the events of that night she clung doggedly to the account she had already given the magistrates, despite the fact that her recollections contradicted Bill Probert's testimony. Though Probert had now admitted helping drag Weare's body to his pond, Elizabeth did not identify him as one of the two men she had seen hauling the corpse, and though he had just described how they brought the dead man to the pond from the back garden gate, she still maintained that the sound of something dragged very heavily seemed to come from the stable to the garden.

When Gurney asked Elizabeth whether she told her husband what she had heard when he came to bed, she became very agitated and asked faintly whether she must answer. Gurney assured her: "No evidence you now give can prejudice your husband. He has been this day put before a jury of his countrymen, and acquitted of this murder." Mrs. Probert responded with a sobbing hysterial shriek: "Oh, has he! Has he!" Her "sudden vehement and tearful joy at the safety of her husband," Herbert noted from the audience, was "late but timely," for to his knowledge, Undersheriff Nicholson had informed her of her husband's immunity at the time of the grand jury proceedings on December 5, "just one month before her hysterics." Herbert opined that "so abominable a farce never was played off in a Court of Justice; but it had its effect, for it touched his Lordship and made Mr. Gurney weep!"[9]

When it was his turn for cross-examination, Platt promptly challenged Elizabeth's pretense that she had not previously been told that Probert was to be acquitted, but she would not budge from her show of spontaneous wifely joy. He had more success when he challenged her ability to have seen the horse led out of the stable by two men on the murder night. She admitted that a high fence partially obstructed her view but claimed that it was a fine moonlit night and, if she wasn't sure she could have seen the stable door, she certainly had been able to look over the fence so as to see the horse emerge from the stable. She also equivocated somewhat on the identity of the men she had seen in the garden. She rather thought that they were Thurtell and Hunt, that is, the short man was Hunt, and she could not positively say as to the other. She also tried ineffectually to explain why her husband's voice had not carried from the parlor as clearly as the voices of the defendants: "I could not distinctly hear the whole of the conversation. I thought I could distinguish the different voices, but cannot be positive; my husband whispered so low that I could not hear him, but I cannot take upon myself to say positively that he did whisper."

Platt then took what at first appeared to be an irrelevant tack: Did the Proberts keep a store of potatoes in the garden? Yes, Elizabeth answered, there was a hole made for them and they were covered over. The reporters who had followed the case closely knew what Platt was after: he wanted to find an innocent explanation for the potato hole in the garden that some had supposed to be Weare's intended grave. The hole was in the center of the garden between the pond and the adjoining barley field of farmer James Wardle. Platt's questioning, however, did nothing to dispel the continuing speculation as to the site of the garden "grave." The magistrates' clerk Jones, in his edition of the trial, maintains that the intended grave was, in fact, in the part of the garden adjoining an orchard, near the spot where Hunt threw the new spade over the hedge on Sunday, October 26. Jones wrote that this grave was pointed out to Clutterbuck and Mason while they were searching the grounds on Tuesday, October 28. A man named Broughall called their attention to a patch of ground around which clay had been thrown up. When the ground was dug by Clutterbuck's order, "it was found that a grave or pit, measuring five feet in length by three in breadth, had been dug to the depth of two feet, and had been again filled in." Jones speculated that the persons who began the grave were deterred when they came to the natural soil, "a stiff clay with stones imbedded in it." They would have had to proceed with a pickaxe, which would have made a noise and created suspicion by throwing out clay that was dissimilar to the upper soil.[10]

Thesiger obtained Mrs. Probert's admission that despite all she had seen from her window she did not attempt to return the watch chain to Thurtell. But for the most part he lapsed into trivia, dwelling on the number of songs Hunt had sung and whether cards had been played on Sunday night. Elizabeth admitted asking Hunt for an encore, but her plea to the offense of cardplaying on the Sabbath was mixed: yes, there had been cards on Sunday night, but she did not play and would swear her husband did not join in the play. (The cardplaying at Gill's Hill Cottage became an obsession with Thesiger, who later obtained an admission from Thomas Noyes that everyone was present during the card game on Sunday night.)

There was little the defense counsel could do to blunt the force of the parade of eyewitnesses to the defendants' journeys to Hertfordshire on the night of the crime. Andrews tried unsuccessfully to obtain an admission by Thomas Wilson that he had made inconsistent descriptions of the colors of Thurtell's horse and gig. It was true, Wilson conceded, that they had passed him quickly on the road, but it was light enough to distinguish between a roan and a gray horse. The policeman, however, had always been cautious, for he had from the outset described the horse as a roan gray. The gig he had never described other than as a dark one. Besides, Wilson was certain that, though he could not identify the men who passed him, he could not mistake the horse when he saw him again at Mr. Probert's stable; he had a very white face. Platt's attempt to throw doubt on James Freeman's identification of the hired horse and carriage in Gill's Hill Lane suffered a similar fate. Freeman would not recognize the gig, though he was sure it was not yellow, as suggested by Platt. However, the horse's white face had shone through the darkness.

Herbert has left us sharply etched impressions of the other witnesses who completed the prosecution's case: Weare's brother, who was truly shocked and whose "sincere grief exposed the art and trickery of many serious and hysterical witnesses"; and the "thoroughbred" pub landlords, all "sleek, sly and rosy." The "little round head" of Field, proprietor of the Artichoke, "with a little round nose to suit, a domestic nose, that would not quit the face, with a voice thin as small ale, was right pleasant to behold."[11]

The innkeeper confirmed that Probert and Hunt left the Artichoke at 8:49 after staying a half hour or thirty-five minutes. William Clarke, proprietor of the White Lion at Edgware, provided a valuable insight into the behavior of Probert and Hunt at that stage of their journey. The two men had stopped at his pub for about a quarter of an hour and had left about twenty minutes past seven. "Probert did not enter the house, and was impatient for Hunt to set off. They must have been nearly three miles behind John Thurtell and his companion." With no apparent axe to grind, this witness at least had received the impression that it was Joe Hunt who was less anxious to overtake the murderer.

Herbert, as he observed the trial, perceived touches of the picturesque and of comic relief in the appearance of Probert's servants. "Little Addis, Probert's boy, was a boy of uncommon quickness and pretty manner. He was a nice ingenuous lad. When you saw his youth, his innocence, his pretty face and frankness, you shuddered to think of the characters he had associated with, and the scenes he had witnessed. His little artless foot had kicked up the bloody leaves; he had seen the stains fresh on the murderer's clothes."[12] Beneath the sentimental trappings that Herbert's description foisted upon him, young Addis turned out to be an effective witness for the prosecution. He recalled that about a quarter before eight o'clock on Friday night he had heard the wheels of a gig going past Probert's house. At first he thought it was Probert's gig; he went outside and found that the gig had passed on very rapidly in the direction of Battlers Green. About nine o'clock he heard the gate bell ring, and when he went to answer it he found Thurtell at the door. After completing his testimony, the young lad was cross-examined by Andrews, who hoped to raise a doubt as to whether the gig that had passed Gill's Hill Cottage was Thurtell's. Addis admitted that the lane at the point where he later saw blood was so narrow that a gig could not turn around; and that in fact it was impossible for a carriage to turn in Gill's Hill Lane except in a corner where there was a heap of mud which would likely cause the carriage to capsize. With these facts in hand, Andrews now sought the pivotal concession: "If then a gig passed your master's house when you heard the noise, it might have gone on to Letchmore Heath before it turned?" But young Addis calmly rejected this suggestion: "No, it might have turned before it came to Battlers Green. It could have turned before it came to Mr. Nicholls's house." Andrews had come out second best in his skirmish with the servant boy; it was now quite clear to the jury that Thurtell, after committing the murder, could have emerged from the far end of Gill's Hill Lane and turned to reenter the lane without making the wide detour suggested by Andrews. It was, therefore, perfectly possible for him to have presented himself at Gill's Hill Cottage within an hour of the crime. Before he retired to lick his wounds, Andrews could extract only one small admission from the tough little witness. Addis had always said that he was not very certain whether Mr. Thurtell had sponged his coat or not.

The cook, Susan Woodruff, proved herself to be a spiritual descendant of Mrs. Malaprop and artlessly spoke the most memorable words of the trial. She was talking about the supper served at Gill's Hill Cottage on Friday night when Mr. Bolland for the prosecution asked her if the supper was postponed. "No!" she replied. "It was pork." [13]

When, past nine o'clock, the laborer Richard Hunt was called to testify about the discovery of the blood and weapons in Gill's Hill Lane, Thurtell intervened, asking Mr. Justice Park for an adjournment until the next day. "I am really so much fatigued and exhausted," he pleaded, "that I particularly wish it may be postponed. I have been up since six o'clock this morning, and unless such a delay be granted, I shall really be unable to enter into my defense." Park responded dryly that according to the law of the land the case must proceed to its conclusion, and he must do everything in his power to complete the trial if the jury was willing to continue; the judge bragged that he had in other cases sat sixteen or seventeen hours in a single day. Taking Park's hint, Thurtell directly appealed to the jury to take his request into consideration.

Showing the first signs of what was to become a remarkable sympathy for Thurtell, the judge then asked the prosecution how much of its case remained and was advised that only a small amount of testimony was left. Park decided that they had better go on in any event with the rest of the Crown's case. After completing a line of testimony of the discovery of the bloody knife and pistol, the prosecution focused on the piece of tangible evidence that most compellingly tied Thurtell to the corpse of Weare: the red shawl found about the dead man's neck. The testimony of surgeon John Pidcock to his removal of the shawl from the neck of Weare's body at the Artichoke was immediately followed by John Fleet's account of his delivery of the same shawl to Hunt at Thurtell's written instruction. The best Andrews could do on cross-examination was to obtain Fleet's admission that he did not know whether the instruction with which he had complied was in Thurtell's handwriting. Platt's attempt at further cross-examination was a ludicrous failure: Did not the witness know that Thurtell was subject to nosebleeds? The witness did not, but the poor taste of the question hovered in the courtroom air after Fleet left the stand. It was not Thurtell's nose but Weare's cut throat that had stained the shawl.

The two final Crown witnesses, examined by Broderick, testified to damning admissions of Thurtell after the crime. Officer John Upson stated that, in the course of a conversation with Thurtell while he was bringing him from London to Watford, he asked what his prisoner had done with Weare's watch and that Thurtell had told him he had thrown it away in the village about two miles on the London side of Watford "among some trees where there were some palings." The last witness, Constable Charles Foster, testified that on October 30, while Thurtell was in custody at the Plough at Hertford, he had said that Hunt was a rascal for "nosing" (incriminating) him, particularly since Thurtell had offered Weare's watch for sale in Hunt's name.

The prosecution now rested, and the jury, on Park's inquiry, indicated a desire to adjourn. The judge, whose attachment to procedural formalities had not been weakened by the late hour, told them that they had relieved him of great difficulty, for he would not have granted the wish of the prisoners for adjournment without their concurrence. The case was recessed until the next morning, and the judge ordered two bailiffs to take custody of the jurors, "to furnish them with every proper and convenient accommodation, and not speak to them themselves, or allow others to speak to them, touching the matter in issue, without leave of the Court." The two prisoners as they were led away, appeared to be exhausted.

When the trial resumed at eight o'clock the next morning, Mr. Justice Park revealed that he had yet another formal quibble up his judicial sleeve. He recalled officer Ruthven to the stand and took him through a lesson in London geography. Perplexed but dutiful, Ruthven recited that Conduit Street, the location of the Coach and Horses, was in the County of Middlesex; that Whitcomb Street (the address of Mr. Cross's stable, where Stephen March testified he had hitched the white-faced horse to a dark green gig on October 24) was in the same county. Apparently, the meticulous Park was making sure that the proof of these details corresponded to the charge of the indictment. Shortly afterwards the Crown case was closed again.

Chapter Twelve

ANOTHER KEAN

———

Mr. Justice Park now addressed Thurtell: "John Thurtell, this is the time that it becomes your duty to make your defence." Thurtell bowed respectfully and turned to speak in low tones to his solicitor Jay. Jay nodded briefly and then told Park that Thurtell wished to call his witnesses first; Park refused the request saying that the prisoner must abide strictly by court rules.

All eyes in the courtroom were on him as Thurtell began to deliver the long-studied speech that he had practiced before Pierce Egan. Herbert's account fixes the moment for all time. "Thurtell," he wrote, "now seemed to retire within himself for half a minute,—and then slowly,—the crowd being breathlessly silent and anxious,—drawing his breath, gathering up his frame, and looking very steadfastly at the jury, he commenced his defence.—He spoke in a deep, measured, and unshaken tone;—accompanying it with a rather studied and theatrical action."[1] The magistrates' clerk Jones was told by "a gentleman of unquestionable veracity, to whom it was communicated by John Thurtell" that the beginning and end of his speech were of his own composition with the exception of two or three passages from the speeches of Charles Phillips but that the intermediate section was the work of others. If the opening was actually his own composition, Thurtell had mined a vein of native eloquence:

> Under the pressure of greater difficulties than, perhaps, it has before fallen to the lot of man to sustain, I now rise, to vindicate my character, and preserve my life. But appalling as are these difficulties, I have been

supported under the impression that the hour would arise when I should
be enabled to defend myself in a land of liberty, before that tribunal
which the free institutions of my country have awarded to the accused;
namely, an enlightened Court and a Jury of twelve fellow-subjects, unin-
fluenced by prejudice and unawed by power. I have been represented by
the public press, which carries on its rapid wings, from one extremity of
the kingdom to the other, either benefits or curses, as a man the most
depraved, the most habitually profligate, the most gratuitously cruel,
that has appeared in modern times.

These descriptions had been given of him not only daily but hourly
by the public journals throughout the kingdom. The jury had no
doubt read them; he would not say they had been influenced by
them but it would "exact too much from the common virtue of human nature" to suppose that they could entirely rid themselves of
the feelings—even creditable feelings—that the press statements,
if true, were calculated to excite. But he was satisfied that they
would decide the case in a manner becoming the character of their
sacred office. He was strengthened in this hope by the basic psy-
chological insight that should guide their deliberations: that a penchant for barbaric crime does not commonly spring up unher-
alded in the years of maturity. "Guilt, of such a complexion as that
imputed to me, is not of the custom of this land; it must have
sprung from an innate principle, which must have advanced to
maturity by a continued practice in crime. It must have 'grown
with my growth, and strengthened with my strength.'" However,
"men of the most unblemished reputation" would testify that there
was a period in Thurtell's life when his bosom "flowed with the
most gentle and kindly feelings of affection and sympathy."[2]

His entrance into life had been auspicious, he told the jury. He
had been reared by a kind, affectionate and religious mother, "who
first taught [his] lips to utter their first accents in praise of that
Being who guides the conduct of your hearts, and of the learned
Judge upon the Bench." His youthful steps had been directed by a
father whose kindness and charity extended to all who came within
the sphere of its influence. Having invoked his respectable origins,
Thurtell lost no time in staking an even stronger claim to the jury's
respect and sympathy: he was a veteran of England's foreign wars
who had served the late monarch without disgrace and had "fought
and bled" for his country. But bravery in battle did not bend his

soul towards cowardly assassination: "I never feared in the open field to shed the blood of [England's] declared foes—but to raise the assassin's arm, and against an unsuspecting friend, believe it not."

Thurtell then tried to expunge another blemish on his reputation, his well-publicized association with sports and gambling. Among many other vices attributed to him it was said he had been a sporting man and a gambler, and to that accusation, with true penitence of heart, he pled guilty. But three years had elapsed since he had entered a gaming house or attended or betted upon a horse race, a fight, or other sporting exhibition, and even had he continued the practice, he could not understand why such a vice was unpardonable only in him. Sounding a central theme of the public furor over the murder case, he asked, "Why am I to be thrust out of the pale of society for this practice, when half the nobility of this land have been my examples, some of the most enlightened statesmen of the country have been my companions in them?" One last emotional appeal remained to complete Thurtell's introduction, the invocation of his misfortunes after he had been mustered out of military service. With the romantic feelings of a soldier's life he had considered his acquaintances in the postwar commercial world in the same light as he was accustomed to view his brother officers: his purse was open and his heart was warm to their demands. Instead of receiving thanks, he was driven into bankruptcy and hounded by his principal creditor. The disaster of the fire followed and even this calamity was made the occasion of a conspiracy on the part of Barber Beaumont to fix on Thurtell the false charge of fraudulently removing the goods that the jury had found to have been destroyed by the fire. Having presumably received from Mrs. Walker the requested copy of a political diatribe against Beaumont, he proceeded to brand him a dangerous radical, "that professed friend of the aggrieved, that pretended corrector of public abuses, that self-appointed supporter of the laws, that champion of liberty, who had the audacity to hoist the standard of rebellion in front of the palace of his Sovereign." The false claims of the press had deepened Thurtell's miseries; he could prove by unquestionable testimony that he was in Norwich at the time the newspapers claimed that he had inveigled Woods into the Manchester Buildings with the intention of murdering him. In short, all the actions of his life had been "ransacked to supply the magazine of slander." Even his days of glory had been sullied, for the public had been told that "when the battle's rage had ceased, and the peril of the conflict was over, the vanquished, unoffending, yielding, nay supplicating foe— . . ." At this point Thurtell broke off and began to cry. Mr. Justice Park kindly told him to sit down for a moment to recover himself. He did so and then completed his denial of the cold-blooded killing and plundering of his prisoner at the siege of San Sebastián.

His masterful opening now nearly over, he expressed regret for any misunderstanding between the Reverend Mr. Lloyd and his solicitor Fenton and offered his thanks to Chaplain Franklin and to the prison governor Wilson. He then turned to a review of the evidence, which, in his words, was "contradictory, inconsistent, and derived from the mouths of persons who have been willing to save their own lives by any sort of falsehood or injustice towards others."

As far as it went, Thurtell's review of the prosecution's case was often effective. His starting point was well chosen: the discovery of the body in the Hill Slough. The jury should find, he urged, that the place of the body's concealment incriminated Hunt and Probert, not him. Why could Hunt point out the location, unless he had deposited the body there himself? What proof was there that the body was not put into this pond on the night of the murder or that it was ever in Probert's pond? There was none but the evidence of Probert himself. Constable Beeson had testified that no one person could have thrown the corpse into the Hill Slough, and what better candidate was there for the second man than Probert? Beeson had pointed out that there was a large pond at Medbourn Bridge near the Hill Slough. Who could have chosen the smaller pond but a person acquainted with the neighborhood? Who would have known that the larger pond was sometimes dry but the small one never? Who but Probert himself?

Yet Probert was the only man whose testimony pointed at Thurtell. "And who is he? What is he? He is himself a murderer. Is it credible that he could have introduced me, just hot from slaughtering, to his wife? Where was the murder committed? A quarter of a mile from his house. Where was the body found? In his pond. Who took it there? Himself." The jury could not possibly reconcile the differences between the statements of Hunt and Probert, and yet these men had been "running a race" to be admitted as witness for the Crown; they had "put up their evidence to auction, hoping to find a bribe in proportion to the length of their consciences." It was not believable that Thurtell would have told Probert that he was going "to do" for Weare "for he had robbed me of several hundreds," when Probert was a previous stranger to the matter. And it was not more credible that Thurtell had ordered him to put Hunt down near Phillimore Lodge, when that part of the country was unknown to Hunt and, as both the Proberts had testified, he had never been at Gill's Hill Cottage before. Still Probert claimed that he had left Hunt at the place where it was intended for the murder to be committed. Why did he do this? Simply because Hunt and Probert thought that "it was the most proper place to commit the murder." He thought it clear that they had arranged to meet Weare at the fatal spot and that Thurtell "was likewise to have been their victim."

The jury's attention was then called to discrepancies between the stories of Probert and his wife. Probert claimed that Hunt and Thurtell had taken the body through the rear garden gate and dragged it to the bank of the pond, but his wife stated that the body was dragged through the stable-yard gate down the dark walk to the pond. Probert contradicted his wife's story that the men had had a lantern, and to add further illumination for her remote and obstructed window view she had claimed that it was a fine moonlit night, which was contrary to all the other testimony. Besides, what faith could the jury put in "the testimony of a female who confesses that she put round her neck a chain which had been plundered from the murdered man; and that after the sanguinary tragedy had been perpetrated, she called upon the blood-stained Hunt to sing her a song?" Could they believe a witness who saw two men bring a horse out of a stable to fetch a body when she subsequently admitted she could not see the stable door? Then too, she had overheard a long conversation later that night in the parlor, though her husband said that immediately after leaving the pond he had gone to bed. Wasn't it clear to the jury that the testimony about the whispered conversation was a scheme settled between the Proberts? Winding up his assault on his principal adversaries,

Thurtell offered some of his own deductions. He expressed the belief that Weare's body was never in Probert's pond at all. He also proposed a timetable that would have permitted Hunt and Probert to have committed the crime comfortably before their arrival at the cottage. Mr. Field of the Artichoke had testified that they had left his inn at a quarter before nine o'clock, and Clarke of the White Lion had put their departure from his establishment at a quarter past seven. If this was true, the two men had time to go to the top of Gill's Hill Lane and return to the Artichoke after they perpetrated the murder so as to enable them to throw the guilt on another. (In his enthusiasm for his own solution of the mysteries of the case, Thurtell seemed to forget temporarily that he had already contended that Phillimore Lodge was the site chosen by Probert and Hunt for the murder.)

Thurtell had now arrived at the end of his review of the evidence, and in the welter of contradictions and uncertainties that he had invited the jury to consider, one huge omission remained in his chain of argument: when had he last seen Mr. Weare, and if they had embarked together on the journey to Hertfordshire, how had they parted company? It was a point that Thurtell and his counsel hoped the jury would miss or discount.

From this point forward Thurtell, having begun promisingly, started to lose his audience. Perhaps inspired by the speeches of Charles Phillips, from which he borrowed, or perhaps at the suggestion of his counsel, he launched into a lengthy tirade on the unreliability of circumstantial evidence, on which he claimed the Crown's case was entirely founded. Circumstantial evidence, he said, "is at best but a fearful guide to human judgment. . . . The annals of our own and of foreign jurisprudence frequently show it. Some of the most melancholy and dreadful instances are to be found of a too fatal adherence to the supposed infallibility of circumstantial evidence." He cited the Jean Calas cause célèbre from eighteenth-century France, in which Voltaire had taken an interest, and invoked numerous precedents from the *Newgate Calendar* and the *Percy Anecdotes*. His listeners for the most part remained such in name only, but one of the stories he recounted from the *Percy Anecdotes* must have, however briefly, revived their attention.

In the reign of Queen Elizabeth a charge of murder was brought before Sir James Dyer, lord chief justice of the Court of Common Pleas. The victim was found lying dead in a field with two wounds in his breast that appeared to have been made by a sharp implement. A pitchfork was found near the corpse marked with the initials of the prisoner, who was known to have previously quarreled with the victim. When the prisoner was arrested, a neighbor followed him to the house of the justice of the peace and attended his examination, during the course of which he observed that the prisoner had changed clothes since he had last seen him in the morning. When the prisoner gave evasive answers about his change of apparel, the justice issued a warrant to search his house and the very clothes that the witness had described were discovered concealed in a straw bed covered with blood. The suspect was charged with murder and brought to trial. Eleven of the jurors who heard the case favored a guilty verdict from the outset, but because of the obstinacy of the foreman they ultimately voted for acquittal, much to the court's displeasure. When the judge learned that the verdict had been due to the stubbornness of the foreman, he called the man before him. In a confidential interview, the foreman explained to the astounded judge that he himself had killed the victim in self-defense in the course of a quarrel that arose over the sharing of crops. To clear the prisoner of the charge which had been wrongly brought against him, he had managed to obtain a summons to serve on the jury and had successfully angled for election as foreman, having determined all along that he would rather die himself than suffer any harm to be done to the prisoner. As Thurtell retold this amazing story, he must have placed special emphasis on the misleading tangible evidence. The Elizabethan prisoner had bloodied his clothes when he came to the assistance of the dying man, and in his great concern and confusion of mind arising from the fear that he would be taken for the murderer he fled the scene, inadvertently exchanging his pitchfork for the victim's, and hid his clothes.

When Thurtell at last finished his law lecture and laid aside his prepared notes, "he seemed to return with joy and strength to his memory, and to muster up all his might for the peroration." One hardly expected such moving words from a man who had gone astray in London's underworld:

Cut me not off—I implore it of your justice, of your humanity—in the very summer of my life. I implore it, not for myself, but for the sake of those whose name I bear, and whose character accusation never stained; for the sake of their home, a happy home, which my death will render desolate. . . . I stand before you as before my God, overwhelmed with misfortunes, but unconscious of crime; and while you decide on my future destiny, I earnestly entreat you to remember my last solemn declaration; I am innocent, so help me God!

Herbert, like an appreciative drama critic reviewing a performance by a new rival of Edmund Kean, was bowled over by the "solid, slow, and appalling tone in which he wrung out these last words." Thurtell had worked himself up into a great actor and his eye turned alive and eloquent. Through the power of Herbert's pen we see him strike an attitude of final appeal to the emotions of the jury and the entire courtroom:

He clung to every separate word with an earnestness, which we cannot describe, as though every syllable had the power to buoy up his sinking life. . . . The final word, GOD! was thrown up with an almost gigantic energy,—and he stood after its utterance with his arms extended, his face protruded, and his chest dilated, as if the spell of the sound were yet upon him, and as though he dared not move lest he should disturb the still echoing appeal! He then drew his hands slowly back,—pressed them firmly to his breast, and sat down half exhausted in the dock.[3]

After this dramatic high point of the trial, the testimony offered in behalf of Thurtell came as a distinct anticlimax, particularly when it became apparent that only character evidence would be offered and the facts of the prosecution's case left undisturbed. A solicitor Samuel Wadeson, who had become professionally acquainted with Probert in July, 1819, as counsel to bankruptcy creditors, said he would not believe him on oath unless supported by additional testimony. By contrast, Langdon Haydon, a land surveyor and auctioneer, had known Thurtell for some years and had never heard anything against his character for humanity; he had always thought him a liberal, kind, and good-hearted man. Perhaps the most impressive character witness was Captain George Mackinlay, under whose command Thurtell had served on the *Bellona* between 1812 and 1814. Thurtell, the captain said, was always correct in his conduct as an officer, and he had never seen anything bad of him or heard anything against his character for humanity. However, the force of his testimony was lessened when, in response to a question from Mr. Justice Park, he said that he had not seen Thurtell since 1814. The time gap was filled somewhat by the evidence of Thurtell's final witness, Joseph Walmesley, an officer serving the sheriff of Middlesex; he had frequently been in Thurtell's company during the last three years and always thought him a "humane, quiet, peaceable, well-disposed man."

It was now Joe Hunt's turn to speak. To the disappointment of the courtroom, however, he could only manage one sentence: "My Lord, I have a defence to make, but from the extreme anxiety of mind under which I labour, I do not feel myself competent to read it." At the judge's direction, Hunt's written speech was handed up to Knapp, the court clerk, who read it. The principal theme of the speech was the broken faith of the magistracy in failing to support Hunt's claim to immunity. Mr. Justice Park was invited to consider whether he had been fairly and candidly dealt with. Hunt claimed that he had no concern for his own life but was moved by pity for his family: "I have no desire to prolong a wretched existence, unless it be to afford the opportunity for endeavouring, by prayer and penitence, to obtain mercy and forgiveness of the Almighty, for the sins and transgressions I have committed. But in pity to the feelings of an aged and respectable mother, a virtuous and amiable wife, and my dearly beloved brother and sister, I do feel most anxious to avoid an ignominious death." When Knapp finished reading the prepared text (thought to have been composed by Hunt's solicitor Harmer), Hunt told the judge that he had another paper that he wished to have read, and Park asked him whether he had not better allow that paper to be read by Knapp as well. Hunt mustered the last poor shreds of his manhood and answered that as the paper was very short he would read it himself. This he proceeded to do in a "poor dejected voice":

> I merely wish to add, that the greater part of Probert's evidence is false, and especially that part of it in which it is stated, that I was acquainted with all the circumstances which occurred previous to the murder. In order to save his own life, Probert has found it necessary to sacrifice mine. One fact which Probert has stated, everybody must see must be false. Probert has said, that I pointed out the place where I was to set down on the road. Now it is in evidence that I had never before been in that part of the country. How then could I point out the spot?

These last words did not seem to impress the judge much, for his mind had already veered away into his own preoccupation with geography. He wanted evidence that Gill's Hill was in Hertfordshire as alleged in the indictment and this burning issue was resolved by testimony by the coroner who happened to be in court. To bring the judge's mind to complete rest, the coroner also stated for the record that the precise place where Weare's body was found was also in the county of Hertfordshire.

Mr. Justice Park's charge to the jury lasted for several hours, but through it all, Thurtell "with an untired spirit superintended the whole explanation of the evidence; interrupting the Judge, respectfully but firmly, when he apprehended any omission, or conceived any amendment capable of being made."[4] By way of prelude, the judge paid tribute to Thurtell's eloquence and at the same time castigated his lawyers for the interpolated lecture on circumstantial evidence.

> Gentlemen, the greater part of what was said by John Thurtell in his defence did him great credit. I must except indeed some part of what he said, but I allude particularly to his observations at the commencement and the close of his defence. This part of his defence, which I take to be his own, did him great credit. It was manly, energetic, and powerful. I cannot help saying, however (although everybody who knows me, knows that I never go out of my way to say anything harsh or severe of anybody), that I did not admire the judgment of those who advised him to introduce the middle part of his address. If the first and last part of his address had any effect—and it could not fail to have an effect upon every sensible mind—that effect must have been weakened by the dreadfully long quotations which he was advised to introduce from such books as the "Percy Anecdotes" and "Newgate Calendar," which, for anything I know to the contrary, may be mere books of romance.

The jury might have been pardoned if it wondered for a moment whether it was listening to a rhetoric professor grading a student's performance rather than a judge giving guidance in the dread assignment of choosing between life and death. Park, however, soon righted his course and dealt with the issue of circumstantial evidence. Neither he nor any judge who knew anything about his profession ever doubted the opinion of Lord Hale cited by Thurtell that before a man can be convicted of murder, it is necessary to prove that "the fact be proved to have been done, or

at least the body of the dead man be found." But if the jury followed Thurtell's argument on the danger of giving too much credence to circumstantial evidence, "there would be an end at once
to the judicature of man"; indeed, circumstantial evidence "is considered as more satisfactory in producing conviction in the human
mind, than the direct testimony of any single individual who saw
the crime in question committed." For his own part, despite the infamous character of Probert, he had never seen a case in which
circumstantial evidence was more useful.

Turning to the question of pretrial publicity, the court found it
distressing that the prisoners were obliged to implore the jury to
dismiss the publications entirely from their thoughts and to avoid
them as they would "the breath of a pestilence." He added that if
these publications "are not checked immediately by authority, I,
for one, shall tremble for the Constitution of my country. We have
long boasted, and I think justly boasted, of the purity with which
justice is administered amongst us; but if the practices which have
recently grown up are allowed to continue, that boast must before
long become a mere idle boast." Nevertheless, the judge was sure
that the jurors would do their duty to the prisoners. He asked
them also to disregard Hunt's point relating to the alleged promise
of pardon, since this was a matter to be considered by him. In no
event should the jury allow any concern about extortion of the
confession blind them to the essential, incontrovertible conclusion
that, even if the confession had been induced by a false promise of
pardon, the recovery of the body from the Hill Slough showed
that in the most important respect Hunt had spoken the truth.

Proceeding to review the evidence in detail, the judge stressed
the importance of accepting and crediting the evidence of accomplices, for it was essential that "men of low degree, who confederate together for the commission of crime, should know that all
friendships which rest upon such a foundation are hollow, treacherous, and perfidious." He also told the jury that they need not
consider whether Hunt actually assisted Thurtell at the scene of
the crime, for if two or more persons prepared together to do a
criminal act, though the act was performed by only one, the accomplices were equally guilty.

For the most part the judge's comments on the testimony were fair and incisive, marred only by an irresistible urge to show off his sensitivity to the use of jargon. Referring to Probert's evidence that Thurtell had told him of Weare's "singing out that he would deliver all that he had won of him, if he would only spare his life," Park triumphantly reasserted his belief that "singing out" was navy slang. Indeed, it had since been established by the evidence of Captain Mackinlay that in fact Thurtell had been at sea. "The question here for you," the judicial linguist enjoined the jury, "will be, whether the use of such a term by Thurtell was not a circumstance to be taken as confirmatory of the truth of the evidence." Though he seized with relish on this questionable evidence of naval slang, the judge proclaimed a fastidious innocence as to the meaning of Thurtell's words that the six pounds given to Probert and Hunt were their share of the "blunt." *Blunt,* he said, "is a cant phrase which, happily, I do not understand." Apart from these linguistic conundrums, the prosecution's case seemed to fit together admirably. (The only point he could not fathom was why so much stress had been placed on the potato pit.)

The judge's compulsive impalement on points of factual detail manifested itself again when he instructed the jury with great seriousness about conflicting testimony concerning the black and white hats in Gill's Hill Lane. On the morning after the crime, he reminded them, the road menders had seen two men in the lane, one wearing a black hat and the other a white one. Herrington had identified Thurtell as the man in the white hat and stated that the other had large bushy hair and black whiskers. Now, proceeded the judge, it had been proved that Thurtell had no white hat of his own but Probert did; on the other hand, Probert denied wearing his white hat that morning. The cook had remembered seeing Thurtell lying on the sofa with a white hat on his head. The judge paused after this disquisition on headgear and posed an "important fact" to be considered by the jury: was Thurtell wearing a white hat or not on the day in question?

When Park came to speculate on the motive for the crime, he could not resist the opportunity for moralizing. No adequate motive could be surmised for such an atrocious and horrible murder, but it had appeared that Weare had won a considerable sum from Thurtell at play:

> If this were so, it is to be considered whether that dreadful, that horrible
> vice, by which he has suffered, and which the prisoner himself has in his
> address most properly stigmatized with the strongest reprobation—that
> vice which destroys the good order of society, saps the foundations of all
> morals, and too often drives men to the commission of crimes that other-
> wise they would never contemplate—whether this has really been the
> motive of the fatal crime that has been committed? If it has been, I sin-
> cerely hope that the event of this day, whatever way the business may
> terminate, will operate as an awful lesson. If what the prisoner has
> stated were indeed true, that the nobility and gentry of this country
> commonly indulged in the destructive vice of gaming, I trust that this
> will have a salutary effect upon them.

After tying up the remaining loose ends of the case, the judge
embarked on a peroration that he was determined would rival
Thurtell's. In concluding, he told the jury that if the facts were sufficient to bring their minds conviction, then, however respectable
the prisoner's family and however much the jury might regret that
such a man should be guilty of the crime imputed to him, the jury's
feeling ought not to influence their verdict.

It was about twenty-five minutes past three o'clock when the
charge concluded. As the jury was about to retire, Joe Hunt requested permission to address a few last words to them. Mr. Justice
Park expressed distress that such a late application had been made,
for he was forbidden to grant it; however, he asked Hunt's counsel
to confer with their client and if they told him it was advisable the
judge would communicate the prisoner's message to the jury. After
Thesiger conferred with Hunt and the court, the judge said that
he had nothing further to tell the jurors.

While the jury was out, Thurtell, free at last from mandated silence, exploded into conversation with all who would listen. Onlookers were shocked as he calmly inquired of his counsel whether
the judge had the power to grant a few days respite from execution, but the tone of his remarks soon lightened. When someone
remarked that his address was very powerful and energetic, Thurtell frankly admitted that he had compiled it from various sources.
"What did you think of the conclusion," he asked, "was it not very
fine? I took it principally from Phillips's speeches; it is in the defence he wrote for Turnor, the bank clerk." He ridiculed Probert's
evidence and took particular offense at the notion that in the death

struggle Weare had nearly got the better of him. He said: "Weare was a very little man; and to think it possible that such a person could get the better of me, is all nonsense." A friend observed that at all events he could not be accused of betraying his companions and he acknowledged the compliment. Before anyone could have got his secret from him, he would have had to tear his heart from his breast. His friend, fearing that this comment implied an admission, hurriedly interjected: "You mean if you had been concerned." As if as an afterthought, Thurtell answered distractedly, "Yes, of course."[5]

At five minutes before four the jury returned; Hunt gave them a look of "intense anxiety," but Thurtell "surveyed them with the same calmness as before." Both men were found guilty. According to Edwart Herbert, the foreman delivered the verdict against Thurtell "in tears, and in a tone which seemed to say, 'we have tried to find him innocent—but the evidence is too true!'"[6]

One last bizarre chapter remained in the trial proceedings. As Mr. Justice Park was preparing to pass sentence, Andrews in a low tone said that he moved in behalf of Thurtell for an arrest of judgment and wished the motion to be argued by Chitty. The argument Park heard reflected a degree of formalism that rivaled his own. Chitty urged that the trial was illegal because it had been held on a day that was directed by statute to be kept holy, the Festival of the Epiphany. Park observed that all the law required was that there be a full church service on that day, but Chitty proceeded with his argument undeterred. He recalled a famous legal anecdote: "Your lordship will recollect a story of Mr. Dunning, who, when Lord Mansfield said, 'I shall sit tomorrow (Good Friday),' replied, 'Then your lordship will be the first Judge, since Pontius Pilate, who did.'" Humorlessly, Mr. Justice Park responded: "But not the last. For the last twenty years it has been the constant practice on the Northern Circuit." A judge had told Park that when he was in an assize town on Good Friday, he intentionally sat after church services because by so doing he prevented many individuals who were called on to attend the court "from closing the day in debauchery or drunkenness." In "humble imitation of him," Park had followed the same course; there must have been five thousand persons brought to trial on Good Friday.

When Chitty finally admitted defeat, the clerk Knapp asked the defendants whether either of them had any reason to put forward why sentence of death should not be passed on them. Thurtell, pursuing the theme of his recent conversation with his lawyers, asked for postponement of the execution until the following Monday so that his friends would have an opportunity to come from Norwich to visit him. Park rejected the request, put on the black coif and addressed the prisoners. With a show of great emotion, he said of Thurtell: "It cannot but give great compunction to every feeling mind that a person who, from his conduct this day, has shown that he was born with capacity for better things—who, according to his statement, received in his childhood religious impressions from a kind and careful mother—who in his youth served his country without reproach—should, notwithstanding, have been guilty of so foul and detestable a crime." He ordered that the two defendants be taken on Friday, January 9, "to a place of execution, and that you be hanged by the neck till you be dead, and that your body be taken down and delivered over to the surgeon to be dissected and anatomized." Thurtell listened to the judge's words with "unbroken spirit." While the directions for the dissection of his body were given, he consumed a pinch of snuff that he had been working in his fingers and then shook hands with a friend under the dock.

Not only the judge but the onlookers were strangely moved by Thurtell's sentence and the courage with which he bore it. Edward Herbert, still mesmerized by Jack's powerful oratory, wrote: "I confess I myself was shaken. I was cold and sick. I looked with tumultuous feelings at that desperate man, thus meeting death, as though it were an ordinary circumstance of his life; and when he went through the dark door [of the courtroom], he seemed to me gone to his fate. It struck me that death then took him! I never saw him more."[7] When Thurtell returned to jail, prison governor Wilson treated him with great kindness. Chaplain Franklin found Thurtell in his cell bathed in tears, but he recovered his composure when Franklin entered. The chaplain thought that he might be in a mood to make a full disclosure of all he knew about the crime but felt that under the circumstances it would be unfair to press him and he did not ask any questions. After Franklin left, handcuffs were placed on Thurtell's wrists and three men came to sit up with him all night. One of them covered him with a rug and Jack soon dropped into a sound sleep. He awoke once or twice and on one occasion called out to one of his guards, "William, are you there?" On being told, "That's right," he again slept deeply.[8]

Chapter Thirteen

THE NEW DROP

The next morning Thurtell awoke at seven o'clock. Sitting on a stool near the fire that had been tended all night, he read briefly from religious tracts that had been left him. About half an hour later he was glad to receive a visit from prison governor Wilson, whose company he always enjoyed; he seemed to have struck a responsive chord in the hearts of Wilson and his family, who respected his courage and regarded him as a model prisoner. When Wilson told him that the execution on the following day would not be as early as he had anticipated, Thurtell expressed regret: "The sooner the better, for I have taken my leave of this world; as my doom is fixed, the sooner I suffer the better." He walked to the chapel with a firm step and looked perfectly composed; Joe Hunt, who was also there, looked a perfect picture of despair. No other persons were allowed to be present; the sheriff, still fearful of the long arm of the "Lemon mob," had given strict orders that no one was to be admitted to the jail without his permission. The service was performed by Chaplain Franklin in an impressive manner. He delivered an eloquent speech that took its text from 2 Corinthians 5:10: "For we must all appear before the judgment seat of Christ; that every one may receive the things done in his body, according to that he hath done, whether it be good or bad." He implored the prisoners to consider the certainty of a future judgment in view of the unequal distribution of happiness and misery in this life. The justice of God seemed to require that at the final consummation of all things this seeming injustice should be rectified and "that there would be held a general assize of all men that ever breathed on the face of the whole earth, when they would all have a fair and open trial, and God would render to each according to his works." Franklin was particularly solemn in dealing with the profligacy of those who were not deterred by a sense of religion from the commission of sin, as if believing that eternal justice were asleep. He said that it would be easy to draw a terrible picture of the great day of judgment but that he preferred the arguments that cool reason suggested. Why did men show such insensibility of human interests, why did they stifle the voice of conscience, and why did they labor to drown its cries "by the din and riot of worldly cares and pleasures"?[1]

Repeatedly, Franklin was moved to tears by his own words. Hunt seemed strongly affected and his head dropped upon the front of his pew, but Thurtell evinced the same blend of emotions that had attracted unusual sympathy from those who had observed him in prison since the trial, an appearance of extreme penitence that yet left his characteristic stoutheartedness intact. The population of the jail, who had seen so many men prepare to die, found a special appeal in this stormy man whom the last comforts of religion appeared to have made wiser but not less brave.[2]

While Thurtell's spiritual welfare was being provided for, the magistrates were meeting to determine the arrangements for the execution. It was decided that Thurtell would be hanged next day at noon in front of the prison's main entrance (which was called the "Mill Door" or "Treadmill Door") and not in the field or gravel pit opposite the prison where the gallows was usually erected. Work on the scaffold, which was being constructed under the direction of Undersheriff Nicholson, had been begun before the opening of the trial, but some objection had been made at the time by the magistrates that "it might be considered indelicate to commence such a work, as it were, in anticipation of the conviction of the prisoners."[3] However, since there was no other fit gallows in the county, Sheriff Sutton had decided that there was no time to be lost. An anecdote that was circulating claimed that Thurtell's contempt for Hertford's antiquated execution practices had led to the decision to erect a thoroughly modern gallows. It was said that one day, while conversing with Wilson, Jack had "jocosely" said: "Why, I understand that when you *round* (hang) people here, you put them in a *tumbler* (cart), and send them out of the world with a *gee-up, gee-ho* [to the horses pulling the cart], and I suppose my ears will be saturated with a smack of the whip; but this is rather an old-fashioned and ungentlemanly way of finishing a man." This comment was supposedly communicated to the magistrates, and "they determined to accommodate him by ordering a new drop gallows to be erected and allowing him to hansel it [initiate its use]."[4]

The same civic pride that dictated the investment in an up-to-date hanging machine made Hertford's leaders anxious to avoid disgrace through the botched performance of a provincial executioner. Even before the trial was over a message had been sent to John Wontner, the keeper of Newgate, "to send down a proper man." For some reason James Foxen, the chief London hangman was unavailable, so the best Wontner could provide was Thomas Cheshire, Foxen's perpetual deputy. Even before the verdict was announced, "Old Cheese" (as someone without much imagination had dubbed Cheshire) bet a oneway ticket on the result; he traveled down to Hertford on the top of a coach. Upon his arrival he engaged a room at a public house and soon gathered a circle of admirers in the bar parlor. They traded drinks for stories of his professional experiences and a peek at the nooses he had brought in his traveling bag. The result of this convivial occasion is described by Horace Bleackley in *The Hangmen of England:*

> Unfortunately, too, Tom always grew quarrelsome when in his cups. After giving pantomimic displays of the correct way to tie up a "party," he proceeded to wrangle with the other folks in the bar, a quarrel with a coachmen leading to a fierce fight. While the hangman and his adversary were pummelling each other the hangman's ropes were stolen by one of the bar-loafers, and finally the landlord interfered turning Cheshire into the street. Fuming with rage, he went at once to Hertford gaol to complain of this wrongs, whereupon the turnkeys locked him up in an empty cell, so that he could be kept out of mischief and might sleep off the effects of his carousal. And here they made him stay until the day of execution.[5]

The gallows that Nicholson and his men erected received a favorable review from even such an inveterate Londoner as Pierce Egan:

> The drop was ingeniously suited to the purpose for which it was intended, and was calculated to terminate the existence of the unhappy

culprit in the shortest possible period. There was a temporary platform with a falling leaf, supported by bolts, and upon this the prisoner was to be placed. The bolts were fixed in such a manner as to be removed in an instant, and as instantaneously the victim of his own crimes would be launched into eternity. Above this platform was a cross-beam, to which the fatal cord was to be affixed. The whole was solidly and compactly made, and capable of being taken asunder and removed in a very short time. The inclosure consisted of boards seven feet in height, and dove-tailed into each other, so as to close every crevice. The extent of the place thus embraced was about thirty feet in length, and fifty in width.[6]

During the whole of Thursday afternoon people of every social rank were seen driving into Hertford from all directions to witness the execution, their expectation sharpened by the hope "that some extraordinary declaration would be made by Thurtell, in his dying moments." All the local inns were completely filled, for the place of the crowds that had departed after the trial had been taken by the hordes of new arrivals. Pierce Egan, already on the scene, de-duced from the very appearance of some of the travelers and the jaded state of their horses that they had come long distances "and indeed we know that many hundreds of them actually come from Worcester, the scene of the late extraordinary contest between Spring and Langan."[7]

On Wednesday, before upwards of thirty thousand spectators the English champion, Tom Spring (born Tom Winter) had defeated the Irish champion Jack Langan in an epic match of seventy-seven rounds. In the last round Spring had administered heavy punish-ment with both hands and Langan fell quite exhausted. When time was called, the Irishman was insensible and Josh Hudson, his second, gave in for him. Half a minute later, Langan opened his eyes still sitting on the knee of his second. Hudson had no right to give in for him, he insisted, he could fight forty more rounds.[8] When the news of Spring's victory came to the ear of Jack Thurtell on Thursday, his enthusiasm put his own desperate situation com-pletely out of his mind. He remarked to one of his jailers that he would dearly love to read Pierce Egan's account of the fight.[9]

For the most part, however, Thursday was a day punctuated by interviews and leave-takings. Up to the last moment, the public clung to the notion that Thurtell must in some way be responsible for all the unsolved crimes of the age. Mr. Richards, a fellow of one of the colleges at Cambridge University, arrived at Hertford Gaol and told the authorities that the Reverend Mr. Colton, of whose mysterious disappearance much had been recently written in the press, had been a member of his college and that, having heard of Thurtell's conviction, he had come to Hertford to ask him whether he had any information about Colton's fate. Chaplain Franklin dutifully put his question to Jack, who said he knew nothing of Mr. Colton. Franklin had been unwilling to allow the visitor to speak to Thurtell directly, for High Sheriff Sutton had given orders that no person should be admitted to ask the prisoner questions "lest such interruptions should divert his mind from the solemn preparation it was undergoing."[10]

An exception from this order was made for Tom Thurtell, who came to visit his brother in the evening to take a last farewell before he himself was reconveyed to Newgate where he was imprisoned on the fire conspiracy charge. It was only with the greatest difficulty that the chaplain could tear the brothers apart when the interview ended. When his brother was removed, Thurtell expressed regret that Tom had come: "Poor fellow, he had quite unmanned me." He also spoke of his mother more than once with great tenderness. Referring to the part of his sentence by which he was ordered to be dissected and anatomized, he expressed a wish that only the minimal formalities of that operation would be complied with and that his body might thereafter be delivered to friends for interment so that his mother might be able to visit her son's grave: "I know my mother's tender heart; she will search for the grave of her darling son, and will find a melancholy pleasure in weeping over a stone engraved only with the initials of his name." He also explained his refusal to have a cast made of his head: "I do not wish that a cast should be taken of my head, lest from that cast a bust should be made, which might, at some future time, meet the eyes of my family, and serve to perpetuate the remembrance of my unhappy fate."[11]

About nine o'clock Chaplain Franklin, after a short absence, returned to Thurtell's room bringing a few oranges (for which Jack had a passion) and after some conversation on religious themes found the prisoner's mind calm and collected. When Franklin was about to leave an hour later, Jack expressed the wish that Joe Hunt be permitted to pass the night with him. The chaplain saw no objection and in fact felt that the experience might make a favorable impression on the feelings of Hunt who, in his view, did not exhibit the same spirit of repentance that he had seen with gratification in Thurtell. Wilson's son, who had become especially fond of Thurtell, replaced Franklin in the cell and read to the prisoner from the Scriptures and from sermons furnished by Franklin, and the prisoner also read extracts from religious works. When young Wilson retired for the night, Joe Hunt was led in. Thurtell took him by the hand and said: "Joe, the past is forgotten. I stand on the brink of eternity, and we meet now only as friends. It may be your fate to lose your life as ignominiously as myself; but I sincerely hope the Royal mercy will be extended to you, and that you will live to repent of your past errors, and make some atonement for the injuries which you may have done to me or others. Although you may have been my enemy, I freely forgive you." Hunt, who had entered the room with understandable apprehension as to how he would be received, was greatly relieved by Thurtell's words and, grasping his hand vigorously, burst into his ever ready tears. Joe was indeed hoping for mercy. In the meantime he was benefiting from the two-week deferment of execution ordinarily granted to accessories.

Acceding to Jack's wish that they spend his last hours together, Joe sat down by the hearth and the two men continued to pray and read religious works together until one o'clock. Jack had previously taken tea and occasionally during the night sucked an orange, but in the early hours of the morning he became fatigued and fell asleep, leaving Hunt reading by the fire.[12]

As day broke an immense crowd began to gather before the prison, occupying every elevated spot. Among the visitors from the metropolis, the *Times* reporter "observed many of that pernicious race, who are *par excellence,* we suppose, denominated 'the fancy'—that race to his connexion with whom Thurtell would, we doubt not, have attributed all his misfortunes and all his infamy, could he have been induced to speak his mind openly." Two features of the crowd struck the *Times* reporter as unusual: the vast number of riders most of whom were apparently "small farmers intermingled with sporting butchers, bakers, and mealmen" and the throng of women, "who, to their shame be it spoken, appeared on the ground."[13]

By eleven o'clock the onlookers extended in a dense mass for about a furlong on the London side of the jail and the same distance on the Hertford side, and beyond, a less closely packed gathering straggled along a small bridge over a rivulet that ran up to the Blue-Coat School. The spectators found that the best accommodation was afforded by a cow house and a place for rearing swine that stood near a hedge immediately opposite the gallows; these humble outbuildings were lightly constructed with boards and covered with thatch and did not appear capable of supporting any great weight. Nevertheless, throwing caution to the winds, jostling spectators soon filled both roofs. The inevitable mishaps were soon to follow. About eleven o'clock a portion of the cow house roof gave way, but since there were no injuries, the warning was not taken and nobody was willing to abandon such a favorable viewing position. Then, a half hour later, both roofs completely collapsed; a boy's thigh was broken, and other spectators were hurt, but even greater injuries would have been suffered if governor Wilson had not taken the precaution of filling the fragile structures with straw.[14]

At half past six that morning, Wilson's son had entered Thurtell's cell to find him fast asleep and snoring vigorously; Joe Hunt, in a deep slumber, was still sitting near the fire. At seven o'clock he came back with his father, who, approaching Thurtell's bed, found that his face was covered with a blanket and that the prisoner was sleeping so profoundly that his breath was not audible. When he called his name, Jack was startled awake and seemed disoriented; he told Wilson that he had dreamt "several odd things" but had never dreamt anything "about this business" since he had been in Hertford. After he had bathed his face, he was brought tea and bread and butter instead of the traditional hearty breakfast, but only sipped a bit of the tea. At eight o'clock Chaplain Franklin arrived and expressed satisfaction at finding him in a firm and composed frame of mind. When Wilson and the three attendants left them alone in the cell, Thurtell told the chaplain that he regretted the short time remaining for penitence and mentioned that he had written on the previous day to his father and had dealt with all his worldly concerns. Afterwards, he wrote two more letters, one to his brother Tom in Newgate, and the other to his solicitor Fenton.

When Undersheriff Nicholson came to see him, Jack thanked him for his kindness and declined High Sheriff Sutton's offer of a visit. He and Joe Hunt were then taken to the prison chapel. During communion Jack was heard to read the prayers in a distinct voice; afterwards he turned to Hunt and grasped his hands repeatedly with renewed assurances that he forgave him. When Wilson and Thurtell remained alone in the chapel, the governor could not resist one last jab at the truth. "Now, Thurtell, as there is no eye to witness what is passing between us but that of God, you must not be surprised if I ask you a question." Thurtell turned to face him with a look that was surprised and wary, but Wilson was not disconcerted. "If you intend to make any confession, I think you cannot do it at a better time than the present." Pausing for a few moments and hearing no reply, Wilson quickly lowered his expectations. "I ask you if you acknowledge the justice of your sentence." Thurtell immediately took Wilson's hands and, pressing them warmly, gave him his final words on the murder of Weare, words that fell short of confession but accepted his treatment at the hands of the law: "I am quite satisfied, I forgive the world; I die in peace and charity with all mankind, and that is all I wish to go forth upon this occasion. . . . I admit that justice has been done me—I am perfectly satisfied." At this point the chaplain rejoined them, and Wilson broke off the conversation.[15]

At noon precisely, Nicholson tapped at the chapel door with his wand of office. It was now Jack Thurtell's turn to become comforter, for noticing an expression of deep sorrow on Franklin's face, he said firmly, "Sir, I am ready." As he thanked Franklin not only for his charity but for the contrite spirit in which he was now about to die, the chaplain, who was not new to death, burst into tears.

The way from the chapel to the Mill Door leading to the scaffold was mercifully short, not more than ten yards along a paved passage. Jack walked along the passage with his hand on the chaplain's arm. His step was firm and his demeanor unagitated, and he seemed less affected by his fate than those around him. He cordially shook hands with young Wilson to whom earlier in the morning he had given a lock of his hair for lack of a better memento; now as if recollecting himself, he said, "Oh! Here's my snuff box. It is now empty and I have no further occasion for it; keep it for my sake." When he arrived at the foot of the gallows, he also shook hands with Chaplain Franklin and mounted the steps to the scaffold, preceded by High Sheriff Sutton and the executioner Cheshire and followed by Wilson and the head turnkey.[16]

The scaffold was surrounded by a body of javelin men, but neither they nor their staves were necessary to restrain the crowd, which was reported to have been extraordinarily well behaved. When some spectators in an elevated place signaled Thurtell's approach to the gallows, there was a sudden exclamation from the surrounding crowd, but then almost everyone present took off their hats as if in respect for the doomed man. Pierce Egan, as he intently observed Thurtell's appearance under the gallows, thought he had received a bow of recognition from his old acquaintance:

> Thurtell . . . looked round with a countenance unchanged by the awfulness of his situation.—His manner was firm and undaunted, at the same time that it betrayed no unbecoming levity. After regarding the crowd for a moment, he appeared to recognize an individual beneath him (we believe Mr. Pierce Egan) to whom he bowed in a friendly but dignified manner. He afterwards bowed generally to all about him. Previously to his mounting the scaffold, he had begged of Mr. Nicholson that as little delay as possible might take place in his execution after his appearance upon the platform.[17]

Dressed in a dark brown greatcoat, black velvet collar, white corduroy breeches, and drab gaiters, Thurtell had his hands confined with handcuffs instead of the usual cord; at his request his arms were not pinioned. Spectators near the scaffold could see his black kid gloves below the cuffs of his coat, and he wore the same white cravat that he had sported on the last day of the trial. These elegant details of his dress clashed with the very heavy chains that bound his legs and were tied round his waist by the emblem of the Fancy—a Belcher handkerchief. To the *Times* reporter he looked careworn; "his countenance had assumed a cadaverous hue, and there was a haggardness and lankness about his cheeks and mouth, which could not fail to attract the notice of every spectator."[18]

The moment Thurtell placed himself under the beam, Chesh-

ire, complying with the prisoner's previously expressed wish, proceeded without delay to perform his duty. As he took off Jack's cravat and shirt collar, the condemned man stood perfectly calm and
still, holding out his neck to make the hangman's task easier. A
white cap was placed upon his head and drawn down over his eyes,
the fabric so thin as to permit Thurtell to continue scanning the
crowd. Jack remained unmoved when the rope was placed round
his neck, but while the executioner was attaching the other end to
the beam above, he turned to him with a last request: "Give me fall
enough." The hangman replied with professional confidence that
he might be assured he should have plenty of fall and that all would
be right. But Jack, desiring a second opinion, repeated the request
to Wilson and received the same promise; these oddly assorted
friends, jailer and doomed man, exchanged blessings, and Wilson
retired to the boards that had been placed immediately behind the
drop. The undersheriff then gave a signal with his wand, and the
new drop fell quickly without the slightest noise. Outside the enclosure, some of the spectators, fifteen thousand strong, fainted
from the pressure of the crowd, but "upon the whole, . . . the mot-
ley assemblage, vast as it was, was characterized by the most or-
derly and decorous behaviour." [19]

Thurtell had been granted his wish of an easy death for only "a
slight convulsion of the mouth" was observed the moment after
the trap opened, followed by a single groan and then silence. The
crowd, however, thought that he had struggled greatly, for the
hangman, to make his job doubly sure, had pulled the dead man's
body towards the ground more than a dozen times. When the bolt
had been drawn, an involuntary shudder seemed to run through
the crowd, and the *Times* reporter saw one man faint and several
trying to hide their emotions.

Still, the outpouring of sympathy for Thurtell did not wholly
overwhelm a competing emotion: the dread that the unseen presence of the mysterious gang leader Lemon was among them. At
the very moment of Thurtell's death, the *Times* asserted, "four
horse-expresses proceeded at full gallop towards London, for the
purpose, it was said, of informing some of Thurtell's late associates
that he had died without making any confession to their prejudice." Camden Pelham, in his *Chronicles of Crime; or, The New New-*

gate Calendar, reported that an even darker plot had been attempted among the Fancy: some fighting men had volunteered "to bear him away from the scaffold, before his execution, in defiance of the law, and in the face of the vast mob, which, it was known, would be collected on the occasion of his execution, the confusion produced by which, however, they well knew would aid rather than oppose their object." According to Pelham, the number of willing pugilists was so small that money was needed to procure outside assistance; with this object, the conspiring bruisers opened negotiations with Thurtell's friends for a war chest, "but the sum demanded, which was said to be £500, not being forthcoming, the plan was given up." Pelham attributed Thurtell's calmness on the scaffold to his hope of a last-minute rescue.[20]

Thurtell's body remained hanging for one hour before the eyes of most of the crowd, which quietly stayed at the scene. Then it was carried into the prison chapel, where a platform had been prepared to receive it in one of the pews, and was immediately stripped under Nicholson's direction. When the cap was removed, the face appeared somewhat discolored but in short time assumed the waxen tone of death. The hangman's trademark on Thurtell's neck seemed unusually strong, and Pierce Egan offered the explanation that this was because of "the violence of the fall, by which it appeared that the vertebrae were completely dislocated." He added admiringly, "The form of the unfortunate deceased was, in the highest degree, symmetrical and muscular, and was spoken of by the surgeon who was present, as distinguished for every indication of strength and activity."[21]

With the trial and execution over and no fear left of the wrath of Mr. Justice Park, the newspapers, which had grown fat on the case, were filled with editorial appraisals of John Thurtell. Fitting the surprising pattern of most of the commentary, the *British Press,* a London daily, was so full of admiration for the courage and eloquence Thurtell had displayed at Hertford that it had to remind itself, as if unwillingly, of the barbarity of Gill's Hill Lane:

> Thus perished John Thurtell, in the thirty-second year of his age; a memorable example of the evil consequences of that attachment to sporting by which so many young men are ruined, and so many more depraved. May some of those who are entering on the path that led to his destruction take warning by his fate!

... his fortitude had inspired into the public mind no small share of sympathy for his suffering. . . . He looked at death steadily, and met it unshrinkingly. Had the determination of character, the self-possession in danger, and the bold intrepidity which he displayed during the whole trial, and to the moment of his death, been enlisted in a good cause, he would have been an invaluable citizen. . . .

The most affecting part of his address to the jury was the contrast which he drew between what he then was and what he might have been. His expression of regret, that he had not fallen in the field of defence of his country was manly, natural, and energetic.[22]

The *Times,* too, had to repress by main force its enthusiasm for Thurtell's last days and for the "amiability" he had shown his warders:

We must guard against admitting our admiration of his fortitude to overcome our moral abhorrence of the barbarities he committed. It is evident that he was a man of uncommon energy of mind, and the sympathy of his gaol-attendants, men unused to melt, shows that he must have possessed some kind, and generous, and amiable qualities. . . . At the same time society must feel relieved by casting off from its bosom a being who, having chosen the path of crime, was equally formidable from the laxity of his principles and the strength of his passions, from the unbounded influence his mental vigour gave him over his associates, and from his utter fearlessness of danger and of death.[23]

The *Morning Chronicle* echoed the *Times*'s sentiments, opining that, if anything could have made reparation to mankind for his crime, "it would be the exemplary piety, and the moral fortitude with which he met his untimely fate."[24]

It was perhaps predictable that Pierce Egan would stand apart from this chorus of praise because of his acquaintance with Thurtell and the blatant press-agentry in which he had engaged through the publication of his prison interviews. He commented, "All cases of crime portray various *shades* of guilt; but in no instance do I recollect, during my life, nor in the course of reading the memoirs of numerous criminals, a murder of a more, if of so cold-blooded nature as the one before me." But the force of his observation was muted by Egan's self-seeking explanation: "I think it necessary to make this assertion, that no misconception may afterwards arise respecting my opinion of the late John Thurtell."[25] Edward Herbert, despite his emotional response to the sentence, retained a clear-eyed vision of Thurtell's villainy; he saw him as a man whose life had been "one long vice" but who "had iron nerves and sullen low love of fame,—even black fame,—which stimulated him to be a hero, though but of the gallows." Herbert assumed that the much praised defense speech was actually written by Thurtell's lawyer friend, Charles Pearson, and then learned by rote. He reminded his readers that Thurtell had rehearsed it a month before to Pierce Egan and had probably thought that, embellished by gentlemanly dress and a pathetic manner, it would bring him through to safety or at least "insure him a gloomy immortality." For the admirers of Thurtell's courtroom showmanship, Herbert, despite his own unbridled praise, had a disdain that was mixed with the hope that they would at last come back to their senses. "His ordinary discourse was slang and blasphemy; but he chained up his oaths in court. The result of all this masquerading, for a short time, has been public sorrow for his fate, and particularly among women! The re-action is, however, again coming round, and although it is impossible not to admire this man's courage and his intellect; it is also as impossible not to rejoice in the death of so much revenge, cruelty, and bloody power!"[26]

In the view of *Blackwood's Edinburgh Magazine,* perennially disapproving of things English (including crimes), Thurtell's case had prospered in public favor because it had come on for trial in the boring winter months, when newspapers had nothing else to publish. It was certain that "from the latter end of February, through the merry months of spring, and the merrier months of summer, Thurtell would have been tried without a whisper outside the walls of the Court, and hung with no other consideration than that which the Ordinary and the Hangman give to the family of Cut-throats." No language could be too strong for the horror of the crime and "no contempt too bitter for the miserable sympathy that attempted to turn [Thurtell] into a victim or a hero."[27]

As in the early days of the investigation, newspaper diatribes were briefly relieved by a recognition of the sufferings of Alderman Thurtell. An exchange of correspondence was published between the unhappy father and Sheriff Sutton, in which Thomas Thurtell thanked the sheriff for forwarding Jack's last letter and asked the Hertford magistrates, Lloyd, Franklin, and Wilson to accept his warmest acknowledgment of their kind attention to his son. Chaplain Franklin, at Jack's request, wrote to Alderman Thurtell's friend Nathaniel Bolingbroke an account of the prisoner's sincere repentance and in response received a small silver platter "as a slight token of the gratitude" that the elder Thurtells "must ever feel to him for his unremitted attention to our son's spiritual welfare, and our sincere wish for his earthly and heavenly happiness."[28] With this communication, Alderman Thurtell disappeared from the news reports of the case, only to reemerge a short time later as the defendant in a suit brought by Jack's lawyers, seeking recovery of their unpaid trial fees.

The retribution for the Gill's Hill murder did not end with Thurtell's hanging. At six o'clock on the evening of the execution day his body was put into a sack and transported to St. Bartholomew's Hospital; it was widely noted with ironic satisfaction that the conveyance used was a gig, "the same kind of vehicle in which the murderer carried, on that day eleven weeks, the body of the unfortunate Mr. Weare."[29] Undersheriff Nicholson had declined an application by Thurtell's friends to have the body buried at Norwich, stating that he was bound by the terms of Mr. Justice Park's sentence requiring a dissection. Mr. Colbeck, the surgeon of Hertford Gaol, together with this assistant, made a slight beginning in the dissection process so as to comply with the letter of the law but was only too glad to dispatch the body to St. Bartholomew's for the rest of the grisly work to be done.[30]

Great crowds assembled at St. Bartholomew's shortly after the corpse arrived and, following an ineffectual attempt at restricting entry, an almost indiscriminate admission of the public was permitted to continue for three or four days. Among those who viewed the remains were about twenty persons belonging to the establishment of Thomas Kelly, the publisher of *The Fatal Effects of Gambling Exemplified in the Murder of William Weare* (1824). With this delegation,

> an eminent artist attended for the purpose of verifying to the extremest possible point of fidelity our portrait of the great criminal. The result of his efforts has been highly satisfactory; for we are thereby enabled to add to our excellent portrait of Thurtell while living, a faithful representation of his countenance when dead. It was finished from a cast taken from his face, in proof of the accuracy and genuineness of which

we can assure our readers, that while in the possession of our artist, many hairs from the eyebrows and whiskers of the deceased, which had detached themselves with the plaster mould, were still adhering. . . .

This very curious relic, has not, we believe, been accessible to any other publisher.[31]

Thurtell's corpse had at first been placed in a small room contiguous to the theater of anatomy, which could accommodate no more than ten or twelve persons. Subsequently, it was moved into the theater for convenience of the surgical lectures of Mr. Abernethy and other eminent colleagues. The body was five feet, ten and a half inches, long, remarkable for its muscularity and symmetry and clearness of skin. From the appearance of the limbs it was difficult for observers to imagine that they had lost any of their living strength and elasticity. The features were not distorted by death; the principal change that had come over them was the relaxation of the cheek muscles, which had been powerful and massive in life. Publisher Kelly's men thought that death had proved flattering to Thurtell's eyes, which now seemed larger than in life and shone a fine blue. The head, with its hair removed, seemed well formed and the low forehead was less noticeable. Day after day the visitors witnessed the gradual dilapidation of the body: "On one day a finger, on another an eye, was missing; and as the surgeons, in the intervals of their admission of the public proceeded with their work, the body progressively presented such appearances as to render it both a matter of prudence and of public decency finally to close the door against farther admission."[32]

Thurtell's contemporary, the French crime journalist and novelist, Henri de Latouche, wrote that the absurd can save men from the horrible. This salutary function was served on the occasion of Thurtell's dissection by the phrenologists. In *The Fatal Effects of Gambling* it was reported that "these worthies were all a-gog to find a very common prominence behind and above [Thurtell's] ear, which they are pleased to call 'the organ of destructiveness,' or murder." Unfortunately for the "dabblers in this science," no such bump was found on Thurtell's head, but what was still worse, the "organs of benevolence" and of "caution" were very strongly marked. The savants beat a retreat, consoling themselves with the discovery that Thurtell's organ of "courage" was very large. The author of *The*

Fatal Effects of Gambling quoted (or invented) an anecdote to show the stupidity of these pseudoscientists:

> Some time ago a gentleman found a large turnip in his field, of the shape of a man's head, and with the resemblance of the features of a man. Struck with the curiosity, he had a cast made from it, and sent the cast to a Society of Phrenologists, stating, that it was taken from the head of Baron Turenpourtz, a celebrated Polish professor, and requesting their opinion thereon. After sitting in judgment, they scientifically examined the cast, in which they declared that they had discovered an unusual prominence, which denoted that he was a man of an acute mind and deep research, that he had the organ of quick perception, and also of perseverance, with another that indicated credulity. The opinion was transmitted to the owner of the cast, with a letter, requesting as a particular favour that he would send them the head; to this he politely replied, "that he would willingly do so, but was prevented, as he and his family had *eaten it the day before with their mutton at dinner.*"[33]

Long after the curiosity seekers had gone, Thurtell's remains were an object of more serious study at St. Bartholomew's. In late 1829, after becoming apprenticed to a surgeon bound for western Australia, the fifteen-year-old John Pocock was taken to the St. Bartholomew's dissecting room and looked over its museum; subjects, he noted, "were very scarce and disjointed members were lying on the dissecting tables with the tickets and price of each affixed." There he saw the skulls of Thurtell and of John Bellingham, who had assassinated Prime Minister Spencer Perceval in 1812. The young Pocock, like many other students, received his first introduction to the structure of human life from the bones of men who had destroyed it.[34]

Chapter Fourteen

THE FATAL EFFECTS
OF THE FAST LIFE

———

Boiled Beef Williams, the manager of the New Surrey Theatre, was not a man to waste time. On January 12, 1824, only three days after Thurtell's hanging, he advertised in the *Times* that on that evening a "re-production" of *The Gamblers* would be presented, followed by an entirely new comic operetta with a strangely relevant title, *Four Inside; or, Off by the Night Coach.*[1]

The playbill promised the appearence of "the "identical horse and gig alluded to in the daily press in the accounts of the late murder, together with the table at which the party supped, the sofa as described to having been slept on, with other household furniture, as purchased at the late auction." Despite all these added touches of realism, the attempt to portray the recently convicted murderers was ruined by hurried casting that selected for the part of Thurtell "a little gentleman . . . who is not quite five feet high." The *Times* review snobbishly noted that, when repetition of the play was mentioned, "severe disapprobation was announced, by several gentlemen in white hats and drab great coats in the pit, but three chimney-sweepers in the gallery, who had from the beginning of the piece testified their love of justice by their loud plaudits, soon drowned the opposition, and brought over the majority to their side, and in favour of the new piece."[2]

On the same evening, the Royal Coburg opened a rival production, *The Hertfordshire Tragedy; or, The Victims of Gaming.* This play, according to the *Times*, "portrayed (as far as scenic arrangements could effect it) the whole of the revolting transactions which led to the late trial and execution," and even the disposal of the body was represented with "disgusting exactness." Unlike his counterpart at the Surrey, the Thurtell figure of the Coburg play (named Freeman) was given a partially sympathetic characterization as an innocent young provincial whom a gang of blacklegs introduced to the vice of gambling and persuaded to murder Weare to settle their own scores. The *Times* was repelled by the entire spectacle and particularly by the allusions in Thurtell's dock speech to his respectable father, which "are in violation of every common feeling of humanity."[3] The *Times's* outrage was not shared by the general public, for the two plays were staged during the next two years under a variety of titles in cities and towns all over the country, including Manchester, Nottingham, Tamworth, and Leamington.

The trial and execution of Thurtell also reopened the floodgates to a new spate of street literature. As usual, Jemmy Catnach led his competitors in ingenuity; he brought out an inconsequential broadside that was headed *WE ARE ALIVE AGAIN!* but left so little space between the words *WE* and *ARE* that it appeared to announce the resurrection of Jack Thurtell's victim.[4] Vying with the broadsides for the small change of the public was a heavy supply of books and pamphlets on the trial and Thurtell's last days. One of these productions, the account by Watford clerk G. H. Jones, garnered an endorsement from a surprising sponsor—magistrate Robert Clutterbuck, who had spearheaded the early investigations. In a letter from Watford of February 1, Clutterbuck reveals how quickly his mind had turned from justice to commerce: "I have been mindful of Mr. Jones's pamphlet during my absence [in Chichester], and have spoken upon this subject to a bookseller there of the name of Jacques whom my sister employs, who thinks that he can sell a good many copies for Mr. Jones, I having certified at the foot of one of the prospectuses 'that I have revised the whole of it, and can certify that it is authentick.'"[5]

The balladeers were moved, as always, to draw inspiring lessons from the scaffold. A Catnach ballad bearing the edifying title *The Hertfordshire Tragedy; or, The Fatal Effects of Gambling* invoked the legend of vampirism that had begun to attach itself to lurid accounts of Thurtell's brutal attack on Weare:

> The helpless man sprung [*sic*] from the gig,
>   And strove the road to gain,

> But Thurtell pounc'd on him, and dash'd
>   His pistol through his brains.
> Then pulling out his murderous knife,
>   As over him he stood,
> He cut his throat, and, tiger-like,
>   Did drink his reeking blood.[6]

The broadside was embellished with cameo portraits of Thurtell and Hunt and a series of eight scenes associated with the crime, among which the central place of honor was given to the scene of the murder in Gill's Hill Lane. The opening verses of a second Catnach "execution song" about Jack Thurtell were quoted by a street seller to Henry Mayhew over thirty-five years later.[7] However, it was another verse, attributed after years of controversy to William Webb, that has survived all the ephemera of the Thurtell-Hunt case and taken a permanent place among classic murder ballads. Webb, otherwise known as "Flare Up" (slang for cheap gin) or "Hoppy," had, at the height of his career, been an acrobat in a traveling circus, but he tumbled right out of show business to become a linkman or torchbearer on city streets. He was later transported for "stealing the jewels of a *prima donna* while she was leaving the Opera-House" and died on his way to Australia. The first three stanzas of Webb's verse end with the lines that achieved immortality by juxtaposing the gruesome with the matter-of-fact:

> They asked him down from London town
>   A-shooting for to go,
> But little did the gem' man think
>   As they would shoot him too.
>
> So Ruthven went, from Bow street sent,
>   Searching the country over,
> Until he pitched into Joe Hunt,
>   John Thurtell, and Bill Probert.
>
> His throat they cut from ear to ear,
>   His brains they punched in,
> His name was Mr. William Weare,
>   Wot lived in Lyon's Inn.[8]

Other popular literature followed the same formula as the Catnach ballad in portraying the murder case as proof of the fatal effects of gambling and the sporting life. One of the principal accounts of the murder case, published by Thomas Kelly, *The Fatal Effects of Gambling Exemplified in the Murder of William Weare*, ap-

pends to the trial narrative an exposé of London's gambling underworld called *The Gambler's Scourge*. The book's introduction draws
the following moral from the crime:

> The murder of William Weare will hereafter stand upon record as one
> of the distinguishing features of the present era; as a great and painful
> effort by which society has relieved itself of a huge load of vice and
> crime. . . . The murder of Weare has doubtlessly resulted from an ad-
> hesion to the principles engendered in that school of *fraud* and *flash*
> [underworld], to which not only the victim but his murderers also were
> attached. Weare, Thurtell and Probert, were all *sporting blades*, ultra *flash*
> *men*, and gamblers—preying alike upon each other, and upon society in
> general.[9]

Similarly, in *A History of the Gambling Houses and Gamesters of the Metropolis,* attached to another edition of the trial, the author asserts
that nobody "that has read the details of the murder of Weare,
with the requisite attention, can doubt for a moment that to the
accursed desire of obtaining the property of others by means of
the Gaming Table, is to be ascribed that loss of character in those
persons which led eventually to the loss of life in one of them, and
to a miserable existence of the survivors."[10] The same message is
conveyed in a pamphlet sermon of the Reverend John Wooll, head-
master of Rugby, with the chastening title *The Dangerous and Irresistible Progress of Habitual Sin, as Exemplified in the Murder of Mr.
Weare.* In this sermon originally delivered in the school chapel on
Sunday, November 2, 1823, before the indictments and postponement of the trial, the Reverend Mr. Wooll did not feel the slightest
inhibition about prejudging the case, which, to his mind, provided
a clear warning against the moral evils of gambling:

> Had these men remembered their Creator in the days of their youth,
> had their minds willingly imbibed the studies of godliness and sound
> learning—had their time in the dawn of life been profitably and laud-
> ably employed, they would not have chosen evil associates, nor taken ref-
> uge in dangerous amusements; had they not cultivated an intimacy with
> such associates, and derived gratification from such amusements, they
> would not have become professed gamesters; and had they never been
> gamesters, they would not have closed the guilty scene with the appall-
> ing crime of murder.[11]

Many of Wooll's contemporaries agreed that the Thurtell case was
a dark mirror that reflected, for all who would see, the unlovely
reality of Regency life—with all its surface glitter extinct. In his

memoirs written seventy years after Thurtell's execution, George Augustus Sala remembered the case as a prime exemplar of the "fast life of the past," which had exposed the "almost immeasurable mischief" caused by common gaming houses. "Midnight gambling," wrote Sala, "sapped the very vitals, economically speaking, of the community, and directly and indirectly led to innumerable tragedies."[12]

The newspapers that had pulled out all stops on pretrial publicity were not disposed to cede the exploitation of Thurtell's trial and hanging to the pamphleteers and street sellers. It is reported that each of the major London papers had four to six "horse expresses" carrying fresh news from Hertford to the metropolis. Unlike the catchpenny presses, the *Times*, in its editorial comment on the execution, directed most of its fire not against gambling (which it had thoroughly flayed in the previous months) but against boxing and its followers. In its account of the hanging, the *Times* referred to speculation among the witnesses as to Thurtell's interest, even on the point of his execution, in the result and details of the Spring-Langan fight. Towards the conclusion of the article, the *Times* expressed disgust at the insensitivity of Thurtell's former associates among the Fancy; it was extraordinary that though they were aware that "Thurtell's first plunge into crime was occasioned by his predilection for prize-fighting and similar savage amusements; many of them were wondering at the very moment before his death whether he had heard news of the recent [Spring-Langan] fight near Worcester." The article ended with a tirade against the fight crowd:

> We know not what the feelings of such men may be; but we should have expected, that if they entertained the slightest regard for the good opinion of their fellow-countrymen, they would have refrained from venturing upon such a topic at such a moment. No words can describe our disgust at conduct so revolting to decency, humanity, and all proper feeling. We shall only say, that it was in perfect keeping with the parties from whom it proceeded: we mean the gentlemen of the fancy—the ruffians of the ring.[13]

The words further inflamed the resentment of the sporting newspaper the *Weekly Dispatch*, which, already stung by the *Times*'s earlier assaults on boxing, had been publishing an apologia for its favorite sport in a series called "The Philosophy of Pugilism." In its first installment of January 4 the *Weekly Dispatch* invoked the example of the gymnastic institutions of the ancient Greeks and in its next issue claimed similar benefits from English boxing contests, which had had "the effect of inspiring the inferior, and many of the middle classes, with courage and with instinctive feelings of justice and humanity." There was naturally inherent in mankind a hostile spirit to which no civil power or legislation could put a total stop. This spirit, the *Weekly Dispatch* claimed, had been implanted by God for the wisest purposes and was nothing more than the exuberance of certain passions carried to an improper excess. Clearly boxing provided the best way of quelling the wrath that men may feel towards each other. In the England and France of a hundred years ago quarrels had been resolved by dueling; pistol fighting was still common in Ireland; and in Italy the spirit of revenge was stifled until it could be "satiated by the secret stiletto." But in England, and particularly in those parts near London where boxing flourished, there were very few instances of people stabbing each other from anger or for revenge, and secret assassination had never been less known.[14]

After the second installment in its series, the *Weekly Dispatch* read with indignation the *Times*'s new assault against the "ruffians of the ring," and it responded in kind in the January 18 installment of "The Philosophy of Pugilism." The column began by rejecting as unproved the assertion of the *Times* writer that Thurtell had become a murderer by reason of his fondness for the ring. No gentlemen of the Fancy had been named as associates of Thurtell, and none had come forward as a character witness at the trial. The *Times*'s report that boxing fans were speculating at the moment before Thurtell's death about his interest in the Spring-Langan match was a "refinement in absurdity." How could anyone know the secret thoughts of an immense mob? But suppose that someone in the crowd had wondered whether Thurtell had heard of the champions' fight: what unfeelingness or spirit of ruffianism would the question suggest? It was well known that for some time before the match, Thurtell had been talking with great animation about its probable outcome, and nothing could be more natural "than for persons to allude to the very circumstance which proved the culprit to be so hardened and so indifferent to his fate."[15]

The *Weekly Dispatch* rejected as charlatanism the claim that the frequent boxing matches that took place in England had the effect of converting men into murderers. To the contrary, there was a time in the history of the country when pugilism was unknown and murders were alarmingly frequent. In 1823, however, there was only one person committed for murder in the county of Middlesex, which was the place where all the great pugilistic matches were arranged and was unquestionably the most enlightened part of the kingdom. What then was significant about Thurtell's love for the ring? "Thurtell and his associates were murderers: of that there is no doubt: but how can it be shown that the practice of pugilism made them so? They attended at boxing matches; and so did many other infamous characters: but they never themselves took a part in those contests: they attended them only with the same view that infamous black-legs attend at horse-races—to win money by fraudulent devices." The effect of boxing, concluded the *Weekly Dispatch*, was precisely the reverse of that asserted by the *Times*, "for numerous instances can be produced to show that it has been most effectually instrumental in disarming our countrymen of that treacherous and vindictive spirit, which prevails over most of the Continent of Europe, where it generally terminates in murder."[16]

Despite all the rhetoric and ancient history marshaled by the *Weekly Dispatch* and kindred journals in defense of prizefighting, the golden age of the sport drew to a close in the year of Thurtell's execution. Although the impact of the trial and the bad name it gave to boxing cannot be measured, there is little doubt that the decline of the prize ring was accelerated by many of the factors that reportage of the case had underlined: the intimate bonds between boxing and the gambling underworld and the profusion of rowdy and criminal elements in the crowds at ringside. Before the year 1824 had run its course the withdrawal of "respectable" patronage for boxing was heralded when Gentleman John Jackson closed his training rooms in Bond Street and the Pugilistic Club, which had upheld the integrity of bouts and maintained order in the fight audience, disbanded. The month of December brought new troubles. On December 19, writing in the *Weekly Dispatch*, which remained one of the main citadels of the Fancy, George

Kent blamed the decline of boxing on the fixing of fights by gambling interests:

> Alas the golden age of pugilism is gone. It cannot be denied that prize-fighting is on the decline . . . owing to the bad conduct of its professors. While some of them carry on in the same spirit of the olden time, others seem to be fond of "X's". At this period when a host of enemies are arrayed against the prize-ring, when the big-wigs are threatening, canting hypocrites are preaching, and many a scribe is dealing forth invective against milling [boxing] and millers,—as if to assist these efforts, the Kingdom is divided against itself. If the real friends of pugilism do not exert themselves to put an end to *baulks* and *crosses* [fixed fights], the consequences must be fateful.[17]

One of the hostile bigwigs against whom George Kent inveighed—Mr. Justice James Burrough of the Court of Common Pleas—was soon to be heard from. On December 19, the same day as Kent's article appeared, Ned Neale (or O'Neale), the "Streatham Youth," decisively defeated Jem Burn in a fifty-four-round bout at boxing's favorite locale, Moulsey Hurst. The holding of the illegal fight with the acquiescence of local authorities in the midst of the Christmas season roused the considerable ire of Mr. Justice Burrough. When the Kingston Assizes opened on December 28, Burrough immediately announced his intention to bring the constabulary to account for its failure to enforce the law. Remarking that the names of the constables had not been called at the opening of the day's sessions, he "asked of the Under Sheriff the reason, as by law they were bound to give their attendance at the Assizes." When the undersheriff replied that it was not usual to summon them, Mr. Justice Burrough snapped impatiently, "But they ought to be summoned; the law requires their attendance, and upon the present occasion I wanted particularly to see the constables of Moulsey; all the constables must be summoned at the next Assizes." The judge, in his address to the grand jury, expressed outrage over the fight at Moulsey; the event was particularly intolerable to him because in an earlier part of his circuit he had been required to call the attention of the grand jury of another county to a case of manslaughter "occasioned by a man having been killed in consequence of a pugilistic encounter." That case, however, had extenuating circumstances, for the evidence indicated that "it was a fair fight, arising out of a quarrel." By contrast, the Neale-Burn fight was a commercially arranged match scheduled to take place in the Holy Season. Mr. Justice Burrough asked the grand jury:

> Gentlemen, after what had previously passed, is this to be endured? Is such conduct to be tolerated? It is well known to be contrary to the laws of the country, and must be put an end to. We are all aware that these fights are made up for the purposes of indulging the propensities of the vicious, and encouraging the betting of gamblers. Even the men themselves fight for money; and sorry I am to perceive, that even those who have some pretensions to the rank of gentlemen are found to encourage them. . . . These fights are frequented, it is well known, by all the rabble of London; who, instead of worshipping their God and rejoicing in the birth of a Saviour, . . . assembled on a day devoted to holiness for the indulgence of vice and subversion of order.[18]

The grand jury, Mr. Justice Burrough instructed them, was not powerless to deal with such unlawful assemblies. It was notorious that these pitched battles were generally arranged at public houses; the grand jury had strong power to refuse renewal of the license of any publican who had allowed such transactions to take place in his house. Other courses were also available to discourage boxing: the indictment of each of the boxers for assault upon each other and indictment of their seconds as aiders and abettors of a breach of the peace.

After he released the jury for its deliberations, he recalled them to suggest an additional remedy—pressure on the local law enforcement establishment. He recommended that they would do well to send for the constables of Moulsey to justify their conduct in connection with the recent prizefight. The *Times*, in an editorial of December 30, was prompt to hail Mr. Justice Burrough's action:

> It is gratifying to observe how the press, or at least the respectable part of it, precedes the ordinary authorities of the land in the correction of abuses. It is now some time since we stigmatized prize-fights as brutal exhibitions, disgraceful to the country, and abstained, in consequence, from giving any account of them. The practice immediately drooped, and many subscribers to what was called the Pugilistic Club withdrew their names. The Judges have at length followed the current of public opinion, denounced boxers and their abettors as guilty of a breach of the peace, and pointed out how they may be rendered amenable to the

law. We have no doubt but that the opinion of Judge Burrough is that of his learned brethren on the bench, who may have conferred together on the occasion. If Magistrates and Grand Juries, therefore will do their duty, public prize-fighting is at an end; and it can hardly answer to the combatants to sell their blood in private circles.[19]

The *Times* did not report any subsequent action by the grand jury or any trial court against Neale and Burn and, in any event, their careers do not seem to have been interrupted, for they were soon reported to have been arranging new matches. However, Mr. Justice Burrough's intimidation of the local magistrates had the effect of permanently closing Moulsey Hurst as the country's leading safe harbor for boxing.

On October 2, 1825, Vincent Dowling, editor of *Bell's Life in London,* cited as additional evidence of "the decline, we might also say fall, of the Fancy" the end of support for boxing by the upper classes: "The Corinthians . . . have ceased to grant either the light of their countenances, or the aid of their purses towards the encouragement of the Ring, and without such support, it is hardly necessary to note that prize-fighting can no longer have a local habitation or a name. . . . when honour and fame cease to influence the combatants a system of low gambling is substituted."[20] However, the sport proved hardier than such gloomy prophets as Dowling could have predicted. It fell on hard times after the retirement of Tom Spring, but in due course a great new champion, Tom Sayers, arose to revive the national enthusiasm for bare-knuckle boxing. The international encounter in 1860 between Sayers and the American champion John Heenan was billed as the "fight of the century." However, their struggle was marred at the end when Heenan attemped to strangle Sayers on the ropes. The contest was declared a draw, and constables were compelled to clear the crowd from the ring.[21] Later in the century, the world champion's palm passed to John L. Sullivan of America, where today are again heard voices that call for the abolition or reform of the sport.

Whatever its contribution may have been to the demise of boxing's golden age, the Thurtell-Hunt case delivered only a glancing blow to England's gambling establishment. As the uproar over gambling hells continued in the press, it was only a matter of time before governmental officials would be tempted to take remedial actions. The need to appease the public wrath was particularly clear, for as Leon Radzinowicz has noted in *A History of English Criminal Law*, "The [Thurtell-Hunt] case focused public attention on the fraudulent practices, deceit and bribery which maintained the Metropolitan gambling dens, and in particular on the complicity of the police. It now became public knowledge that many police officers were in the pay of the keepers of the worst gaming houses, often thinly disguised as dining clubs." [22] In 1824 the London authorities, under the pressure of inflamed public opinion, brought a series of prosecutions against the keepers of a notorious gambling house in King Street, St. James. John Wade in his *Treatise on the Police and Crimes of the Metropolis* (1829) noted indignantly that the proceedings came to nothing and that the ruined players who instigated them and key witnesses were quieted by bribes. The "settling" of the cases, wrote Wade "cost under £2,000, which, it was boastingly said, was more than three times repaid to the defendants by the first throw of the dice on the night following." [23] Far from being ready to crumble, the gambling world of the West End was about to enter a new era of glory, with the opening in January, 1828, of William Crockford's sumptuous gambling club in St. James's Street, designed by a fashionable architect Benjamin Wyatt. In addition to providing handsome surroundings, Crockford buttressed the claims of his establishment to respectability by hiring a world-class chef Louis Eustache Ude, and assembling a "Management Committee of Noblemen and Gentlemen." Crockford's Club became a favorite resort of Talleyrand and the diplomatic corps and of literary dandies including Bulwer Lytton and the young Disraeli; it featured play, according to its member Captain Gronow, "on a scale of magnificence and liberality hitherto unknown in Europe." [24]

The death knell for Regency-style gambling was finally sounded after the advent of Victoria. In 1844 select committees of both houses of Parliament held hearings on gaming, and the star witness, Police Commissioner Richard Mayne, testified on the cleverness of gaming-house keepers in hiding gambling devices in advance of police raids and the difficulty of obtaining evidence and search warrants. As a result of the hearings, Parliament in 1845 passed an act "to amend the law concerning games and wagers," which effectively shut down the gambling hells that had been frequented by Thurtell and his associates.[25] Crockford's Club closed on January 1, 1846, and ultimately degenerated into a cheap dining house called the Wellington.[26]

Chapter Fifteen

PROBERT'S MARE

———

After the execution of John Thurtell, bad fortune continued to dog his brothers. On June 3, 1824, Tom Thurtell went on trial in the Court of King's Bench for conspiracy to defraud the County Fire Office. Facing the charges with him was his agent John Snowden, who had allegedly resold insured goods the Thurtells claimed had been in the Watling Street warehouse at the time of the fire, and the Thurtells' porter, William Annison. The defendants were not charged with arson, but evidence was offered that John Thurtell had kindled the fire after altering the premises to prevent its timely discovery. One of the principal witnesses for the Crown was the formidable Barber Beaumont, who detailed his investigations, which had traced the insured goods into the hands of Margraves & Company, a firm that had been willing to buy them at a discount though advised that "there was a grand explosion to take place." A highlight of Beaumont's testimony was his account of his questioning of Tom Thurtell after submission of the insurance claim. The concrete details of this interview convincingly render the delirious failure of Tom's nerve and his reliance on Jack's superior ability to brazen out the fraud: "I asked him some other questions, when he stopped short and put his hand to his forehead, and said that he had just left his wife, who was at the point of death, and that he verily believed he should not find her alive when he went home—that he had no doubt she was dead, and that he could not answer any more questions, but would send his brother John to give every particular."[1] The jury charge of Lord Chief Justice Abbott was eminently fair; he took special pains to caution the jurors against allowing the Hertford trial to influence their decision. After deliberating for about ten minutes, they found Tom Thurtell and Snowden guilty but acquitted the porter Annison. On July 2 the two convicted defendants were sentenced to two years' imprisonment in Newgate.

Jack Thurtell's young sailor brother Henry returned to London in the fall of 1824 after having been at sea for over four years. On March 19, 1825, the *Times* reported that on the day before Henry had been brought up before Thomas Halls, the sitting magistrate at Bow Street, charged with stealing a silver watch belonging to Mr. Bradbee, the landlord of the White Swan public house in Chancery Lane. Bradbee's testimony made Halls feel at once that there was something distinctly odd about the prisoner's conduct. On the previous evening, Bradbee was sitting at his bar when Henry walked in and coolly took down a watch that had been hanging up behind the publican's chair. "I say, sir," said the disconcerted Bradbee, "what are you going to do with my watch? I shall not allow you to play any lark with it." Henry's answer was unresponsive, "I am only going to your friend Mr. Fean's of the White Lion, and you must come with me or follow me, for he wants to see you." Since there was nobody else in the bar, Bradbee could not follow Henry when he left but he later went over to the White Lion, which was close by; there he learned that Fean knew nothing about his watch and had not sent anyone to him with a message. Young Thurtell was later taken into custody at a third pub, the Red Lion in Covent Garden, and the watch was recovered. As he finished his testimony, Bradbee still did not know what to make of the incident: "I don't want to go any further with the business, for I believe it was done in a joke."[2]

Mr. Halls asked whether he thought the night before that it was a joke. When the witness said he didn't know about that, Halls was exasperated. If Bradbee was in doubt, why did he come here? Was it a joke to have a man taken into custody? The questions were rhetorical, for Halls said that "he saw pretty plainly into the case" but would not allow the Bow Street office to be made a plaything of or a man to play fast and loose with a matter of the kind before him.[3]

The suspicion that was beginning to form in the magistrate's mind was confirmed by the testimony of Fean. When Bradbee had informed him of the loss of his watch, Fean went to a pub run by the retired boxers Randall and Belcher and learned there that Henry would most likely be found in the neighborhood of Covent Garden. Fean went there and came upon Thurtell in Hart Street. When he seized the young sailor by the collar and accused him of stealing Bradbee's watch, Henry openly admitted the theft: "I know I did it; I took it because I want to be sent out of the country—the public point at me, and I am sick of the world." Magistrate Halls was greatly moved when Henry confirmed these feelings and added that he was ready to go wherever Halls might choose to send him. He spoke to the young man kindly, and Henry's lip quivered as he thanked him for his expressions of understanding:

> I feel your kindness, Sir, and I thank you. I came home some months ago, after an absence of four years in the service of my country, during which time . . . I conducted myself as a British seaman ought to do. When I came to this country, I wrote to my father and friends, and the answer I received was, that they did not wish to see me—they wished to have nothing to say to me. Since then I have cared very little about myself, I am pointed at wherever I go, and the sooner I am disposed of the better.

At this point the prisoner broke down and could not continue. The complainant Bradbee stepped forward and asked for the case to be dismissed, saying that "he would rather lose his watch ten times over." Magistrate Halls acceded to his wish, addressing Henry: "Thurtell, you are yet a fine young man, and may live to earn an honourable fame. Will you go to sea?" When Henry said he would, Halls discharged him and expressed the hope to hear a good account of him in the future.[4]

Bill Probert did not have the good fortune of the young Henry Thurtell in surviving the consequences of the public opprobrium that resulted from the Weare murder case. Before his execution, Jack Thurtell said that he forgave Probert from the bottom of his heart and hoped he would live to repent of his past sins. But the condemned man would not trade his gallows for the fate of the craven confederate he was leaving behind: "Notwithstanding the awful situation in which I am placed, were I to be offered life for one hundred years with 20,000 pounds, I would rather die, as I am about to do, than live degraded and disgraced like him: a vaga-

bond walking about the streets, pointed at by the finger of scorn."[5]
The *Times* held out no higher hopes for Probert: "Where can this
unhappy wretch hide his head? The grave is his only refuge. . . .
In the midst of mankind, he will find himself more than in soli-
tude. In the latter he would, indeed, be inflicted by the pangs of
conscience, by the gnawings of "the worm that never dies;" but,
should he appear in society, he will, in addition, have to encounter
'the slow and moving finger' of public scorn, which will point out
at him every step and turn."[6]

On Thursday, January 8, the day before Thurtell's execution,
the Reverend Mr. Lloyd was shocked to come upon Probert and
his wife seated at the White Hart in Hertford with a bottle of wine
"and apparently callous to the [shame] with which the former had
been covered." His finely tuned sensibilities jarred by the possibility that the crowd at the hanging would include one of the criminals, Lloyd urged upon Probert the impropriety of his remaining
in Hertford. Probert assured the clergyman that they were leaving
that evening by the public coach. This was most indelicate, Lloyd
replied, for he would be recognized at every stopping place. He
firmly recommended that the Proberts hire a private carriage (post
chaise), and when told that they had no money for this, he gave
them two pounds. This small windfall must have pleased Probert's
heart, for ever the petty sponger, he had departed from prison
without repaying a few pence he had borrowed from a wretched
fellow prisoner. That evening the Proberts left Hertford in a post
chaise with the blinds drawn.[7]

In the weeks that followed, it seemed that Probert himself was
determined not to let his notoriety wane. He brazenly threatened
the *Times* and other newspapers with libel, and an attorney wrote
in his behalf to Pierce Egan's publishers advising them of his intention to "take instant proceedings against them" for publishing
Egan's *Recollections of John Thurtell*.[8] Even had he tried to forget
the past, however, the public would not have had it so. The newspapers must have awarded Probert seven-league boots, for they
spotted him everywhere. At one time it was "confidently asserted"
that he had taken passage on a vessel in the Thames, chartered for
New York. A provincial newspaper insisted that he had passed
through Chester on his way to Liverpool "from which port he

meant to embark for the western world."[9] Londoners also claimed the hounded man for their own and spread rumors that he had rented the lower part of a house at the far end of Oxford Street to resume his old business as a wine and spirit merchant. In January, 1824, it was disclosed with appropriate indignation that "Probert has had the impudence to appear on the Royal Exchange," but some months later Probert was seen in Gloucestershire, exhibiting a horse for sale at Newnham Fair. This last report, whether or not the most accurate, contained the seeds of Probert's future.[10]

Thurtell's disclaimers had not quelled the widespread belief that his "gang," including Probert, knew what had become of the missing Reverend Mr. Colton. On January 18, 1824, the *Weekly Dispatch* reported a new rumor sweeping London—that Probert had been arrested on suspicion of involvement in the mysterious disappearance of a Regent Street ironmonger named White, who vanished two years earlier after leaving home to collect six hundred pounds at the Board of Works. The newspaper made inquiries, but all that could be verified was that Probert, who had been living since his release at a Lambeth public house, could not be found and that the police were on the "alert" for him.[11]

By the spring of the following year, fact had substituted itself for surmise. Probert, on April 5, 1825, was indicted at the Middlesex Sessions for a capital offense of a distinctly lesser order—the stealing of a mare worth twenty-five pounds. The trial on the charge was held at the Old Bailey two days later before Lord Chief Justice Charles Abbott of the Court of King's Bench, and an old acquaintance of Probert's, Sir James Alan Park. Directing the prosecution was one of the Crown counsel in the Thurtell trial, Mr. Bolland. The prisoner, genteelly dressed in black and appearing to be in good health and free of fear, addressed the lord chief justice: "My Lord, I have not been able to employ counsel for my defense. I have therefore prepared, within a few days, a brief for that purpose, and I trust your Lordship will assign some gentleman at the bar to undertake my defence." The court assigned a barrister named Barry to advise the defendant "in matters of law"; under the same rules that prevailed in Thurtell's trial, defense counsel could cross-examine the Crown's witnesses but could not address the jury.[12]

As the tale of the crime was unfolded by the Crown's witnesses, the courtroom recognized the same pattern of betrayal of trust, clumsiness, and misdirected cunning that had characterized the Weare murder. In late 1824 Probert found lodging with a Mrs. Meredith of Gloucestershire. On February 8 of the following year, during a visit to the farm of her son William and her daughter-in-law Mary, Probert, true to form, found a way of abusing the family's kindness. Seeing a black mare in the fold at night, he asked Mary whether that was where it was kept; she said it was, but that sometimes the mare was turned out into the orchard. She was not aware that their visitor considered equine resting places as anything more than a subject for rural small talk.

A week later Probert turned up at the livery stables of Mr. Francis in Phillimore Place, Kensington, leading a black mare saddled and bridled. Handing her over to the ostler James Stanmers, Probert commented, "She has had a hard day's work. I have rode her forty miles." He added mysteriously that he was not sure he would fetch the mare himself but might send an associate the next day with a note addressed to "James the ostler."

Somewhere in Probert's weak but labyrinthine mind lurked the idea that he would be shielded from detection or culpability by reclaiming the mare through an intermediary; he presumably discounted the fact that he had delivered his prize to the ostler in person. His first call in his elaborate quest for camouflage was on an acquaintance of five months, James Frewin, a greengrocer of Carnaby Street. He approached his purpose by easy stages, seeking Frewin's recommendation of a lodging for the night and then sharing a supper of bread, cheese, and porter, which ended with his inviting Frewin to call on him in the morning. When the greengrocer appeared, Probert finally came to the point: he had a mare to sell and if Frewin would take it to the auction repositories, he would pay him a sovereign for the favor. After Frewin agreed, Probert gave him three notes, one of which was open, directing Stanmers to release the mare; the others were sealed notes addressed to William Cousens, a Kensington linen draper (apparently the same man identified as "Cozens" in Thurtell's prison letter to Mrs. Walker), and to the auctioneer Dixon. It was Probert's less than brilliant scheme that he would hide his gigantic but cowardly bulk behind his friend Cousens, who was to give the order for the mare's sale in his own name. But Cousens, after receiving Probert's note from the greengrocer-turned-go-between, burned it in his presence. He declared that he did not know the sender, and literally speaking he was quite right, for Probert, with an added twist of stupid deception, had signed this note "Thompson." But Probert, for all his blundering, had a certain degree of foresight. To arm his emissary in advance against Cousens' refusal, the third note he had entrusted to Frewin was an instruction to the auctioneer to sell the mare, written by Probert in Cousens' name.

Of course, the flimsy fabrication fell apart. Soon after the mare was sold, a Bow Street officer arrested Probert and found on him a pair of scissors and a bill for refreshments on the back of which was written in pencil "Dixon's Barbican, on Friday." The notation led the officer to the auction house and to the mare's innocent purchaser, who displayed the stolen animal, fatter in spite of her adventure but her mane trimmed and tail docked by Probert's scissors in yet another futile gesture of deceit.

Against all this evidence, Probert's court-assigned counsel Barry could muster nothing more than a feeble challenge to the mare's identity, to which William Meredith, with pride of restored ownership, responded: "Turn her among a thousand, and I will pick her out." Barry's inconsistent suggestion, in his cross-examination of Mrs. Meredith, that the mare might have been lent to Probert was equally unsuccessful.

The defense offered no evidence, but the prisoner spoke in his own behalf. Like Thurtell, he rose magnificently to the occasion and displayed the surprising eloquence that is observed in many British criminal defendants of the nineteenth century. If he had pleaded not guilty, Probert began, it was not from a wish "by subtleties to evade or screen myself from the verdict and sentence which my country may award against me, if convicted, but that I might have an opportunity to say something in this Court, to evince to the public, that whatever may have been the unhappy circumstances of the latter days of my life, I was not driven into my present crime from depravity of disposition, but from a species of fatal necessity, which had placed me far beyond the reach of all human assistance and charity." As he proceeded to reflect on his life since he left Hertford Goal, the miseries he had suffered showed Thurtell to have been more adept at fortune-telling than gambling:

> It cannot have escaped your notice, my Lord and Gentlemen of the Jury, that immediately after, and ever since my discharge from Hertford, the public animosity has been kept alive against me by the public press, which has reached every part of England. Wherever I went, even to the remotest village throughout the kingdom, I was spurned as an outcast of society; and the chief instrument which prevented my obtaining employment, or indeed to effect reformation, was the public press, which has not slackened to follow, and portray me to the world. As the victim of prejudice, I can scarcely move from one place to another without seeing myself noticed in the daily papers. Those of my former friends, who might otherwise have wished to continue their services towards me, shrunk back from an apprehension of public reprobation for being connected with one such as myself. Every door was shut against me, every hope of future support blasted. My country had spared my life, but individuals rendered that life of no value or utility to me. I was hunted down like a wild beast of the forest.

The public hatred, he added, had followed him into Newgate Prison, for while he was being transferred there from the police office his ears were stunned along the way by "the horrid yells of the populace" and threats against his life. Since the "calamitous event that took place at Hertford," he had been a lost man, and at times on the verge of self-destruction.[13]

Probert read his address with great composure but in a somewhat low tone of voice. Shortly before noon the lord chief justice commenced his charge to the jury by instructing them to dismiss from their minds anything they might have heard respecting the prisoner. Without retiring from the box, the jury consulted together for five minutes and returned a verdict of guilty, without a recommendation of mercy. Shortly after the trial, Probert appeared before the recorder for sentencing. Asked whether he had anything to say in his own behalf, Probert read, in a faltering voice, a speech again urging the sufferings of his last two years and his poverty and asserting his innocence of contriving the Weare murder, which was the principal source of his subsequent miseries. He also considered that he should not have been pursued so severely for the horse stealing, "when it is considered that no violence was used [and] the mare the property of a relation."[14]

The recorder, observing that Probert's claims for mercy were a matter for the king's consideration and beyond the court's authority, sentenced him to death. On Tuesday, June 14, Probert's execution was set for the following Monday. He was then thirty-six years old.

On June 19, Probert's distraught wife (who, he had told his jury, had recently given birth) and his mother visited him for the last time. Although he had been rejected by society as tainted with Weare's murder, he was observed to be "pertinaciously clinging to life to the last" and hoped for a last-minute reprieve.[15] He may have written an appeal to the earl of Uxbridge, who, during a visit with friends to Newgate (a popular excursion, which the young Charles Dickens was to make early in his journalistic career), had stopped to talk with the famous Probert and had given him some money to assist his family.[16]

At half past ten in the morning of June 19, Probert, with three other men also sentenced to hang the next day, was conducted to the prison chapel to hear the condemned sermon to be delivered by the Reverend Horace Cotton, the ordinary (or chaplain) of Newgate.[17] The ordinary's persistent ministrations to condemned prisoners up to the very moment when the drop fell had led some wag to remark that many a criminal had departed this world "with Cotton in his ear." Mercifully, Probert was to be spared Cotton's heaviest barrages of fire and brimstone, for the prison committee had laid his chapel oratory under tight restraint. The ordinary's chapel sermon before the execution of the forger Henry Fauntleroy in November, 1824, had been roundly criticized as "harrowing the prisoner's feelings unnecessarily."[18] The prison committee had responded to the furor by adopting new regulations intended to dampen the ordinary's pulpit ardor: the public was to be barred from services for the condemned, and the ordinary was prohibited from commenting on the specific offenses of which the criminals in his literally captive audience had been convicted.

The *Times* reporter, grumbling at his exclusion from the service, was yet able to give a vivid second-hand account. Probert, he wrote, "exhibits one strong evidence of a 'mind diseased.' His hair, which was quite dark when he appeared with his brother murderers at Hertford, is now almost completely gray. Calamity and crime have changed it." The chastened ordinary took as his scriptural text

Luke 15:10: "Likewise, I say unto you, there is joy in the presence of the angels of God over one sinner that repenteth." Probert appeared unshaken until the ordinary alluded to the prisoners' wives and children; then he moaned and some thought he wept. He seemed as lonely among the condemned as in the society that turned its back on the survivor of Hertford. As soon as the ordinary concluded, Smith, one of Probert's fellow condemned, who had been praying fervently during the service, called on prisoners around him to look on the next day's executions as their inevitable end should they persevere in their course of profligacy. Several female prisoners screamed aloud at his words, and men were also moved. But Probert returned quietly to his cell.[19]

It was not that Probert was numbed by the prospect of hanging; to the contrary, he had never reconciled himself to dying. He was not ready to hear the last clear call of religion, for surely the authorities would finally awake to the injustice that had been meted out to him. In the words of the *Times,* "Probert's love of life was so intense as absolutely to incapacitate him, until almost his last minutes, from paying attention to the religious admonitions of the chaplain of the gaol. Until a very short time before his end, he entertained hope that some representation might be made to the Secretary of State with success. He considered himself as unfairly treated: all the good deeds of his life had, he said, been forgotten by those in whose hands his fate rested." Finally, the word came to him that the Privy Council would not interfere with his scheduled execution. He was surprised, having somehow satisfied himself that, though he had been an outcast, "the public voice was in his favour." On being admonished by visitors that he bore his fate with less fortitude than his condemned companions of tomorrow, he had a ready reply: was that to be wondered at, since they could have supported themselves by honest means, but he was compelled by dire necessity to commit the theft for which he was to hang—or to have starved? His thoughts leapt back two years to the crime for which he believed he was being belatedly punished; he declared that he was completely ignorant of the circumstances of Weare's murder until after it was committed.[20]

The scaffold ended these dialogues. Newgate's bell began to toll at eight o'clock in the morning, signaling the start of the march to the gallows. The crowd assembled at the prison must have been one of the largest ever to witness the execution of a thief. Three hours earlier "every position or point adjacent to that part of the prison where the fatal platform was erected, was occupied by persons whose appearance denoted respectability, and many of whom, by a well applied *douceur,* got within the enclosure, and consequently took up positions closely under the scaffold." Following a burglar (the prison chapel revivalist) and two other horse thieves, Probert ascended the steps last, his limbs "palsied" and his agitation "dreadful." After the noose was tied, he moved as far as he could and turned himself about, raising his hands in quick and tremulous movements. This he continued to do until the ordinary took his leave and the platform fell.[21]

The press was divided as to the justness of Probert's punishment. An unascribed newspaper clipping in a contemporary collection reads: "We assume (as most people we meet with seem to admit), that had his fate depended upon that one act [the horse stealing] alone, and nothing else been known of him, he would not have been executed." The hanging, then, was a breaking of "public faith" with a man admitted in the Weare murder trial as king's evidence. But another editorial strongly disagreed: "A mistaken idea prevails that the execution of Probert for the offense of horse stealing was owing to his having been concerned in the murder of Weare. The fact is that . . . horse stealing has of late become so frequent, that Government have determined to make examples of offenders . . . That Probert was not particularly singled out, is proved from this, that two other horse stealers were hanged along with him."[22]

The theory that Probert had fallen victim to an accelerated enforcement campaign against horse stealing appears to be borne out by statistics published in the *Annual Register.* During the six-year period from 1819 through 1824 only thirteen persons had been executed for horse stealing in England and Wales with the high point being reached in 1823, when four thieves were hanged. By contrast, eight horse thieves were executed in 1825, the year of Probert's trial and hanging.[23] The increased frequency of horse stealing in 1825 is evidenced by an article in the *Times* of March 3, which reports that it was no longer safe to leave horses in the streets: "Several horses which were left in the streets while their masters went into public or private houses, have lately been stolen. It is now usual with thieves, the moment they see persons alight from their horses, to take their places and drive off. Information was given at the Mansion-house [police station] of numerous robberies of the kind."[24]

If, however, we are to believe a note from the *County Herald,* some were willing to leave the debating of right and wrong to others and to capitalize on Probert's new fame. A coach proprietor, fighting off a new competitor, purchased the mare stolen by Probert and harnessed her to his conveyance, thereby attracting great numbers who preferred to be drawn by "the animal for stealing which Probert suffered the awful penalty of the law."[25] The ghost-faced horse that starred in *The Gamblers* had found a worthy successor.

Probert was buried in the churchyard of St. Martin's, with none of his family in attendance except his mother. Instead of pallbearers, he had to make do with the undertaker's retinue and the turnkey of Newgate who was charged with seeing his prisoners safely into the ground. The report of the *Times* indicates that the funeral was marred by a macabre error. By mistake, the ground that was originally opened to receive the hanged man's body "belonged to another family, which being discovered, the grave was filled up, and another dug. During the delay occasioned by this operation, it became known that Probert was to be buried, and an immense crowd was collected: and so great was the noise, that the voice of the clergyman was scarcely audible."[26] Poor fool to the last, Probert couldn't even find the right grave.

Chapter Sixteen

THE SURVIVAL OF HUNT

———

In his application for reprieve, presented to Home Secretary Robert Peel, Joseph Hunt began by declaring that he would not deny his guilt or seek to extenuate its enormity "but most humbly rests his claim for mercy on the ground of his having, upon promise of favour, furnished the only means and groundwork of the prosecution against himself and his companions." In this respect the petition was well founded for, under Lord Hale's doctrine, cited at the trial, no murder charge could have been brought if the body had not been recovered, at Hunt's direction, from the Hill Slough. As to the criticism of his incomplete confessions, the application continued, Hunt had never been admonished about the necessity of revealing every minute detail within his knowledge, nor was he ever questioned by the prosecution after the inquest. If he had been interrogated again, Hunt tardily assured Peel, he "would have readily disclosed everything as he has now done to his own Solicitor." It was the height of injustice that the prosecutors, without any hint that they were dissatisfied with his statements, had granted immunity to Probert, "who, as your Petitioner most solemnly asserts, was even more deeply implicated in the crime than your Petitioner, and who had not entitled himself to the least claim to merciful consideration, inasmuch as he denied all share in the guilty transaction until after he learned that your Petitioner had confessed, and even then he only admitted himself to be an accessory after the fact." Only on the eve of trial had Probert for the first time stated any knowledge of the previous intention to mur-

der Weare, and in his trial evidence "he as falsely presented igno-
rance of the wicked scheme." [1]

On Tuesday evening, January 20, prison governor Wilson received notice of a week's respite for Hunt and then on the following Tuesday a reprieve was delivered to Hertford commuting the
death sentence to transportation to Australia for life. On the next
day, January 28, Wilson accompanied his prisoner to Woolwich
and put him on board the "hulk" (floating prison) *Justitia,* which
lay at anchor a little below the arsenal. [2] Since the passage of the
Act of 1799, ordering ships to be used for penal discipline in relief of overcrowded jails, the *Justitia,* an old Indiaman, had been
stationed at Woolwich for the detention of criminals. Breeding
grounds of disease, the hulks had been denounced as death traps
as early as 1801 by Jeremy Bentham, and George Cruikshank
drew a scene of a prisoner dying in a dormitory of the *Justitia.* [3] In
this unsalubrious environment Hunt would remain in detention
until he was removed to the convict ship that would take him to
Australia.

While Joe underwent the initiatory rite of changing his dress
and having his hair and whiskers clipped, newspaper gossip hovered nearby. The *Weekly Dispatch* regarded it as "remarkable" that
Hunt was wearing a shirt that was suspected to be Weare's because
some remains of his initials were visible despite the efforts that had
been made to obliterate them. When Hunt was spoken to about
the shirt, he acknowledged that it belonged to the murdered man
but explained that his wife had inadvertently sent it down to him at
Hertford with his clothes and linen and that he had tried to remove the marks with his teeth. [4]

Although the first sight of the *Justitia* depressed him, Hunt had
been in high spirits and in an expansive mood during the journey
from Hertford. His escort Wilson claimed that in the course of the
trip Joe had confessed to him that he had assisted Thurtell in
throwing Weare's body into the Elstree pond. [5] Other confessions
attributed to Hunt appeared in four installments in the *Weekly Dispatch* between February 1 and 22, 1824.

Like many other so-called criminal confessions, Hunt's revelations were short on admissions of guilt. Instead, they tended to

denigrate his confederates and mitigate his own misdeeds. Hunt's statements were supposedly made to his solicitor Harmer prior to the trial but in a mood of pessimism about its outcome. As the issue of the prosecution was extremely uncertain, he began, and as the consquences to him were "very likely to terminate fatally," he felt a debt to society to make a full and true confession of the circumstances of Weare's death, and his "acquaintance with, and knowledge of, the parties implicated in his murder."[6]

He attributed his acquaintance with Probert and Thurtell to two-thirds of the great worldly trinity—wine and song. When Hunt was keeping the Army and Navy Coffeehouse in St. Martin's Lane, Probert's brother-in-law, Noyes, had obtained his order for port and sherry and had introduced Probert as the proprietor of the wine business he represented. Three months later, Joe's pub had failed and he was in Fleet Prison as a bankrupt. After his release, he became a regular customer of another pub, where he often met Probert and Noyes. While he was there one day a man named Leach struck up a conversation with Joe, saying that he had often been in his company and had heard him sing "very excellent songs." During the conversation Mr. Ensor came in and reminded Leach that it was time to go to court; they had both been subpoenaed to testify at the trial of Tom Thurtell's case against the County Fire Office. Hunt went along with them. After the verdict was returned in Tom's favor, the Thurtells and all their friends went to the Cock in the Haymarket for a celebration dinner. Hunt, at Probert's request, sang for the company, and was introduced to the Thurtells. The final links in the chain that bound these ill-fated men had been forged.

After recounting the origins of his acquaintance with his two associates, Hunt devoted the balance of the first two installments of his confession to elaborating the previously published rumors of John Thurtell's other murder plans. Thurtell had told him he had a hit list of three or four men who had mistreated him, but his rival suitor Woods stood first. According to Joe, Thurtell's famous dumbbell attempt on Woods had been preceded by a plan to shoot him in Castle Street where Woods, Probert, and Noyes had lodgings in the same house. When Woods was asleep, Thurtell, disguised in a boat cloak, was to enter the house by means of Probert's street-

door key, proceed to Woods's room and shoot him through the
heart with the airgun Jack had borrowed from a friend in Norwich. A small discharged pistol was to be placed in Woods's hand to
simulate suicide; and Probert was to testify at the inquest that
Woods had been in embarrassed financial circumstances. This
plan, however, was not carried out immediately because the airgun
had to be sent to a gunsmith for a new valve, and when a date was
finally set for the murder, the lucky Woods slept away from home.
At this point the airgun was put aside for the more exotic dumbbells. It was Hunt who had acted as lure in the new death plot;
dressed as Tom Thurtell's servant, he led Woods to 10 Manchester
Buildings on the pretext that an elderly lady with whom Woods
was friendly wished to meet him there. On his arrival Woods had
been frightened off by the sight of Jack Thurtell standing at the
foot of the stairs, his head covered by the ubiquitous red handkerchief, dumbbells in hand. Undoubtedly much to Joe's relief,
Thurtell now told him he would put off Woods's murder for a
month or two.

But Joe was not to be dismissed so easily from his service as murderer's Leporello. Jack's mind was now set on the murder of his
nemesis Barber Beaumont, whom he blamed for the nonpayment
of the Thurtell fire "loss." For several days and nights Jack lurked
in the neighborhood of the Fire Office, airgun on the ready. He
stationed Hunt at the office door to look out for Beaumont's coming and going. If Joe saw him leave, he was to run to Jack and to
tell him which way Beaumont was taking; Thurtell was to follow
and shoot him. But the feckless Hunt could never make out which
of the callers at the Fire Office was Beaumont, for he never knew
what he looked like until someone pointed him out at the Weare
inquest. It would have been reasonable to suppose that by now
Thurtell might have doubted Hunt's (and perhaps his own) talent
for murder, but he continued to tell Joe of other possible victims:
Captain Kelly, who had made a nuisance of himself to Thurtell's
underworld friends by his violence at gaming houses, and a Norwich attorney named Springfield who had mistreated Thurtell
during his bankruptcy proceedings.

The name that ultimately rose to the top of Thurtell's murder
agenda was, of course, Weare. In turning to his account of the plot

against the gambler, Hunt announced at the very outset his intention to assign Probert a more prominent role than his own:

> Probert and John Thurtell were almost continually in company to-
> gether, either in London or in going backward and forward to the Cot-
> tage; and I believe they arranged and settled the plan of Mr. Weare's
> murder before the particulars were communicated to me; for although
> I heard it mentioned several times that it was to be done, I was not in-
> formed of the manner in which it was to be perpetrated until just before
> the murder took place, but although I was ignorant, Probert, from the
> observations he made, and the directions which he gave, appeared to
> know every particular. It was not until the Friday morning that the mur-
> der was committed at night that I was let into the secret as to several of
> the arrangements.

Hunt attributed Probert's willingness to participate in murder to
financial distress: unless he got some money immediately Probert
would be compelled to leave the cottage secretly and he was in
daily fear that his landlord would come to seize the place. Hunt
asserted that Probert therefore pressed Thurtell not to delay the
murder any longer than he could help and suggested the Gill's Hill
neighborhood as the scene of the crime, saying: "If it is done
there, it can never be found out, because it is so out of the way and
private a place; for I kept a private jigger [still] there, and it was
never discovered." Thurtell accepted Probert's suggestion. He said
he would tell Weare that he had become acquainted with a young
gentleman who had just come into possession of a large property
and who had an inclination for gaming but could be tempted to
play only for large stakes, that this gentleman had asked him to
come down to his country house and to bring a friend with him for
two or three days' shooting. Thurtell would persuade Weare to accept the pretended invitation and urge him to take a large sum,
because "as [Thurtell] had no money to entice the gentleman to
play, Weare must provide it, and if he did so, they could introduce
cards, hazard or backgammon after dinner, and make a famous
thing of it." About two nights before the murder Probert had told
Thurtell that he had better make it Friday night because Probert
was usually down at the cottage on Saturday and no suspicion
would fall on him if he appeared at that time.

It was arranged that Probert and Hunt were to wait at the Artichoke until Thurtell and Weare passed and then to follow them at a little distance to prevent interruption of the murder and to give Thurtell notice if anyone approached. Thurtell was to pass Probert's cottage out of the hearing of pistol shot and then to shoot Weare while sitting beside him in the gig. According to Hunt, Probert told Thurtell precisely how to do it, even specifying the direction in which the victim's attention should be distracted. "He said, 'Jack, if the man has any suspicion about the Lane, you can tell him you think you have missed your way, and when you have got to a convenient spot, as you are the driver you can make some remark, and point his attention to make him look to the left, and directly he turns his head, that is your time to shoot him.'" After the murder, the body was to be put into a sack and brought to Probert's and thrown into the pond by him and Thurtell, while Hunt (safely away from the scene) was to be engaged in amusing the people in the house with his vocalizing.

Hunt now asserted for the first time that on the road to Gill's Hill Cottage he and Probert saw Thurtell and Weare pass twice, first at Edgware, while they were stopping at a corn chandler's where Probert had got out to purchase corn, and then at the Artichoke. When Thurtell's gig drove by the Artichoke, Probert nudged him and whispered: "There they go; we must be after them." But it was Probert's fault that they set out late in pursuit; his companion had insisted that they had time for another brandy and water. On Hunt's exhibiting anxiety to be off, Probert said: "Never mind, we shall be time enough; for as their horse is a hired horse, he must be nearly knocked up, and as ours is fresh, we shall soon overtake them." Hunt held to the story he had told to the authorities that it was Probert who insisted that he get off and wait at Phillimore Lodge, with which Hunt claimed he was then totally unacquainted. In his recollection of the remaining events of the crime, there was little new except an expression of suspicion that Thurtell had cheated him in the division of the spoils:

> I have now reason to believe that either one or both of them must have deceived me as to the money found on the deceased, because it was not likely Mr. Weare should have brought so small a sum down, considering

the object he had in view: nor was it probable that he would carry his notes loose, when he had a silk note case in his possession. This note case had been taken by Thurtell from the deceased before Probert and me arrived; and besides how should he have been able to tell Probert that the man had not so much money about him as he expected, unless he had made a complete search. My opinion is, that he had got the money, and kept it in his possession, except the 20 pounds which he put into the pocket as a blind to us; and I am the more confirmed in this opinion because he afterwards had plenty of money, and has boasted that he could give 300 pounds to get witnesses to clear him.

Basking in the public attention his confession brought him, Hunt was by late February restored to a more sociable temper.[7] It was reported that, on request, he had sung to his fellow prisoners in chapel the tenor part of the duet "All's Well," which he had performed for Mrs. Probert after the murder. Improving on the charges against Thurtell that had appeared in the first two installments of the confession, Joe now claimed to casual visitors that Jack had disposed of three or four people in the house at 10 Manchester Buildings.[8] His levees continued until March when he was transferred to the convict ship that was to transport him to Australia, the *Countess of Harcourt*. Built in India in 1811, the *Countess* was a two-decker of 517 tons and on her maiden voyage as a convict ship in 1821 under her master, George Bunn, had sailed from Portsmouth to Hobart in ninety-nine days, a record that held up until 1837. On March 23, 1824, the *Countess* left the Downs, a well-sheltered roadstead off Deal on the southeastern coast of England, on its third voyage to the Australian penal colony, with Joe Hunt and 173 other male prisoners on board.[9]

Later that month, it was reported that the ship had been forced by contrary winds to put into Tor Bay on the Devon coast. "It excited so great a sensation in Brixham, that many of the inhabitants went off on the following day, to see the delinquent whose name stands so high in the calendar of crime." After this last audience in England, Hunt's name dropped out of view, but only for about a year.[10] In April, 1825, it was reported in several newspapers, including the *Dublin Warder,* that Hunt had died on his passage to New South Wales.[11] A more lurid version of the rumor was that Hunt had been shot in a mutiny on board the convict ship on her passage out to Australia. The *Times,* in its issue of April 30, 1825, quoted an evening newspaper's report that the rumors of Hunt's death were unfounded: "It happens, unfortunately for the foregoing statement [of Hunt's death], that the *Countess of Harcourt* has returned to England, having disembarked her living cargo (Hunt among the rest) at their ordered destination, and that the captain of the said convict-ship states, that the whole of the report is utterly destitute of truth."[12]

Despite this prompt disclaimer, the tradition of Hunt's death in a convict ship mutiny survives in John Alexander Ferguson's *Bibliography of Australia,* which contains the following entry under the name Joseph Hunt: "Hunt was killed in the quelling of an insurrection among the convicts upon the convict-ship Marquis of Huntley when 17 convicts were shot or hanged."[13] It is curious that this entry found its way into Mr. Justice Ferguson's work for it appears erroneous on its face. In the first place, Hunt sailed on the *Countess of Harcourt,* as we have seen, and not on the *Marquis of Huntley,* which apparently made its maiden voyage to Australia in 1826. Moreover, Charles Bateson, in *The Convict Ships,* has pointed out that few convict ships reached Australia in the 1820s without reporting a suspected mutiny among the prisoners but that "it is doubtful . . . if in any single instance the danger of a rising was really serious."[14]

Strangely, Ferguson accepted the mutiny rumor that attached itself to Hunt's name without substantiation. It appears that he gullibly accepted the wild fabrications of a catchpenny chapbook in his collection. Published by Chubb, of Long Lane, London, the pamphlet bore a breathtaking and paper-consuming title: *The Full Particulars of the Sudden and Awful Murder of Hunt! The Associate of Thurtell & Probert with a Narrative of the Mutiny on Board the Marquis of Huntley* [sic], *on Which Occasion 17 Convicts Were Shot and Hung.* The bogus production, dating from 1825, was an obvious attempt to capitalize on the impending execution of Probert, to which the author refers in the first paragraph; he claims to see the interference of the "hand of heaven" in bringing to violent ends the three men "who planned and put into execution one of the most cold blooded Murders perhaps the annals of crime ever related." The *Marquis of Huntley,* according to the pamphlet, set sail from England with over two hundred convicts aboard, including Hunt.

"Perhaps there were never a more depressed set of villains in one vessel before," and the captain, had he not had an incurably "mild and peaceable disposition," would have been justified in having some of them hung at the yardarm. The convicts soon bound themselves by dreadful oaths to mutiny and murder the captain, but the plot was given away by the deathbed confession of a lad named Melluish, who had been taken ill and was placed in what the sailors called the "dying pit." The mutiny broke out on the fourth night of a roaring gale, but the ship's crew were on the alert and their musket fire repelled the attempt of the mutineers to force the main hatchway. As the dead convicts were removed, Hunt was found among them; "a musket ball had entered the top of his head and pierced directly through his brain." If providence had not been taking deferred revenge, Hunt's end would have seemed unjustified to the pamphleteer, for he had not taken an active part in the convicts' "tumultuous proceedings" but "was always looked upon by the crew as a well behaved and gentlemanly man." [15]

In fact, the *Countess of Harcourt* arrived at Sydney on July 12, 1824, after a direct crossing of 111 days. The Archives Office of New South Wales preserves a description of Joe Hunt on his arrival in Australia. Out of the mercurial past of this ne'er-do-well, the archivist was able to distill a profession, that of hotel keeper. Joe, then aged twenty-nine, was 5 feet, 8 ¼ inches, tall; had hazel eyes, a pale complexion, and hair that, despite his recent tribulations, remained dark brown. Following the physical description is an enigmatic phrase "very well," which may refer either to his health or, more likely, to his good conduct during the passage. [16] In a record of the colonial secretary's office, Hunt is listed among eighty-six male convicts from the *Countess* who were forwarded to Parramatta on the outskirts of Sydney for distribution. [17] Hunt's name next appears among a detachment of eighteen prisoners assigned for unspecified government works to Bathurst. The town of Bathurst was located on the south bank of the Macquarie River in a fertile rolling plain hospitable to farming and grazing. It had been founded in 1815, two years after an exploring party under a free settler, Gregory Blaxland, opened up the outback for development by finding its way across the Blue Mountains, which separated the Bathurst Plains from the coastline settlements to the east.

In late 1813 assistant surveyor George William Evans had completed Blaxland's mission by discovering the plains beyond the mountains as well as the westward-flowing rivers.[18]

Before long Hunt was transferred to a pleasant inland agricultural and cattle-raising area called Wellington Valley, located farther up the Macquarie River northwest of Bathurst. Tighe Hopkins has referred to this remote settlement as prime proof that for some fortunate convicts Australia in the early nineteenth century could turn out to be a "felons' paradise": "It was the 'gentleman lag' who found out the soft spots in the colony. There was an elysium called Wellington Valley where many of these elegants were received on their arrival in the colony, and from which they were drafted to comfortable stools in the offices of the Government. The clever ones among them seldom underwent any real punishment."[19] A muster roll of population of the district of Wellington in early 1826 lists Hunt as among five men at a government agricultural and livestock station in the valley, located seven miles from the principal settlement.[20]

After a short stint in Wellington Valley, Hunt moved back to the district of Bathurst. In 1832 his good behavior there won him a "ticket of leave," under which a convict obtained the right to seek free employment within the district to which he was assigned; on Hunt's ticket it is noted that he was permitted to remain in the Bathurst district on the recommendation of the local magistrates.[21] It was about this time that Joe's path crossed that of a distinguished witness of his Hertford trial, Roger Therry, who came to the colony in 1829 and was to become a judge of the Supreme Court of New South Wales. In his *Reminiscences of Thirty Years' Residence in New South Wales and Victoria*, Therry recalls that Hunt, when he fell in with him, was "a trusted, and, I believe, a trustworthy storekeeper, assigned to the service of a Government contractor on the Blue Mountain Road."[22] (Perhaps the contractor was Jonathan Slattery, who appears as Hunt's employer in the 1837 convict muster.)[23] Therry recognized Joe at once when the mail coach by which he was traveling stopped at the contractor's store at an early hour on a winter morning. The kindly and jovial judge, who minimized Hunt's role in the Weare murder, has left us a favorable impression of the exiled convict: "It may be easily imagined what a contrast was presented in his cheerful and healthy countenance to the woe-begone visage he wore in the dock at Hertford. His conduct in the colony was correct and even meritorious. So unobtrusive and humble was his demeanour, as if every moment he was abashed and sensible of the great crime he had committed, that he was not even once annoyed or taunted with a reference to it."[24] Nevertheless, it is recorded that Hunt had at least one minor scrape with the Australian authorities. In December, 1834, his ticket of leave was suspended for six months on the ground that he had harbored a prisoner of the Crown illegally at large. This sanction proved only a temporary setback, for in 1842 Hunt was granted a conditional pardon (effective the following year) under which he regained his liberty on the condition that he not return to the British Isles.[25] Even before this final restoration of freedom, Joe, like many other Australian convicts, had gone over to the service of law and order. He became a constable and the court keeper of the old courthouse at Bathurst and, Therry reports, "by his respectful demeanour and general good conduct enjoyed the favourable opinion of all who came in contact with him."[26]

Love smiled upon Joe as sweetly as the law. The registry of marriages discloses that in July, 1850, the exile, now using the name "Joseph Blaine Hunt" (instead of the less elegant official designation as "Hunt, Countess of Harcourt" under which he chafed in his early days of servitude), married Mary Rogers.[27] Since she is identified in other official records as Mary Quinn or Quin, it is a fair assumption that she was a widow, and indeed, Judge Therry describes her as "the respectable widow of a medical practitioner in Bathurst."[28] The baptismal records report that the Hunts had two children, Angela Mary, born in 1852, and Joseph Henry, born three years later.[29] Therry, waxing eloquent over Hunt's evolution into a middle-class householder, assures us that "by attention to his several duties [he] became quite an exemplary person."[30]

When Judge Therry left New South Wales in 1859, Hunt was still living in Bathurst. Later in the century, another memoirist, James T. Ryan, paid a special visit to Thomas Jones, former chief constable of the town. In his *Reminiscences of Australia*, Ryan recalls that he and his host talked of many things, but that his principal object in calling on the policeman was to find out what had become of Hunt. Jones told his visitor that Hunt had served under him for many years as a constable at Bathurst and described him as "a remarkable man, handsome in person, fine company, and a good singer." The chief constable confirmed that Hunt had married the widow of a doctor and thought (erroneously, as we have seen) that Joe had had two daughters by her. He gave Ryan the additional report that Hunt had met a death by water ironically suitable for the conspirator of the Elstree pond: he had "drowned at Cowra."[31]

So far as I know, Ryan's report of Hunt's death has remained unchallenged to this day. However, a review of death records demonstrates that on this point at least the memory of the old policeman had failed. Joseph Blaine Hunt, described as district constable, died a natural death in 1861. The cause of death is described in the register as "decay of nature and disease of kidneys and bladder."[32] This Regency roisterer had died respectably in a mid-Victorian bed.

Chapter Seventeen

A RETURN TO HERTFORDSHIRE

———

What remains today to remind the world of Thurtell and his crime? Through the century and a half that separate us from the murder of Weare, many famous landmarks of the case have disappeared.

Among London's lost Thurtell-Hunt sites is the Coach and Horses Public House. The point of Thurtell's departure on his murder ride survives in name only; running off Old Burlington Street near the junction of Conduit Street and New Bond Street is Coach and Horses Yard, originally the stable yard to the old inn where Thurtell entered his immortal gig. Another vanished building that had been associated with the case is Lyon's Inn, the last residence of William Weare, whose name is enshrined in the famous doggerel verse of William Webb. According to Walter Thornbury, writing in his *Haunted London*, "It degenerated into a haunt of bill-discounters and Bohemians of all kinds, good and bad, clever and rascally, and remained a dim, mouldy place till 1861, when it was pulled down. Its site is now occupied by the Globe Theatre." Thornbury recalled that when he visited the inn just before its demolition "a washerwoman was hanging out wet and flopping clothes on the site of Mr. William Weare's chambers."[1]

Probert's cottage, which had already felt the ravages of tourism at the time of the murder investigation, apparently survived a little longer. In a contribution to *Notes and Queries* of August 15, 1885, William Fraser reported a pilgrimage he had made not long before to the scene of the murder. He found "an old man clipping the very hedge through which Weare's body was dragged," who showed him the spot on which the victim was killed "close to what is now a tree of some size." At this time, Fraser commented, Gill's Hill Lane was still "the narrowest roadway in England; the brambles intertwine across it." He visited Probert's cottage, sat in the kitchen in which the pork chops were cooked, and saw the stairs on which Mrs. Probert listened. The parlor had been pulled down and the pond was now dry. Fraser's guide claimed to have known the three conspirators and captivated his visitor with a tale that Probert's servant boy Addis had, only a few months before, "come as an old man to the scene of his early notoriety." In *Notes and Queries,* September 9, 1893, another correspondent wrote that Probert's cottage had finally been demolished about 1888.[2]

When I set out as a latter-day pilgrim to retrace the paths of the Thurtell-Hunt case, I knew that my journey must begin in London. The obligatory first visit was to the Royal College of Surgeons, whose Hunterian Collection preserves for the view of visitors the skull of John Thurtell. After Thurtell's dissection, his skull and bones had come into the possession of Thomas Wormald, demonstrator of anatomy at St. Bartholomew's Hospital. In 1874, after Wormald's death, his widow presented Thurtell's remains to the Royal College of Surgeons. They have proved sturdy survivors, having remained intact after the German air raid of May 10, 1941, which destroyed two-thirds of the Hunterian Collection. Displayed at the far end of a gallery above the main level of the museum, Thurtell's skull shares a single showcase with the remains of three other famous murderers: the skull of Eugene Aram and the skeletons of the archgangster of eighteenth-century London, Jonathan Wild, and of the "Red Barn murderer," William Corder. Jessie Dobson, former recorder of the museum, has, with pardonable pride of ownership, dubbed the four malefactors the "College Criminals," a title that would almost suggest that their crimes had consisted of cheating on their examination papers. Dobson's description of Thurtell's skull was indeed accurate: "The outstanding features of the skull are its large size, heavy build and almost exaggerated features of masculinity: the bones of the cranial vault are thick and all muscular prominences and impressions are particularly well-developed. . . . the mastoid processes are exceptionally massive and the brow ridges are prominent. The mandible is heav-

ily built, with a well-developed chin."[3] I noted that only four teeth
remained in the skull, but Dobson's account told me more than
could meet the naked eye: three were decayed during his lifetime,
and root abscesses marked the majority of those he had lost. Had
dental agonies contributed to Thurtell's famous rages?

I bent down to take a close look at Thurtell's skull, which is
placed low in the display case. An earlier visitor, the novelist and
crime historian Rayner Heppenstall eloquently complained of the
arrangement of the skulls, particularly the low placement of Aram's
small skull: "To my mind, it is hard that you should have to squat
like a miner or sit on the floor in order to examine the marks left
by the rusted iron of the gibbet and the sharply projecting mastoid
processes. . . . To gaze into those orbits, you would need to lie
prone in such a position that other visitors (admittedly, the traffic
is not heavy) might tread on your spine or trip over your legs."[4]
I luckily avoided the fate feared by Heppenstall. As I turned to
leave the gallery, the curator offered to show me a box of Thurtell's
bones that have been patiently awaiting rearticulation, but I declined with thanks.

My ultimate destination was, of course, Hertfordshire but the
road that took me there opened up by sheer chance. Shopping one
day in the basement of a Cecil Court bookstore that specializes
in law, I noted without special interest that the alphabetically
arranged crime collection contained the standard edition of the
Thurtell-Hunt trial in the Notable British Trials series. What immediately caught my eye, however, was the slim unlettered spine
of a clothbound pamphlet wedged between the trial volume and
the next full-sized book on the shelf. Inspired by a personal super-
stition that books not immediately identifiable must be more closely
examined and on the off chance that this small item might also re-
late to the Thurtell trial, I took the booklet down and found that
for once my compulsive habits had been rewarded; the plain tan
cover bore a title in red letters: *The Elstree Murder.* I turned the
pages and found that the author was J. R. Avery, senior history
master, Haberdasher's Aske's School, Elstree and that the work had
been published by the boys on the school's press in 1962. The text
of the brief account of the crime added little to what I already

knew, but it was one of the author's acknowledgements that gave me new enthusiasm for a trip to Hertfordshire: Avery thanked C. A. Stott, Esq., Librarian of Aldenham School, who had allowed him to see "his fascinating collection of contemporary newspaper cuttings, drawings and playbills."[5] I sent off a letter immediately to Stott asking for permission to examine his collection. Within two weeks I received a response from his successor, the Reverend David Wallace-Hadrill (also second master of the school) not only granting my request but offering me an additional favor of value at least as great. He wrote: "We are, of course, very near the site of the murder, which is not now as it was in 1823, though the Elstree pond is still there and a good deal of the surrounding countryside and lanes can hardly be much different. Let me tempt you by offering a personally-conducted tour!"

A time for our visit was soon arranged, and in the fall of 1981 my wife and I, after a brief train trip from London, arrived at Radlett (which a Hertfordshire antiquarian asserts has a meaning that Thurtell's crime has rendered prophetic: "red millstream").[6] We hired a local taxi and called for the Reverend Mr. Wallace-Hadrill at the Aldenham School. After showing us around the school grounds and buildings, he joined us for a tour of the Thurtell-Hunt landmarks.

We left the school and headed back towards Radlett, along Common Lane, a pleasant rural road across Letchmore Heath. Lined with trees and hedges, the road quite closely matched my mind's image of Gill's Hill Lane; I had seen contemporary engravings of the lane, which had seemed to survive strangely unchanged in a photograph made by Michael Hardwick around 1960. As we neared Gill's Hill Lane, I recalled the report of the topographer Gordon Maxwell that on October, 24, 1923, he had been present at a commemoration meeting held at the murder scene at nine o'clock in the evening, "exactly one hundred years to the very hour when the evil deed was done." Despite the promising subject of the occasion, Maxwell had confessed modest disappointment: "I should like to write that the night was a typical one suitable for murder and sudden death; with a clouded sky and a fierce east wind blowing chilly and blusteringly over a scene of desolation—it

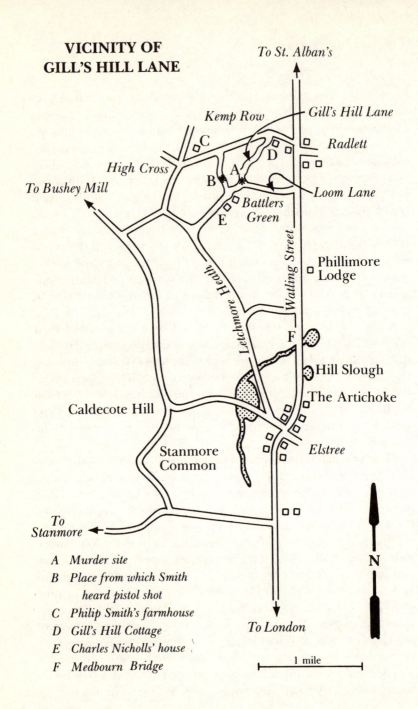

VICINITY OF GILL'S HILL LANE

To St. Alban's

Kemp Row

Gill's Hill Lane

C

Radlett

High Cross

D

B A

To Bushey Mill

Loom Lane

Battlers Green

E

Watling Street

Phillimore Lodge

Letchmore Heath

F

Hill Slough

The Artichoke

Caldecote Hill

Stanmore Common

Elstree

To Stanmore

A   Murder site
B   Place from which Smith
      heard pistol shot
C   Philip Smith's farmhouse
D   Gill's Hill Cottage
E   Charles Nicholls' house
F   Medbourn Bridge

To London

N

1 mile

would have been so much more dramatic, but it would have been untrue. As a matter of fact, it was one of the most lovely nights I have ever seen."[7]

Our first stop before we reached Gill's Hill Lane could not have been more encouraging to my hope that I would recognize the setting of the crime. The taxi had halted for a moment in New Road alongside Battlers Green, where Philip Smith had heard Thurtell's pistol shot. The wide stubbled green fields broken only by occasional trees standing alone or in small huddles could have been a nineteenth-century landscape were it not that a single strand of barbed wire strung along the roadside gave sign of an unfriendlier age. However, our first glimpse of Gill's Hill Lane, at its junction with Loom Lane, told us immediately that the scene described by Maxwell in 1923 and photographed by Hardwick only two decades ago was no more, that the hedges and the brambles were gone and suburbia had triumphed. A long white sign spelling out "Gill's Hill Lane" in neatly printed black letters and supported by two tall posts stood before an artificially weathered wooden fence, which, aided by a careful selection of varied foliage, shielded an elegant house from the view of passersby. About fifty yards up the lane, where Wallace-Hadrill told us the murder had been committed, the roadway had been greatly widened and was bordered by flat lawns; an electric light pole gave illumination where a deed of darkness had once been done. Near the murder site, commodious houses have risen to shame Probert's gloomy dwelling. Further along Gill's Hill Lane a public footpath runs off into a wooded area. As I looked along this more picturesque byway, I remarked to our guide that, according to Maxwell, Gill's Hill Lane in the 1920s was still referred to by local residents as "Murder Lane." I wondered whether this was still so. Wallace-Hadrill suggested that we test our taxi driver on the subject. Asked whether he knew of a famous murder that had been commited at Radlett, the driver was a little vague. No, he couldn't say that he did, but he seemed to remember talk of a murder at Elstree. I was disappointed but only for a moment, for the driver then volunteered that for some reason unknown to him Gill's Hill Lane was sometimes called Murder Lane and the same nickname was given to the footpath at which we had stopped.

After we continued along the lane a little distance, Wallace-Hadrill asked the driver to stop again: we had arrived at the site of Probert's cottage. In place of this infamous dwelling there now stands a respectable two-story old people's home, the Tredinnock, whose arched wooden doorway is framed by a peudo-classical pilastered portal. I wondered whether the smell of the famous pork chops still lingered in the kitchen, but we did not enter. Instead we drove off in the direction of Elstree along Watling Road, the ancient highway that had once echoed to the sound of Thurtell's gig. We stopped again as our guide pointed out a narrow stream that wound its way through a field at the roadside. This, it was thought, was all that remained of the Hill Slough to which Weare's body was transferred from Probert's pond. A bit farther up the road towards Elstree was a white-painted brick pub that needed no commentary from our host. Its sign, consisting of a green vegetable on a white field, proclaimed it to be the Artichoke, the last stage of the pub crawl of Probert and Hunt and the place to which Weare's body was taken from the Hill Slough. A placard on the ground before the entrance invited the traveler to a cold buffet (always available) or hot meals (served between noon and two o'clock).

Only one stopping place now remained on our itinerary: in a few minutes we were walking through the Elstree churchyard where Weare's body was buried (as well as that of Martha Reay, the mistress of the earl of Sandwich, who had been murdered by the lovesick cleric James Hackman in the eighteenth century). The wafer-thin gravestones leaning to all points of the compass reminded us of a scene from Alfred Hitchcock's late film *A Family Plot*. We speculated in vain as to the location of Weare's unmarked grave and were unable to enlist the assistance of the rector, for Wallace-Hadrill, inquiring at the church (that had replaced the structure that witnessed Weare's burial service), found that he was away. On this note of mild disappointment our tour ended, and we returned Wallace-Hadrill to the Aldenham School, where he deepened my debt of gratitude by lending me the school's precious collection of Thurtelliana for review and copying on my return to the United States. Shortly after we returned, we found that our host, with his characteristic courtesy and thoroughness, had completed our inquiry at the Elstree church. He wrote: "The other day I was in conversation with the Rector of the church, Dr. W. J. Elliott, who told me that the stone was certainly not identifiable now, and that drawings and engravings made at the time of the burial show the church from such diverse points of the compass that even at the time there seems to have been doubt about where in the church-yard the burial took place."

Though our visit had shown us that the murder of Weare has long since melted into the changing landscape and the fading memory of Hertfordshire, the question persists: apart from the fact that Weare died by the hand of Thurtell, how much do we know about what actually happened on the fatal night in Gill's Hill Lane? Even for contemporary journalists, who had vied with each other in recording every discoverable fact or conceivable fantasy of the Thurtell-Hunt case, the story ended with a row of question marks. While modern accounts of the crime have borrowed copious narrative details from the Regency newsmen, we have forgotten their doubts.

The principal question raised by the contemporary press is the same that we have often heard in our own time when the public is appalled (and intrigued) by a secret assassination: was there a single assailant acting alone at the scene of the crime? The *Observer* reported in January, 1824, that Clutterbuck and his fellow magis-trates had spared no pains to test the feasibility of the theory that all three men were together at the murder site:

> It will be recollected that Probert and Hunt did go to the Artichoke pub-lic-house on the night of the murder, and a question has arisen as to whether it was not possible for them to have gone by one of the back ways which we have described, to Gill's-hill-lane—to have been present at the murder, and then to have returned to the Artichoke in such a way as to make it appear that they had come direct from Clarke's house at Edgeware, where they had previously been. To decide this question, the distances were all accurately measured, and a person with a horse and gig drove in the various directions, and minuted the time which he was in performing the journey at a quick pace by them all. Nothing, in fact, was omitted by Mr. Clutterbuck and the other Magistrates, which could in any way throw light on the subject.[8]

According to Pierce Egan, Bow Street officer Ruthven thought that both Probert and Hunt were on the spot when Thurtell committed the murder, that Hunt held the horse belonging to Thurtell's gig and Probert restrained the head of his own horse. In an historical anticipation of Sherlock Holmes's deduction concerning the "dog who did nothing in the night-time," Ruthven argued that his theory accounted for the curious passivity of Thurtell's horse. The policeman reasoned that few horses "will stand still at the report of a pistol, fired off close to their heels, more especially strange or hired animals." Egan conceded that Ruthven's opinion was "merely conjecture."[9]

In a more detailed reconstruction of the crime, which appears at the end of his sketch of the trial in *London Magazine*, Edward Herbert concurred with Ruthven in placing all three of the conspirators at the murder scene. He asserted that the trial had left the public mind dissatisfied and in doubt and that the general opinion was that "Probert, the worst and the most dastardly of the gang, has improperly escaped. That he merited death, who can deny?" Noting that Thurtell and Weare were last seen a little before eight o'clock by James Freeman near Probert's cottage, Herbert speculated that "they were then waiting, probably for the arrival of Probert and Hunt, but the sight of Freeman disturbed Thurtell, and he drove down the lane to the place where the crime was perpetrated." The time appointed for the crime was eight o'clock; this schedule accounted for the rapid pace maintained by Thurtell (who supposed himself late) down Edgware Road and for the waiting and drinking of Probert, who feared that he was ahead of time.[10]

Herbert traced the course of Probert and Hunt:

1. They were first seen at the Red Lion in the northern outskirts of London about 6:00. Probert apparently wished to fix his presence there in the mind of the landlord Harding, for he said to him, "You forget me, my name is Probert."

2. They were recognized about 7:00 at the White Lion at Edgware. Their horse was a very fine one, capable of going eleven or twelve miles an hour with ease, and, according to the pub keeper Clarke and his ostler Bingham, seemed quite cool and fresh. Probert yielded testily to Hunt's request for a second glass of brandy and water, but Clarke was certain that they left on the road to Elstree no later than 7:15.

Murder Route and Chronology
Friday, October 24, 1823

Probert and Hunt	Place (approximate number of miles from London)	Thurtell and Weare
Probert and Hunt depart between 5:15 and 5:45 P.M.	Tyburn Turnpike, Marble Arch, London	Thurtell departs, 5:00 P.M.
Probert and Hunt pass Thurtell	(4)	
	Welsh Harp (Harp Hill) (5.5)	Patrolman Wilson passes Thurtell, 6:40[d]
Probert and Hunt stop "between 5:30 and 6:30" for five minutes[a]	Red Lion, Hyde (6)	
Probert stops alone	Bald-Faced Stag (7)	
Probert picks up Hunt	(8)	
Probert and Hunt arrive 7:05, depart 7:20[b]	White Lion	Thurtell passes Probert and Hunt
	Corn Chandler	
	Edgware (8.5)	Clarke sees Thurtell, 7:00[b]
	Elstree (11)	
Probert and Hunt arrive 8:14−8:19, depart 8:49[c]	Artichoke (12)	
	Gill's Hill, Radlett (14.25)	Murder, approximately 8:00

a Harding deposition
b Clarke testimony
c Field testimony
d Wilson deposition

3. The White Lion was only three miles from the Artichoke in
Elstree, and yet, Herbert emphatically pointed out, "it was nearly
twenty minutes after eight when Probert and Hunt arrived there—
Probert's fine horse very much distressed and bathed in sweat.
Thus one hour is consumed in going the three miles!" In the
hour's interval, Probert and Hunt could have driven to their murder rendezvous with Thurtell at Gill's Hill Lane. They might then
have returned a considerable way towards Elstree along the high
road, turned and taken a circuit by Aldenham Common and then
reentered the high road at Elstree below the Artichoke so that they
could reach the inn with the appearance of coming from London.
In confirmation of the supposed route by Aldenham Common
back to Elstree, Herbert cited the statement of a "poor woman of
the name of Mary Hale" that between 8:00 and 9:00 "she heard a
gig 'tearing by,' in front of her cottage, the horse apparently gal-
loping." Herbert concluded: "From this statement I should say all
three were at Gill's-hill-lane on the fatal night and at the fatal hour
of eight o'clock."[11]

Although Herbert's reconstruction is congruent with the hour
and place of the murder and with testimony as to the progress of
Hunt and Probert from pub to pub, it ultimately fails to be persuasive because of its inconsistency with the characters of the two
men and their relationships with each other and Thurtell. If the
record of the trial teaches us anything about Hunt and Probert, it
is that they were cowards. Capable of procuring the implements of
the crime and providing the murder locale, neither showed enthusiasm for direct participation in the deed of blood. It is likely that
neither intended to appear in time at the murder scene and that
the bouts of brandy and water provided a double remedy of assur-
ing late arrival and stilling their fears. External evidence suggests
that at Edgware, Hunt was the principal cause of delay: the proprietor Clarke testified on cross-examination that Probert did not
enter the house and was impatient for Hunt to set off. However,
Probert, who was driving, had not refused to make the stop or the
others along the way, and perhaps was hoping to draw some comfort (in the face of Thurtell's future anger at their desertion) in
being able to put the blame on Joe. Both men later showed their
faintheartedness by their rush to confess, and if Hunt's revelations

in the *Weekly Dispatch* after the trial are to be believed, he had once before failed Thurtell in a murder rendezvous when appointed to stand watch over Barber Beaumont at the door of the County Fire Office. Mixed with the craven streak that Hunt and Probert shared was another trait that would have impelled them to miss the scene of the murder even though they had laid the ground for its commission: both were "jailhouse lawyers" whose brushes with courts and prisons had given them highly technical (and mistaken) notions as to how to avoid or mitigate punishment. Hunt persuaded himself that he would not hang for hiring the horse and furnishing the sack and rope, and Probert was betting that aiding the concealment of a body would not make him Thurtell's partner on the scaffold. Probert repeated such a pattern of criminal hairsplitting in 1825 when he attempted to shield himself from detection and punishment for horse stealing by offering the animal for sale through an intermediary. In his instructions to the jury in the Weare trial, Mr. Justice Park shrewdly identified a tendency of cowardly confederates to find salvation in nice distinctions between the actual perpetrator of a criminal act and his accessories:

> It appears manifest, in various cases which have recently been decided, that it is very common for men of low degree to flatter themselves, that if theirs were not the hand which committed the fatal deed, they were perfectly safe from all consequences, even though they were present at the murder. Nothing can be more fallacious than such an idea. In point of morals it is wrong, and in point of law it is equally wrong. For if two persons go to commit a robbery, or to break open a house, and one party commits the felony with his hand, and the other stands idly by, both are equally guilty in the eye of the law; and it is laying a false and dangerous unction to their souls, to suppose that both will not be equally liable to punishment. I make this observation for the sake of public morals, and hope it will have due effect.[12]

The presence of Hunt and Probert at the murder scene not only is inconsistent with their cowardice and low cunning but is strongly belied by their behavior towards each other during the investigations and trial. Although both men tried their hardest (Probert with the greater success) to exculpate themselves and throw the blame for the crime on their confederates, neither ever accused the other of aiding Thurtell's attack on Weare. If only one of them had been present and the fact had been known to the other, it is difficult, given their great hostility to each other, to account for a reluctance to disclose such a damning involvement. If, on the other hand, it is assumed that both were at Thurtell's side in Gill's Hill Lane, their mutual silence on the point could be explained only by an implied compact of silence that hardly seems to sit well with the unrestrained attacks they made on each other in court and in the press. Finally, the Herbert theory that places Hunt and Probert in Gill's Hill Lane prior to their arrival at the Artichoke appears to founder on the rock of Jack Thurtell's dominance over the two men. Is it likely that Thurtell after prevailing on them to help him murder Weare and find a makeshift place of concealment for the body would permit them to gallop back by a circuitous route to the Artichoke for the sole purpose of establishing an alibi that would leave him in an unwanted spotlight as the lone assassin? With a bow then to the investigative persistence of Officer Ruthven and to Herbert's ingenuity in reading inconclusive testimony, I prefer to maintain the view that Jack Thurtell acted alone in Gill's Hill Lane and was intentionally deserted by his co-conspirators.

Another unanswered question left by the Thurtell-Hunt trial is the place of ambush arranged by the conspirators. It is commonly assumed that the appointed place of rendezvous was the site where the murder was in fact committed—in the dark and little-traveled byway of Gill's Hill Lane. In fact, Joe Hunt, in his posttrial confessions, claimed that Probert had not only suggested Gill's Hill Lane as an ideal place for the murder but had instructed Thurtell how to commit the crime. There is ample reason, though, to doubt that Gill's Hill Lane was anything more than an accidental murder locale hit upon by Thurtell after he realized that his confederates had failed to turn up at the agreed place. It seems to strain belief that the pusillanimous Probert would have tolerated, much less suggested, a murder site so close to his own cottage, and in fact, he was frantic in his insistence that Weare's body be promptly moved after it was unceremoniously dumped into his pond.

Where then should we look to find a murder site that the three confederates would have found more congenial? I can think of no better place than the vicinity of Hill Slough, the inconspicuous Elstree pond to which the body was transferred from its first watery grave. It is noteworthy that this pond is extremely close to Phillimore Lodge, located about a mile north of Elstree, where Hunt got out of the gig, saying, according to Probert, that he would wait for Thurtell. It was likely near the lodge that Hunt and Probert were to meet Thurtell, assist in the murder, and transport the body the short distance to Hill Slough. However, the two accomplices, by their slow progress and brandy consumption, made certain that they would arrive at the rendezvous too late, and Probert drove on hoping to find Thurtell (as indeed he did) with the dirty work already done. It is obvious that Thurtell, because of his frequent visits to Probert's cottage in the past, was familiar with Gill's Hill Lane and did not require an escort to lead Weare to his death under its overarching branches. If these conclusions are correct, then it is only because the original murder plan was thwarted by the defection of Thurtell's confederates that the town of Radlett, rather than Elstree, claims the Weare murder as its own.

The suitability of the area near Phillimore Lodge as a murder site in the early nineteenth century is confirmed by F. D. Maggs in a paper read before the Radlett Literary Society on December 2, 1946, and included in the Thurtell collection of the Aldenham School. Maggs noted that in those days a "narrow winding lane" ran across the fields adjoining the high road to the farm halfway up Butterfly Lane, which forms the northwest border of present day Aldenham Park. Maggs felt "pretty sure that it was Thurtell's intention to turn up that lane and commit the murder there, away from any witnesses and beyond the hearing of any dwellings, and then to return to the opening of the lane, nearly opposite Phillimore Lodge, where Hunt would be waiting to give him a hand in disposing of the body." [13]

A final mystery is the proper judgment to be passed on Thurtell's skill and forethought as a criminal. Both his contemporaries and subsequent commentators have scoffed at the clumsiness of this murderer who had only a few pounds and a gold watch to show for his pains and found himself in custody and facing a mounting tide of evidence only a week after the murder. These customary assessments cannot be sustained with full confidence in light of a fair examination of the record of the case. Since Weare usually carried a considerable amount of money with him and thought that he was headed into the country to fleece a gambler who played for high stakes, there is good reason to sympathize with Hunt's suspicion that Thurtell had pocketed the lion's share of the booty for himself before he split a few miserable pounds with Hunt and Probert. (The prepetration of this fraud on his confederates, if it took place, would, of course, be further confirmation of the hypothesis that Thurtell was acting alone at the murder scene.)

Moreover, if we consider the possibility that Thurtell not only cheated his comrades out of their fair share of the spoils, but had plans to do so prior to his commission of the murder, we may have come close to explaining one of the central enigmas of the case: how and where had Thurtell ultimately overtaken and passed Hunt and Probert on the way to Gill's Hill Lane? In his paper F. B. Maggs offers the explanation that Thurtell, for reasons of his own, had wanted to give his collaborators the slip. In his opinion, Thurtell had passed Probert's gig in Edgware about a quarter past seven, while they were at the White Lion or at the corn chandler's. (The testimony of Clarke and Bingham, however, suggests that Thurtell must have passed earlier since they place him at the White Lion before the arrival of his unreliable confederates.) Pressing on to the top of Elstree Hill, Thurtell, according to Maggs, must have turned off the highway to the left, and proceeded via Letchmore Heath and Kemp Row to approach Radlett and Gill's Hill Lane from the southwest. By this route he would not have passed the Artichoke, which lay on the high road to the north of Elstree.[14]

Two reasons assigned by Maggs for Thurtell's detour fail to ring true. His suggestion that Thurtell made this wide circuit because he had not yet finally decided to commit the crime seems strained in light of the elaborate preparations for the murder. His second explanation that Thurtell, by seeking a new isolated site rather than the ambush agreed upon with his henchmen, was seeking to avoid witnesses to the murder seems excluded by his prompt announcement of the murder to Probert and Hunt and his insistence that they aid him in the concealment and disposal of the body. However, if Maggs's speculation about Thurtell's improvised route is correct, a more characteristic and persuasive motive (the possibility of which Maggs also acknowledges) suggests itself: that somewhere along the way, or perhaps even in the original conception of the scheme, Thurtell had decided to deceive his accomplices by stationing them at a false point of rendezvous and then proceeding to commit the crime at a different place, where, safe from the observation of Probert and Hunt, he could strip Weare's corpse of the major share of the victim's "bank." Having pocketed the fruits of the murder, he could then call on his gullible friends for help in disposing of Weare's body. Certainly, it would have been true to the mean and disloyal relationships among the three men that each in his own way had found a means of betrayal.

Finally, it should be recognized that traditional appraisals of the crime are in error in holding that the speedy arrest and conviction of Thurtell were the result of clumsy planning. Despite the eye-witness testimony placing Thurtell and Weare along the road to Hertfordshire on the night of the crime, Thurtell could never have been prosecuted if Hunt and then Probert had not betrayed him to the authorities and Hunt had not led them to Weare's body, which, under the legal doctrine of the time, was essential evidence in a murder prosecution. Indeed, the most sobering aspect of Thurtell's criminal design is that, inept as he is often seen to have been in execution of his plan, he had hit upon the ingredients of what in our times has too often come to be the perfect professional crime. In devising a scheme in which one underworld figure takes another for a ride into the country, murders him in a secluded place, and drops his body weighted with stones into a watery hiding place, Jack Thurtell became the father of the modern gangland slaying. Little has been done to improve upon his concept, except to replace the gig with a black limousine and his flintstones with a shroud of cement.

Chapter Eighteen

BLOCKHEADS IN A DARK LANE

———

Like the patricide of Beatrice Cenci and her brothers in late sixteenth-century Italy, the Thurtell-Hunt case presented an unusual blend of strong melodrama, picturesque characters and scenes, and agitating social issues that has continued to stir the literary imagination from the time of the murder to our own day. John O'London (Wilfred Whitten) cites the case as the supreme example of "the appeal which [murders] often make to the literary mind," and Gordon Maxwell has observed that "the fascination this crime had over literary men was extraordinary."[1]

The impact of the murder on English artists, though less spectacular than its literary aftermath, was also noteworthy. The Thurtell-Hunt case attracted the keen attention of many of the artists of its era. One of the most ardent followers of the case was William Mulready, who drew the three defendants during the trial at Hertford. Mulready's special interest in Thurtell may have been due in part to their shared passion for boxing. As early as 1800 Mulready had gained admission to the Royal Academy Life School with a black and white drawing of a classical statue of boxer-wrestlers, the *Pancrastinae*, and his masterpiece of 1816, *Fight Interrupted*, shows the aftermath of a street brawl; he also contributed drawings of boxing matches to Pierce Egan's *Boxiana*. The artist was himself trained in boxing by the famous pugilist Mendoza and, confident in his mastery of the manly arts, often would go down to the riverside to pick fights with the tough bargemen; like Thurtell, he was well known for his violent temper, which, according to his friend the painter Richard Redgrave, ultimately made his wife decide to leave him.[2]

Mulready's letters to Sir John Swinburne reveal that his sketches of the three Hertford prisoners were based on an effort to capture his impression of the feelings of the prisoners in reaction to their ordeal:

> There is one thing upon which I unfortunately cannot agree with anybody, the feelings expressed by the countenances & actions of the prisoners. I dare not venture to begin a detailed description of all that I thought I saw, but I must say, that Thurtell appeared to me to be ever, with the exception of a very few moments, on the watch, anxiously on the watch and ready to seize upon any little slip in the evidence of the witnesses against him or any trifling contradiction, or appearance of contradiction amongst them: but he never had a single chance & it was extremely painful to me to see towards the closing of the evidence for the prosecution, the agony, & death of his watchfulness & the "gathering up of himself" to hear the worst.

The artist's powerful attraction to his subjects was shown by the extreme personal discomfort that he had to bear to view the trial, where all seats were taken. "I stood," he reported, "for 15 hours with hat & without any refreshment except two biscuits, and this I believe is the cause of a large boil that appeared the day after upon the inside of my left leg, & which continues to give me very great trouble & inconvenience.[3]

The Victorian painter W. P. Frith asserts in his autobiography that Mulready, in the course of the trial, turned his sketchbook and his knowledge of anatomy to the service of the prosecution. According to Frith, the surgeon Ward during his testimony, "vainly tried to piece together [the fragments of Weare's skull], so as to fit them into that part of the skull that had escaped fracture. Seeing that the surgeon's nervousness rendered him quite incapable of obeying the Judge's order [to assemble the fragments], Mulready offered his services; and on the back of his sketch-book he fitted together the pieces of bone 'as you would a puzzle'—he said to me—and handed them to the jury." Frith claimed that Thurtell, in return, had furthered his anatomical studies, since casts taken from different parts of him had been used as models at Sass's School, which Frith attended. The painter recalled the macabre detail that "all new students were introduced to Thurtell's eye-lashes, which had adhered to the plaster when the cast was taken, our practice being to rub the newcomer's nose into them."[4]

According to an article in *All the Year Round,* a cast of Thurtell's back also figured as a study piece in Victorian ateliers: "A cast of the murder's powerful back, bowed as when the strangling bent it convulsively, we have seen in studios side by side with Madam Vestris's foot and the hand of Lucrezia Borgia.[5]

Solomon Hart of the Royal Academy wrote in his *Reminiscences* (privately published in 1882) that the murder of Weare had inspired designs by Sir Edwin Landseer, who is better known for more pleasing subjects:

> Once at a dinner table, Landseer told Professor Owen that, in early life, he was fond of making drawings of any tragical event, and that in 1824 he had made a series of designs of the particulars of the murder of Weare, at Elstree, by the brothers Thurtell [*sic*]. Upon the Professor expressing surprise, that he should have taken an interest in that dreadful murder, he exclaimed, "Oh, but I like murders"; what had become of the designs, he added, he had never been able to discover, but that some day or other they would produce a great deal of money.[6]

Sketches of the Gill's Hill property were also made as illustrations for George Henry Jones's book on the trial by the landscape painter and lithographer, James Duffield Harding.

The name of Sir Thomas Lawrence was brought into the case by a journalist who is to be praised more for his enterprise than his accuracy. On December 2, 1823, the *Times* reported a "curious application" that had been unanimously rejected by the visiting magistrates with authority over Hertford Gaol:

> About a fortnight ago Sir Thomas Lawrence, the President of the Royal Academy, caused an application to be made to one of the visiting Magistrates at Hertford, for permission to take a cast from the head of the prisoner Thurtell. The Magistrate to whom this request was conveyed instantly replied, that the order of the Magistrates (so often referred to) was imperative against admitting anybody but the legal advisers to see these prisoners, and it was thought that the answer to the President's application would have been deemed conclusive. Such was not, however, the fact, for the request has just been formally renewed to the visiting Magistrates acting in their collective capacity.

It was stated that the renewed request came before the magistrates at the very moment when the sheriff was communicating Thurtell's complaint about his compelled confrontation with the coachman Kay. The *Times* was certain that the prisoner could hardly have welcomed this new proposed intrusion on his privacy:

> In what light he would have viewed the visit of the President of the Royal Academy, to cover his face with wet plaster, it is not easy to conjecture. The fact is, that some half-idle and half-ingenious people have been describing the organic form of this prisoner's head, with a direct reference to the development of supposed passions, according to Gall and Spurzheim's fanciful theory [of phrenology], and Sir Thomas Lawrence was perhaps struck with the opportunity afforded of endeavouring to illustrate the system.

Only a day later the *Times* was "happy to find" that the story of Lawrence's application was "totally erroneous."[7]

The interest shown by artists in the case was matched by all who could read or write. The thirteen-year-old James Milnes Gaskell, who wrote home to his mother about rumors of Thurtell's mass murder plans, was no more preoccupied with the Gill's Hill crime than the other schoolchildren of his generation. In fact, G. M. Trevelyan reports that after Thurtell's execution children were known to write as copybook exercises an amazing sentiment that turned the murderer into a victim: "Thurtell was a murdered man."[8] Perhaps the fascination with the case even had some pedagogic value if we are to believe William Cobbett's account, in *Rural Rides,* of his son Richard's education. He noted that Richard "had learned from mere play to read, being first set to work on his own accord to find out what was said about Thurtell, when all the world was talking and reading about Thurtell."[9] Another young boy, Robert Browning, twelve years old in the year of Thurtell's execution, never lost his delight in the case and in the famous street ballad about William Weare of Lyon's Inn. Sixty years later, at the table of Lord Leighton's father, Browning, according to the memoirs of publisher Kegan Paul, quoted the "ghastly stanza" and "was rather piqued that another guest was able to finish the lines."[10] Like Browning, a host of British writers, whether or not they lived through the events of 1823 and 1824, have found a unique attraction in the Thurtell-Hunt case that supports its claim to being the most "literary" of Britain's murders.

From the time of his execution, Thurtell became a common subject in literary correspondence and diaries. The earliest commentator was the noted murder fancier, Charles Lamb. For some reason, Lamb was strongly moved by Thurtell's execution. Perhaps he knew him or his family, for he mentioned meeting at Shacklewell a "Miss H., the counter-tenor with a fine voice, whose sister married [Tom] Thurtell." There are many curious allusions to John Thurtell's fate in a letter Lamb wrote to Bernard Barton on January 9, 1824, the day of the hanging. Before referring to the execution, Lamb made a completely gratuitous slur on the intelligence of Thurtell's judge by confessing a feeling of lethargy that had left him "emptier than Judge Park's wig when the head is in it." So world-weary was Elia that nothing interested him: "'Tis twelve o'clock, and Thurtell is just now coming out upon the New Drop, Jack Ketch [generic name for the hangman] alertly tucking up his greasy sleeves to do the last office of mortality; yet cannot I elicit a groan or a moral reflection." Despite his protestation, the figure of the executed Thurtell reappears at the close of Lamb's letter. As Lamb summons up the scene of the executioner bargaining with a second-hand dealer over the dead man's clothes, which were one of the perquisites of his office, it seems possible that the writer's black mood has half-translated the murderer into a sacrilegious parody of the crucified Christ: "It is just fifteen minutes after twelve. Thurtell is by this time a good way on his journey . . . ; Ketch is bargaining for his cast coat and waistcoat. The Jew demurs at first at three half-crowns; but, on consideration that he may get somewhat by showing 'em in town, finally closes.[11] In view of his odd empathy with Thurtell, Lamb must have sorely envied his friend Franklin, the Hertford prison chaplain, who had been given the condemned man's watch as a keepsake.[12]

Lamb's interest in the case was easily surpassed by that of Sir Walter Scott. In a letter of January 23, 1824, to Miss Clephane, Scott wrote disdainfully of the newspapers' preoccupation with Thurtell: "No public news—except the more last words of Mr. Thurtell, whose tale seems to interest the public as long as that of Waterloo, showing that a bloody murther will do the business of the newspapers when a bloody battle is not to be heard." He also retailed the latest gossip that a lady had fallen in love with Thurtell in the courtroom.[13] Despite his ridicule of Thurtellmania, Scott quietly collected every book and pamphlet on the case that he could lay his hands on. The catalogue of his library at Abbotsford lists five related items, including Pierce Egan's account of the trial and his recollections of John Thurtell; Scott was also a great admirer of Webb's street ballad.[14] In his journal entry for July 16, 1826, he notes that he "slumbered for three or four hours over a variorum edition of the Gill's-Hill's tragedy." Nonetheless, he maintained even in this private moment a pretense of contempt for the English fascination with the murder, which "led John Bull into one of his uncommon fits of gambols, until at last he became so maudlin as to weep for the pitiless assassin, Thurtell, and treasure up the leaves and twigs of the hedge and shrubs in the fatal garden as valuable relics—nay, thronged the minor theatres to see the very roan horse and yellow gig in which the body was transported from one place to another."[15]

Even in the case of a writer, however, actions speak louder than words; two years later Sir Walter proved that he was every bit as avid a Gill's Hill tourist as the English. In May, 1828, he made a detour on his route from London to Scotland for the purpose of visiting the murder site. In his journal entry for May 28 he described his impressions of Probert's home: "The principal part of the house has been destroyed, and only the kitchen remains standing. The garden has been dismantled, though a few laurels and garden shrubs, run wild, continue to mark the spot. The fatal pond is now only a green swamp, but so near the house that one cannot conceive how it was ever chosen as a place of temporary concealment for a murdered body." Scott had by now been bitten by the same bug of unaccountable sympathy for Thurtell that had afflicted his literary confreres. For him the "one single shade of redeeming character" in the desperate and shortsighted crime was "the mixture of revenge which afforded some relief to the circumstances of treachery and premeditation which accompanied it." In Sir Walter's judgment, "Weare was a cheat, and had no doubt pillaged Thurtell, who therefore deemed he might take greater liberties with him than with others."[16]

Another writer whose diary reflects a strong interest in Thurtell
is Washington Irving. As has been noted, Irving in his *Tales of a
Traveller* (1824) had taken a dim view of the Fancy as a link between
the "man of rank" and the "murderer on the gibbet." "Buckthorne,"
the story in which this passage appears, had begun to germinate in
Irving's mind as early as June, 1823, but it was not published until
the summer of the following year, and its negative attitude towards the boxing crowd may, therefore, have been influenced by
Thurtell's trial and execution. That Irving was following Thurtell's
trial closely during his stay in Paris in January, 1824, is evident
from entries in his journal for January 10, 11, and 12. Apparently,
a parsimonious "browser," he stopped in at Galignani's bookshop
on those three days to read the trial and the account of Thurtell's
execution. He noted with disgust, only after completing his reading free of charge, the "ridiculous fuss made about it in Papers—
romantic reporters of newspapers make Thurtell a hero." This
sentiment cannot disguise Irving's deep interest in any morsel of
gossip that related to Thurtell, however. In his journal for November 3, 1824, he recorded at length an anecdote related to him
by General Shaw. The general told him that he had attended
Thurtell's trial and sat opposite the boxer Jack Martin. Martin had
complained of the accounts Thurtell gave of him to the newspapers, in which he had represented that the pugilist spoke in
slang and was a great friend of his. Martin, anxious to get his own
back with anyone who would listen, told Shaw that Thurtell "was a
fellow who would at any time give all the money in his pocket to
serve a friend tho he would cut a mans throat the next hour to gain
as much." Once when Thurtell had committed some fraud or robbery, he deposited his ill-gotten money with Martin who could
have informed on him for a reward and had him hanged had he
not been "too much of a man of honor." Nevertheless, Martin told
Shaw, Thurtell took it into his head that Martin would betray him
and decided to make away with him. One evening Martin saw
Thurtell "lurking about" and invited him into a public house for a
drink. Thurtell agreed, but had such a moody look that Martin
asked him: "What have you got in your head now, you brute?"
Thurtell then "saw by his own frank manner that his suspicions
were unfounded & the wine had had some effect on his heart—He

drew out a great knife from his pocket & threw it in the fire, [telling him] that with that knife, he had intended to murder him." Martin had broken out into a passion, "and even now," he concluded his story to General Shaw, "I cannot imagine how I kept from almost beating the life out of him."[17]

Other references to Thurtell, his family and friends, can be found in literary correspondence and diaries throughout the nineteenth century. In a letter of May 25, 1844, to Edward Bulwer Lytton, John Forster reported that Madame Anna Mitton had fascinated everybody by her acting and singing at a little theater on Oxford Street. He added the following tittle-tattle: "Who do you think she is??—The daughter of Thurtell by the sister of Hunt. Fact. Upon my word."[18] The great Shakespearean actor William Charles Macready, in his diary entry for May 24, 1833, recorded a lunch visit from Sir John Marshall, who "related anecdotes of Thurtell's brother."[19] As late as 1879 Edward FitzGerald, translator of *The Rubáiyát of Omar Khayyám,* included an appreciation of the Thurtell case in a letter to actress Fanny Kemble: "I like, you know, a good Murder, but in its place . . . only the other night I could not help reverting to that sublime—yes!—of Thurtell sending for his accomplice Hunt who had saved himself by denouncing Thurtell—sending for him to pass the night before Execution with perfect Forgiveness—Handshaking—and 'God Bless You—you couldn't help it—I hope you'll live to be a good man.'"[20] In 1831 in a letter to Jane Carlyle, Mrs. Basil Montague, searching for a simile for a willful "determination not to believe facts," called it "as absurd, as to persuade the living Brother of Wear (sic), that Thurtell neither robbed or murdered his nearest relation."[21] A letter of 1844 from the avid traveler Richard Ford to his publisher, John Murray, described his visit to George Borrow at Oulton, during which, he wrote, "we scamper by day over the country in a sort of gig, which reminds me of Mr. Weare on his trip with Mr. Thurtell."[22]

The journalistic hullabaloo over the Thurtell case was an open invitation to the satirist. The wits of *Blackwood's Magazine* of Edinburgh were not slow in making capital out of the English obsession with Weare's fate. One of the *Noctes Ambrosianae,* a series of comic dialogues that was a staple of the magazine, features a discussion of the case among "Christopher North" (John Wilson), James

Hogg, and Robert Sym. Hogg thought that the "English folk gaed clean mad" over Thurtell, and his own judgment was clear-eyed: "I never could see any thing very remarkable about his cutting Weare's craig [throat]. It was a puir murder yon." All three of the humorists laughed at the literary excesses of Edward Herbert's account of Thurtell's trial and at the conclusion of a phrenological study that "Jack would not have cheated an honest man, that he was another [John] Howard in benevolence, and had a deep sense of religion."[23] Another member of the *Blackwood's* circle, Dr. William Maginn in January, 1824, made his own poetic contribution to Thurtell literature. He published two parodies of the *Spanish Ballads* of Scott's son-in-law and biographer, John Gibson Lockhart. The first, in praise of Tom Spring's victory over Langan, was aptly titled "Spring's Return," and the second was "The Lament for Thurtell." In the "Lament" Maginn gives comic vent to *Blackwood's* Tory partisanship. Purporting to see in Thurtell's rapacious designs against Weare's purse an illustration of the principles of English liberalism, Maginn turned the murderer into "Whig Jack Thurtell":

> He was a Whig—a true, true Whig—all property he hated.
> In funds or land, in purse or hand,—tithes, salaried, or estated.
> When he saw a fob, he itch'd to rob, the genuine whiggish feeling;
> No matter what kind was the job, fraud, larceny, cheating, stealing.[24]

A third work, inspired in large part by Thurtell's crime, appeared in *Blackwood's* in 1827. This was Thomas De Quincey's classic essay, the first of a series of three, "On Murder Considered as One of the Fine Arts." The first essay takes the form of a mock-scholarly lecture by a member of a club styled the Society of Connoisseurs in Murder. The lecturer, who purports to appraise murder cases in accordance with rigorous aesthetic standards, observes to his fellow members: "People begin to see that something more goes to the composition of a fine murder than two blockheads to kill and be killed—a knife—a purse—and a dark lane. Design, gentlemen, grouping, light and shade, poetry, sentiment, are now deemed indispensable to attempts of this nature." De Quincey later explicitly confirms what his readers would have understood without his assistance—that the contemptuous reference to blockheads in a dark lane was an allusion to Thurtell and his victim. The close association of the essay with the Gill's Hill case is under-lined when De Quincey's murder critic recalls in detail the bringing of the news of Thurtell's crime to the connoisseurs' clubrooms:

> As to Mr. Thurtell's case, I know not what to say. . . . speaking ingenu-ously, I do really think that his principal performance, as an artist, has been much overrated. I admit, that at first, I was myself carried away by the general enthusiasm. On the morning when the murder was made known to London, there was the fullest meeting of amateurs that I have ever known since the days of Williams [the Ratcliffe Highway murderer, whose slaughters De Quincey described dramatically in the last essay in the series, "Three Memorable Murders"]; old bedridden connoisseurs, who had got into a peevish way of sneering and complaining "that there was nothing doing," now hobbled down to our club-room: such hilarity, such benign expression of general satisfaction, I have rarely witnessed. On every side you saw people shaking hands, congratulating each other, and forming dinner parties for the evening; and nothing was to be heard but triumphant challenges of—"Well! will *this* do?", "Is *this* the right thing?", "Are you satisfied at last?" But in the middle of the row, I remember, we all grew silent, on hearing the old cynical amateur L. S.—stumping along with his wooden leg; he entered the room with his usual scowl; and, as he advanced, he continued to groan and stutter the whole way—"Mere plagiarism—base plagiarism from hints that I threw out! Besides, his style is as harsh as Albert Durer, and as coarse as Fuseli."

The lecturer concurs with the abusive amateur, and reserves his praise for an "unfinished design of Thurtell's for the murder of a man with a pair of dumb-bells, which I admired greatly."[25]

When De Quincey's first essay on murder appeared, even his ad-mirers thought his humorous approach to be in doubtful taste, though it obviously followed in the tradition of Swift's "A Modest Proposal," in which cannibalism was recommended as a remedy for overcrowded orphanages. Perhaps De Quincey's critics were unaware that some of them were, in fact, his real targets; that the principal object of his satire was not crime but closed systems of aesthetics whose adepts showed more interest in their own aca-demic baggage than sensitivity to the realities of their field of study. A second object of De Quincey's lampoons was a well-observed tendency of the human mind to delight in catastro-phes—especially when they befall others. His fictional murder lec-turer defends his fascination with crime by comparing it to the common attraction of the most virtuous of men (including De Quincey's great contemporary, Samuel Taylor Coleridge) to fires. In "Three Memorable Murders," De Quincey asserts that the same reaction seen in observers of fires is also evoked by murders:

> After the first tribute of sorrow to those who have perished, but at all events, after the personal interests have been tranquillized by time, inevitably the scenical features (what aesthetically may be called the comparative *advantages*) of the several murders are reviewed and valued. One murder is compared with another; and the circumstances of superiority, as, for example, in the incidence and effects of surprise, of mystery, etc., are collated and appraised. I, therefore, for my estravagance, claim an inevitable and perpetual ground in the spontaneous tendencies of the human mind when left to itself.[26]

There can be little doubt that De Quincey, despite the dismissive remarks of his fictional murder lecturer, was properly appreciative of the "scenical features" of Thurtell's crime.

A sole surviving example of "serious" poetry based on the murder is a lugubrious verse called "The Owl" written by the Reverend John Mitford, editor of the *Gentleman's Magazine* between 1833 and 1850.

THE OWL
(Scene: The Cottage in Herts.)

Owl, that lovest the cloudy sky,
    In the murky air
    What saw'st thou there,
For I heard through the fog thy screaming cry?
    "The maple's head
    Was glowing red,
And red were the wings of the autumn sky;
    But a redder gleam
    Rose from the stream
That dabbled my feet as I glided by."

Owl, that lovest the midnight sky,
    Speak, oh! speak,
    What crimson'd thy beak,
And hung on the lids of thy staring eye?
    "'Twas blood! 'twas blood!
    And it rose like a flood,
And for this I scream'd as I hurried by."

Owl, that lovest the cloudy sky,
    Again, again,
    Where are the twain?
"Look while the moon is hurrying by:—
    In the thicket's shade
    The one is laid—
You may see through the boughs his moveless eye."

Owl, that lovest the cloudy sky,
    A step beyond,
    By the silent pond,
I heard a low and moaning cry.—
    "By the water's edge,
    Through the trampled sedge,
A bubble burst and gurgled by:
    My eyes were dim,
    But I look'd from the brim,
And I saw in the weeds a dead man lie."

Owl, that lovest the midnight sky,
    Where the casements blaze
    With the faggots' rays.
Look, oh! look! What seest thou there?
    Owl, what's this
    That snort and hiss—
And why do thy feathers shiver and stare?
    "'Tis he, 'tis he—
    He sits 'mid the three,
And a breathless Woman is on the stair."

Owl, that lovest the cloudy sky,
    Where clank the chains,
    Through the prison panes,
What there thou hearest, tell to me.
    "In her midnight dream
    'Tis a woman's scream,
And she calls on one—on one of three."
    Look in once more
    Through the grated door.
"'Tis a soul that prays in agony."

Owl, that hatest the morning sky,
    On thy pinions gray
    Away, away!
I must pray in charity;
    From midnight chime,
    Till morning prime,
Miserere, Domine![27]

This literary oddity was the last work Beau Brummell copied into his poetry album.

The Thurtell-Hunt case has left a strong mark on English fiction. Edward Bulwer Lytton's novel *Pelham* combined facts and legends of Weare's murder with autobiographical and literary source material in a sensational narrative that kept an international readership spellbound. In 1824, the year of Thurtell's hanging, Bulwer Lytton claimed to have had two narrow escapes from would-be murderers with robbery on their minds; the first was a poor cottager with whom he lodged overnight on the way to Keswick, and the other a fellow pedestrian on a Scottish road who, after affronting him with rude remarks, ultimately pulled out a murderous-looking "life-preserver" (a slung shot) behind his back.[28] These hair-raising experiences must have reinforced his interest in the fate of Weare in a lonely country lane. *Pelham,* however, was itself a hybrid creation that drew on a number of literary antecedents. It is regarded as one of the first of the so-called silver fork novels, portraying scenes of English high society, and inspired the later works by Disraeli in the same genre. However, the murder narrative Bulwer Lytton interpolates in the action seems at odds with the book's prevailing light tone. With its dominant themes of revenge, pursuit and detection, the subplot owes a heavy debt to William Godwin's *Caleb Williams* (1794).[29] It is no accident that the murder victim in *Pelham*, Sir John Tyrrell, a dissolute nobleman addicted to gambling, has the same last name (with a slight variation in spelling) as Barnabas Tyrrel, the victim in Godwin's novel, though Bulwer Lytton, perhaps to disguise his borrowing, invokes in a chapter epigraph the example of still another Tyrrell, the assassin of the young princes in *Richard III*. In addition to reflecting Godwin's influence, Bulwer Lytton heavily capitalized on the popularity of Pierce Egan's *Life in London* by ending his narrative with a scene in the murderer's underground hideout, which Pelham penetrates in disguise after being given a lesson in criminal slang.

Within this familiar literary framework, Bulwer Lytton introduces characters and events from the Gill's Hill murder. His readers would have identified the villainous Sir John Tyrrell, despite his high birth, with Weare, and the murderer, Tom Thornton, a boxing enthusiast and crooked gambler, with John Thurtell. Thornton preys on English expatriates in Paris, pickings that will never run short, a friend of Pelham predicts, "because rogues are like spiders, and eat each other, when there is nothing else to catch." This prophecy is fulfilled when Thornton murders Tyrrell with the help of his accomplice Dawson (Hunt or Probert). The passage describing Pelham's discovery of the body would have reminded any English reader of the Thurtell-Hunt news stories of four years before:

> The ground over which [the horseman] passed was steeped in the moonshine, and I saw the long and disguising cloak in which he was enveloped, as clearly as by the light of day. I paused; and as I was following him with my looks, my eye fell upon some obscure object by the left side of the pool. I threw my horse's rein over the hedge, and firmly grasping my stick, hastened to the spot. As I approached the object, I perceived that it was a human figure: it was lying still and motionless; the limbs were half immersed in the water; the face was turned upwards; the side and throat were wet with a deep red stain,—it was of blood; the thin, dark hairs of the head were clotted together over a frightful and disfiguring contusion. I bent over the face in a shuddering and freezing silence. It was the countenance of Sir John Tyrrell!

Pelham brings Thornton to justice by securing the confession of Dawson, in which the Thurtell's rumored vampirism takes on an added horror by being transformed into a calculating scheme to dispose of evidence: "Thornton's linen and hands were stained with blood. The former he took off, locked up carefully, and burned the first opportunity; the latter he washed; and, that the water might not lead to detection, *drank it.*"[30]

According to the author's grandson, the earl of Lytton, *Pelham* won only mild approbation from Pierce Egan, but shortly after the publication of Bulwer Lytton's crime novel *Eugene Aram*, he received a visit from Egan. After "a long, mysterious, and magniloquent exordium, in the purest dialect of the Seven Dials," he bestowed upon him a unique gift that he thought only the author of *Eugene Aram* was worthy to possess—"the genuine caul of Thurtell the murderer."[31]

The personality of John Thurtell—sometimes viewed as sinister and repellent, occasionally as engaging, but always as masterful—dominates much of the work of Norwich-bred George Borrow. As a child Borrow was strongly attracted to boxing and the Fancy, his enthusiasm probably fired by his father's recurrent boast of having fought the formidable Big Ben Brain.[32] George, following in Captain Borrow's footsteps, prided himself on his acquaintance with Thurtell, nine years his senior; not only did he claim that John taught him how to box, but it has even been stated that Alderman Thurtell's house on Ipswich Road near Harford Bridge became a favorite resort of Norwich's fight crowd. Despite his suspicion that these assertions were exaggerated, Borrow's biographer Clement Shorter assumes that the Thurtell and Borrow families were in fact well acquainted; he bases his belief on his conclusion that the names, John and George Thurtell, appearing in a list of subscribers to Borrow's early work, *Romantic Ballads,* refer to Norwich's famed murderer and a brother.[33]

In light of his pretensions to friendship, there has been a good deal of speculation as to whether Borrow attended Thurtell's trial and execution. According to one of the contemporary accounts of the hanging, Thurtell, on the scaffold, "fixed his eyes on a young gentleman in the crowd, whom he had frequently seen as a spectator at the commencement of the proceedings against him. Seeing that the individual was affected by the circumstance, he removed them to another quarter."[34] Some commentators have identified George Borrow as the sensitive "young gentleman" in the crowd. The evidence on the question to be drawn from his own work is inconclusive but does not appear to support this theory. Within a year after the execution, Borrow was to write of Thurtell's last moments, in his anonymous six-volume compilation *Celebrated Trials* (1825). His account of Thurtell's case was, like the balance of this series, primarily culled from other published sources; it contains nothing that appears to reflect firsthand knowledge or experience. Indeed, he describes the hanging in three brief paragraphs, which draw heavily on Edward Herbert's article in *London Magazine;* Borrow does not name Herbert but refers to him simply as an "eye-witness."[35]

Whatever the strength of Borrow's personal bond with Thurtell may have been in their Norwich years, the recurrent appearances of Thurtell in Borrow's major works confirm the fascination that the author felt for his former acquaintance after he was revealed to be a murderer. In the introduction to *The Zincali; or, An Account of the Gypsies of Spain* (1841), Borrow recalls that at age fourteen he attended a prizefight near Norwich that Thurtell had promoted: "The terrible Thurtell was present, lord of the concourse; for wherever he moved he was master, and whenever he spoke, even when in chains, every other voice was silent. He stood on the mead, grim and pale as usual, with his bruisers around." A more menacing Thurtell (now unnamed but identified beyond all doubt) is encountered by the hero of the semiautobiographical novel *Lavengro* (1851); Borrow has left a memorable portrait of the fearsome promoter as he unsuccessfully attempts to bully a country magistrate into making an enclosed farm field available for a prizefight:

> He was a man somewhat under thirty, and nearly six feet in height. . . . he wore neither whiskers nor moustache and appeared not to delight in hair, which was of a light brown, being closely cropped; the forehead was rather high, but somewhat narrow; the face neither broad nor sharp, the nose almost delicate; the eyes were grey, with an expression in which there was sternness blended with something approaching to feline; his complexion was exceedingly pale, relieved, however, by certain pock-marks, which here and there studded his countenance; his form was athletic but lean; his arms long. In the whole appearance of the man there was a blending of the bluff and the sharp. You might have supposed him a bruiser; his dress was that of one in all its minutiae; something was wanting, however, in his manner—the quietness of the professional man; he rather looked like one performing the part— well—very well—but still performing a part.

Undaunted by the magistrate's refusal, Thurtell stages the fight "in the precincts of the old town, near the field of the chapel." A thunderstorm bursts out during the match, and a gypsy friend of the protagonist Lavengro (Borrow) calls his attention to a cloud that resembles a "stream of blood." The gypsy reveals to Lavengro that the cloud foretells a "bloody fortune" for Thurtell, to whom he points, as the promoter, accompanied by the victorious bruiser, drives away from the field with a "smile of triumph."[36]

Dramatic as the scene may be, there is no reason to believe that the incident of the gypsy's fortune-telling is factual; throughout his works Borrow often described meetings with men who were later to be hanged, including the celebrated Scottish jailbreaker and murderer David Haggart, and on each occasion he delights in his retrospective knowledge of their destinies.

The last lines of the chapter of the gypsy's prophecy introduce a strain of Borrow's sympathy for Thurtell. Anticipating that his reader will judge that Thurtell merited the predicted doom as "a bad, violent man," Borrow cautions, "Softly, friend; when thou wouldst speak harshly of the dead, remember that thou hast not yet fulfilled thy own [fortune]!"[37] However, even this word of compassion hardly prepares us for the eulogy for Thurtell that Borrow puts in the mouth of a jockey in *Romany Rye* (1857), the sequel to *Lavengro*. The jockey tells Lavengro how Thurtell, now referred to only as "Jack," lent him two hundred pounds when he was down on his luck. When he was repaid, Jack refused the jockey's gift of a horse and asked him instead to "come and see him hanged when the time was come." The jockey agreed to the request, not knowing that one day he would keep his word, standing up in his gig before Hertford Gaol, removing his hat, and shouting "God Almighty bless you, Jack!" Some men are born to be hanged and some are not, the jockey muses. Accepting the stories of Thurtell's gallantry in war, the jockey contrasts him favorably with a cowardly nobleman he calls Whitefeather, who intentionally fell off his horse at Waterloo on the day before the battle: "Jack was hanged because, along with his bad qualities, he had courage and generosity; this fellow [Whitefeather] is not, because with all Jack's bad qualities, and many more, amongst which is cunning, he has neither courage nor generosity."[38]

   William Makepeace Thackeray and Charles Dickens were, like Browning, children of the Thurtell-Hunt generation, and their recollections of the case have left imprints on their writings. Thackeray, who began his literary career as a journalist, commented in an early article that to newspapermen a "good murder is a godsend," and he rated Thurtell first among their favorite malefactors. In the closing pages of *Vanity Fair*, where he described Becky Sharp's struggle with life insurance representatives after the mysterious death of Jos Sedley, he gave her legal advisers the names of three murderers, Burke, Thurtell, and Hayes. However, Thackeray's literary enthusiasm for Thurtell cannot be ranked with that of his rival, Dickens, who, sharing in liberal measure the great passion of Londoners for lurid criminal cases, was intimately acquainted with the details of the murder in Gill's Hill Lane. There are explicit references to Thurtell scattered throughout Dickens' work. An early allusion appears in Dickens' sketch of "The Out-and-Out Young

Gentleman" (1838). One of the "young" gentlemen, whose youth must have been subject to question, was a "'Mr. Warmint Blake,' who upon divers occasions has distinguished himself in a manner that would not have disgraced the fighting man, and who—having been a pretty long time about town—had the honor of once shaking hands with the celebrated Mr. Thurtell himself."[39]

In his essay "The Demeanour of Murderers" (1856) Dickens compared the cool courtroom behaviour of Thurtell with the similar aplomb of his more famous successor among sportsmen murderers, the mass poisoner William Palmer; he warned against giving credence to their convincing protestations of innocence, which were likely to be projections of the same callousness that made their murders possible. Dickens noted points of strong resemblance between the two murderers: "Each was born in a fair station, and educated in conformity with it; each murdered a man with whom he had been on terms of intimate association, and for whom he professed a friendship at the time of the murder; both were members of that vermin-race of outer bettors and blacklegs, of whom some worthy samples were presented on both trials, and of whom, as a community, mankind would be blessedly rid, if they could all be, once and for ever, knocked on the head at a blow." Referring to the contemporary newspapers in aid of his "previous knowledge of the case," Dickens found confirmation that Thurtell's demeanor was exactly that of Palmer. During his imprisonment he was collected and resolute and received friends with cheerfulness; at the trial his attention and composure were wonderful, and he wrote notes as Palmer did and watched the case "with the same cool eye." In one respect, he distinguished himself from his successor by acting as his own orator and making a speech "in the manner of Edmund Kean." Since Dickens' article was written prior to the hanging of Palmer, he left it to his readers to find out from reports of the execution whether the parallel between the two cool murderers would hold to the very end. It was clear that no degree of courage that Palmer might display on the scaffold would change Dickens' appraisal of him or Thurtell:

> It is surely time that people who are not in the habit of dissecting such appearances, but who are in the habit of reading about them, should be helped to the knowledge that, in the worst examples they are the most to be expected, and the least to be wondered at. That, there is no inconsis-

tency in them, and no fortitude in them. That, there is nothing in them
but cruelty and insensibility. That, they are seen, because the man is of a
piece with his misdeeds; and that it is not likely that he ever could have
committed the crimes for which he is to suffer, if he had not this demeanour to present, in standing publicly to answer for them.[40]

In *The Lazy Tour of Two Idle Apprentices* (which Dickens wrote in
1857 with Wilkie Collins), Thurtell and Palmer become figures of
a sportsman's nightmare. All through the Doncaster Race Week,
which he is attending with his friend Thomas Idle, Francis Goodchild is prey to the delusion that he is in a lunatic asylum peopled
by betting-mad lunatics and by sharpers playing the role of their
keepers. Goodchild sees "an awful family likeness among the Keepers, to Mr. Palmer and Mr. Thurtell. . . . Cunning, covetousness,
secresy, cold calculation, are the uniform Keeper characteristics.
Mr. Palmer passes me five times in five minutes, and, as I go
down the street, the back of Mr. Thurtell's skull is always going on
before me."[41]

Thurtell's crime seems clearly to have been a major influence
on Dickens's portrayal of the murder of the swindler Montague
Tigg by Jonas Chuzzlewit in *Martin Chuzzlewit*. Tigg organizes a
swindling insurance concern, which he gives a grand and disarming name, the Anglo-Bengalee Disinterested Loan and Life Insurance Company. Using his secretly acquired knowledge of Jonas
Chuzzlewit's attempt to poison his father, Anthony, he presses
Jonas to invest in Anglo-Bengalee and to persuade his father-in-
law Mr. Pecksniff to do the same. Jonas meets Tigg's demands, but
his thoughts turn to murder. He questions Dr. John Jobling about
the efficacy of a lancet in cutting a man's throat and learns of a medical murderer who left his victim leaning upright in the angle of a
doorway with only one drop of blood on his waistcoat—stabbed to
the heart with such dexterity that he had died instantly and bled
internally. That night Tigg, in the company of Jonas, takes a fearful carriage ride into the country under storming skies; the epi-
sode must have stirred Victorian memories of Thurtell's gig and
his spectral horse. During the journey Tigg experiences a sudden
vision of Jonas' murderous enmity, when a lightning bolt "presented or assisted a curious optical illusion . . . [of] Jonas with his
hand lifted, and the bottle clenched in it like a hammer, making as

if he would aim a blow at his head." Terrified by the lightning, the horses overturn the carriage; Jonas, with great presence of mind, tries to draw their hooves over the skull of the prostrate Tigg, but the driver intervenes. Ultimately, Jonas waylays Tigg and murders him in a shadowy wood. Although Dickens does not borrow as literally as did Bulwer Lytton from the details of the Thurtell murder scene, Jonas Chuzzlewit's mental image of the victim he left behind him summons up the horror of the butchery of Mr. Weare:

> The body of a murdered man. In one thick solitary spot, it lay among the last year's leaves of oak and beech, just as it had fallen headlong down. Sopping and soaking in among the leaves that formed its pillow; oozing down into the boggy ground, as if to cover itself from human sight; forcing its way between and through the curling leaves, as if those senseless things rejected and foreswore it, and were coiled up in abhorrence; went a dark, dark stain that dyed the whole summer night from earth to heaven.[42]

At least three twentieth-century novels have been inspired by the Thurtell case. In the earliest of these, *Thurtell's Crime* (1906), the prolific thriller writer Dick Donovan (a pseudonym of Joyce Emmerson Preston Muddock) subordinates a sketchy retelling of the murder of Weare to a formulaic melodrama. Thurtell lures to London and installs as manager of the Cock Tavern Dora Melfort, the daughter of a prosperous Norfolk farmer and patron of the Fancy (Donovan's more respectable version of Mary Dodson). She is pursued by her sister Linda, who hopes to induce her to return to their virtuous home. Thurtell and a villainous gambling confederate, Captain Rowland, kidnap Linda and a young nobleman Lord Purbleck and hold them captive in the Manchester Buildings (the locale of Thurtell's dumbbell plot against Mr. Woods). The two prisoners escape together but Lord Purbleck's gallant rescue of Linda is ill rewarded by her fiancé, who accuses them of being lovers. After Thurtell's crime and execution, the misunderstandings are resolved and all ends happily, except for poor Dora, who drowns herself in Probert's pond.[43]

A far superior work is Thomas Burke's *Murder at Elstree; or, Mr. Thurtell and His Gig* (1936). Burke brackets his narrative with allusions to Borrow; the novella begins with a description of a crooked fight near Norwich promoted by Thurtell, in which a verbatim quotation of the gypsy fortune-telling passage from *Lavengro* is incorporated, and ends as Thurtell on the scaffold has the "fleeting satisfaction" of recognizing Borrow in the crowd. Although marred by a heavily doom-laden style favored by the "had-he-but-known" school of crime writing, *Murder at Elstree* for the most part follows the reported facts with reasonable accuracy and provides plausible answers for some of the eternal riddles of the case. According to Burke, it was Hunt who originally suggested to Thurtell both that he murder Weare and that the crime be committed somewhere along the Elstree road. Thurtell is credited with fixing the precise murder locale at Phillimore Lodge and with recalling the "useful ponds" in the neighborhood; he is also freed of the stigma of having murdered without profit, for Burke hypothesizes that Thurtell found Weare's well-filled moneybag on his body and hid it before he brought his confederates to Gill's Hill Lane. Burke blames the failed rendezvous squarely on Hunt "whose zest for the affair had passed out with the planning of it." While drinking at the White Lion in Edgware, Hunt sees Thurtell's gig pass by but does not tell Probert. Unlike Dick Donovan, Burke renders a lenient judgment on Thurtell's character. Before coming to London, Thurtell, a mixture of the bluffer and the gullible, was not a bad man but was drifting to bad: "The kind of life which appealed to him—the life of which the Prince Regent had been the exemplar—had its being on a bad road; a road which only the man of positive good force can safely ride. Under good management Thurtell might have been a negatively decent man. Riding this road, he became, by stages imperceptible to himself, a desperate, but still not a positive, bad man."[44]

A more realistic portrayal of Thurtell's disordered personality is to be found in *The Swell Yokel* (1955) by historical novelist and crime essayist Philip Lindsay. In this novel Thurtell is a thin-skinned man of violence resolved to murder someone so that he can belie his reputation as a gullible provincial who talks a better game than he can play. His choice of victim hardly matters, and ultimately he persuades himself that he has selected Weare so that he can rob the dead man of funds to finance future murders of his other enemies. Lindsay carefully builds his narrative on the foundation of facts drawn from the trial and Hunt's confession but allows himself the license of imagining a romance between Thurtell and Anne Noyes.[45]

The personality and crime of John Thurtell have also furnished a rich storehouse of images, anecdotes, and allusions to be drawn upon by British essayists with confidence that their readers would be familiar with the details of the case. In one instance the melodramatic quality of the murder itself was invoked in a completely unrelated context, when Sydney Smith, reviewing a book on South America, likened the cry of the goatsucker bird to "Weare being murdered by Thurtell." More often, however, essayists have referred to the conduct of John Thurtell to illustrate their analyses of the character of murderers or of personality development. Two articles on these themes appeared more than thirty years after Thurtell's death but continue to reflect the admiring tone of much of the post-mortem journalism of 1824. The agreeable side of Thurtell as the model prisoner of Hertford was emphasized by Archbishop Richard Whately in his edition of *Bacon's Essays* (1856). In his annotation to the essay "Of Goodness, and Goodness of Nature," Whately cites Thurtell's example in proof of Bacon's suggestion that a considerable endowment of natural benevolence is not incompatible with cruelty:

> When Thurtell, the murderer, was executed, there was a shout of derision raised agaist the phrenologists for saying his organ of *benevolence* was large. But, they replied, that there was large *destructiveness,* and a moral deficiency, which would account for a man goaded to rage (by having been cheated of almost all he had by the man he killed) committing that act. It is a remarkable confirmation of their view, that a gentleman who visited the prison where Thurtell was confined (shortly after the execution) found the gaolers, etc., full of pity and affection for him. They said he was a kind, good-hearted fellow so obliging and friendly, that they had never had a prisoner whom they so much regretted. And such seems to have been his general character when not influenced at once by the desire of revenge and of gain.

On the other hand, the Scottish poet, Alexander Smith, in "A Lark's Flight," an essay about capital punishment, referred to Thurtell's fortitude on the scaffold in confirmation of his theory that "criminals for the most part, die well and bravely." Smith, choosing the most theatrical version of Thurtell's inquiries about the Spring-Langan fight, wrote: "When he came out on the scaf-

fold, he inquired privily of the executioner if the result had yet
become known. Jack Ketch was not aware, and Thurtell expressed
his regret that the ceremony in which he was chief actor should
take place so inconveniently early in the day. Think of a poor
Thurtell forced to take his long journey an hour, perhaps, before
the arrival of intelligence so important!"[46]

A subtler speculation on Thurtell's criminality is contained in
Early One Morning in the Spring (1935), a book of impressions on
children and childhood by the twentieth-century poet Walter de la
Mare. As he ruminates on the unseen fork in the road of childhood that leads on to cruelty and crime, de la Mare calls to mind
Thurtell's courtroom speech. Thurtell had reviewed his respectable and promising beginnings and invited the jury to conclude
that such horrible guilt as had been attributed to him "could not
have resulted from custom, but must have been the innate principle of [his] infant mind," and that a few short years could not
have "reversed the course of nature, and converted the good feelings which [he] possessed, into that spirit of malignant cruelty, to
which only demons can attain." De la Mare notes that Thurtell's
theorizing about the "infant mind" was in vain and implies that his
resigned acceptance of his punishment was a final refutation of his
own argument. In de la Mare's view the narratives of the lives and
executions of criminals deepened the mystery of human affairs
but gave little insight into children. The editors of criminal chronicles referred "frequently to early circumstances," de la Mare concluded, "now and then to nurture, but to early nature, so far as I
can remember, not at all. Cruelty, malicious lying, and a kind of
brutal indecency and malignity make a louring human sunrise.
But what was the sun like, before it came up?[47]

Among the British essayists who worked the lode of the Thurtell-
Hunt murder, the place of honor must be reserved for Thomas
Carlyle, who gave his interpretation of the case a characteristically
ideological turn. Although he had undoubtedly followed the news
reports of the crime, his literary response was aroused in a curiously indirect fashion. While he was reading a review in the *Quarterly Review* for January, 1828, of a book about life in Australia, a
footnote caught his eye. The reviewer had commented in the text
that "The progressive improvement and civilisation of the colony

may further be inferred from the state of society in Sydney, where, according to our author, private carriages are kept, and few individuals, if any, who pretend to what in the slang tongue is called *respectability*, are without their gigs or riding-horses." Led to the footnote by an asterisk after "*respectability*," Carlyle read with indignation: "The term was defined by one of the witnesses on the noted trial of John Thurtell. The question was (but we quote from memory) 'What sort of person was Mr. Weare? *Answer*. Mr. Weare was respectable. *Counsel*. What do you mean by respectability? *Witness*. He kept a gig.'"[48] The reviewer's memory was in fact faulty, for the passage in the news stories he had vaguely recalled was the report in a biographical sketch of Probert that appeared in the *Observer* on Sunday, November 2, 1823, and in the London dailies on the following day that Probert "always maintained an appearance of respectability, and kept his horse and gig."[49] However inaccurate its quotation, the book review suggested to Carlyle that the gig, a central feature of the Thurtell-Hunt case, was a wonderfully apt metaphor for bourgeois materialism, and he was quick to embody and develop this concept in his own work.

It may seem remarkable that Carlyle drew his symbolic concept of the gig from a footnote in a minor book review. That obscure allusion must surely have aroused Carlyle's own recollections of the case, which most literary men of his day followed closely. Perhaps the image of the gig was also associated in his mind with the Tom and Jerry mania. Although the fact has gone unnoticed in writing on the Thurtell-Hunt case, the gig was a central symbol of the "good life" as pictured in Pierce Egan's *Life in London*. The frontispiece of the book depicts a "Corinthian Capital" of society; at the top is the royal court, and at the base a poor family before a cellar fire. The three heroes, who mingle with the high and low, are shown appropriately in the very middle of the column, and above their heads is a rakish young gentleman driving a horse and carriage with a gaudily dressed young woman by his side. In his annotations to the illustration, Egan explains his characterization of the young gentleman as belonging to the ups, "that is, to be *up* to 'push along,' and to 'keep moving,' while a *chance* remains, to sport a *natty* gig, a prime *fast* one, and to have a pretty '*piece of goods*' by your side, just to show the world what a gay fellow you are."[50] Thus the gig was delivered to Carlyle ready-made as a symbol not only of middle-class respectability, but also of middle-class hedonism as praised by Pierce Egan; under both these superficial views of life, the Thurtell-Hunt case had shown, lies a spiritual void that can only too easily be filled by immorality or crime.

Beginning in 1830, Carlyle's essays reflect his obsession with the horse-drawn carriage of the Thurtell case as a sign of smug materialism and philistinism; to express his idée fixe he invented a dizzying series of neologisms built on the root of the word *gig*. In his article on the German writer, Jean Paul Friedrich Richter, which appeared in the *Foreign Review* in 1830, Carlyle wrote that Richter had been able to make his voice heard without having landed property or connections with the higher classes, without even keeping a gig; Richter "was not a nobleman, nor gentleman, nor gigman; but simply a man." In a footnote, Carlyle cited the note in the *Quarterly Review* and added, "Since then we have seen a 'Defensio Gigmanica, or Apology for the Gigmen of Great Britain,' composed not without eloquence, and which we hope one day to prevail on our friend, a man of some whims, to give to the public." Two years later, in an essay for *Fraser's* titled "Boswell's *Life of Johnson*,'" Carlyle spoke of Boswell as "a Scottish squirelet, full of . . . 'gigmanity', who was nonetheless magnetically attracted to the English 'plebeian' Johnson." Referring again in a footnote to the supposed Thurtell-Hunt testimony quoted in the *Quarterly Review,* Carlyle commented: "Thus, it has been said, does society naturally divide itself into four classes: Noblemen, Gentlemen, Gigmen and Men." Another allusion to the gigman made in Carlyle's article on Goethe's works in the *Foreign Quarterly Review* (1832) develops at greater length his critique of respectability: "The first fruit of riches, especially for the man born rich, is to teach him faith in them, and all but hide from him that there is any other faith: thus is he trained up in the miserable eye-service of what is called Honour, Respectability; instead of a man we have but a *gigman*—one who 'always kept a gig,' two-wheeled or four-wheeled." For Carlyle, the "first and most stupendous of gigmen" was Phaeton, child of the Sun, who was struck by Zeus's thunderbolt for reckless driving of "the brightest of all conceivable gigs."[51]

Variants of these first coined "gigwords" appear in the correspondence of Carlyle and his wife Jane: *gigmania, Gigmaness, Gigman-hood,* and *county gigmanism.* Other writers took up the fashion. Thomas Hood, in his *Up the Rhine* (1840) described a doctor as "a respectable gigman, who also likes a fast horse," and in 1884 an article in *Harper's Magazine* asserted that "the gigman spells God with a little 'g.'"[52]

The most substantial utilization of Carlyle's concept is to be found in the work of Thurtell's friend, George Borrow. In his appendix to *Romany Rye,* Borrow explained that his portrayal of the independent and incorruptible vagabond Lavengro was intended as a rebuke to the "absurd mania" of all classes of English society for "gentility." In Borrow's conception, which bears the obvious influence of Carlyle's attacks on respectability, "gentility" is a "glittering or gaudy" show of power, status or affluence that has nothing in common with gentlemanliness, since, like Lavengro, impoverished comrade of the lowborn and the gypsies, "a person can be a gentleman in rags." Confirming that he had rallied to Carlyle's banner, Borrow asserted that no admirer of a dishonest millionaire would think Lavengro a gentleman, "for who can be a gentleman who keeps no gig?"[53]

However, the supreme transfiguration of the image of the gig of the Thurtell-Hunt case is in the apocalyptic prophecy that concludes Carlyle's masterpiece, *The French Revolution* (1837):

Higher, higher yet flames the Fire-Sea; crackling with new dislocated timber; hissing with leather and prunella. The metal Images are molten; the marble Images become mortar-lime; the stone Mountains sulkily explode. RESPECTABILITY, with all her collected Gigs inflamed for funeral pyre, wailing, leaves the Earth: not to return save under new Avatar. Imposture how it burns, through generations: how it is burnt up; for a time. The World is black ashes;—which, ah, when will they grow green? The Images all run into amorphous Corinthian brass; all Dwellings of men destroyed; the very mountains peeled and riven, the valley black and dead: it is an empty World! Woe to them that shall be born then! . . . For it is the End of the dominion of IMPOSTURE (which is Darkness and opaque Fire-damp); and the burning up, with unquenchable fire, of all the Gigs that are in the Earth.[54]

In this visionary passage, a brutal murder case, which had revealed the rot at the core of the pleasure-seeking Regency way of life, becomes a broader symbol of an outworn world order.

NOTES

INTRODUCTION

1. George Macaulay Trevelyan, *British History in the Nineteenth Century (1782–1901)* (London, 1922), 170–71.

2. As quoted in Harold Strong Gulliver, *Thackeray's Literary Apprenticeship* (Valdosta, 1934), 195.

3. Richard D. Altick, *Victorian Studies in Scarlet: Murders and Manners in the Age of Victoria* (New York, 1970), 17–40.

4. Albert Borowitz, "Portraits of Beatrice: The Cenci Case in Literature and Opera," in his *A Gallery of Sinister Perspectives: Ten Crimes and a Scandal* (Kent, 1982), 11–20.

5. See Angus Fletcher (ed.), *The Literature of Fact* (New York, 1976).

Chapter One
BRUISERS AND BLACKLEGS

1. Pierce Egan, *Boxiana; or, Sketches of Ancient and Modern Pugilism* (London, 1818–21), I, 57–60.

2. *Ibid.*, 58.

3. J. C. Reid, *Bucks and Bruisers: Pierce Egan and Regency England* (London, 1971), 12–49; John Ford, *Prizefighting: The Age of Regency Boximania* (Newton Abbot, 1971), 65–101.

4. Ford, *Prizefighting*, 35–64, 71–72.

5. As quoted *ibid.*, 149.

6. Washington Irving, "Buckthorne; or, The Young Man of Great Expectations," in Charles Neider (ed.), *The Complete Tales of Washington Irving* (Garden City, 1975), 328–29.

7. C. F. Shoolbred, *The Law of Gaming and Betting* (2nd ed.; London, 1935), 1–4, 193–204.

8. John Wade, *A Treatise on the Police and Crimes of the Metropolis* (1829; rpr. Montclair, 1972), 110–11.

9. As quoted in John Ashton, *The History of Gambling in England* (1898; rpr. Montclair, 1969), 103.

10. *The Gambler's Scourge,* an appendix to *The Fatal Effects of Gambling Exemplified in the Murder of William Weare* (London, 1824), 349–50.

11. *Ibid.*, 375.

12. *Ibid.*, 350.
13. *Ibid.*, 361.

Chapter Two
THE GAS WENT OUT

1. The account of the Hickman-Neat fight and of the careers and personalities of the two boxers is principally based on Egan, *Boxiana*, III, 287–301; and Egan, *New Series of Boxiana* (London, 1828–29), I, 33–58. See also *Selections from the Fancy; or, True Sportsman's Guide* (Barre, 1972), 45–62; Henry Downes Miles, *Pugilistica: Being One Hundred and Forty-four Years of the History of British Boxing* (London, 1880), II, 104–37.

2. *Selections from the Fancy*, 48.
3. *Ibid.*, 46.
4. Ford, *Prizefighting*, 107–109.
5. Egan, *Boxiana*, III, 280.
6. Reid, *Bucks and Bruisers*, 1–92.
7. William Hazlitt, "The Fight," in Alexander Ireland (ed.), *William Hazlitt, Essayist and Critic: Selections from His Writings* (London, [1889]), 266–80.
8. *Ibid.*, 266, 271–72, 275.
9. Egan, *New Series of Boxiana*, I, 47–48.
10. Hazlitt, "The Fight," 276, 277.
11. *Ibid.*, 273.

Chapter Three
THE SWELL YOKEL

1. Eric R. Watson (ed.), *Trial of Thurtell and Hunt*, Notable British Trials (Edinburgh, 1920), 2.

2. B. Cozens-Hardy and E. A. Kent, *The Mayors of Norwich, 1403–1835* (Norwich, 1938), 156–57.

3. Pierce Egan, *Recollections of John Thurtell* (London, 1824), 36; Watson (ed.), *Trial of Thurtell and Hunt*, 2; George Borrow, *The Romany Rye*, in Clement Shorter (ed.), *The Works of George Borrow* (London, 1923), VI, 137.

4. Watson (ed.), *Trial of Thurtell and Hunt*, 3–4.
5. *Ibid.*, 5; Egan, *Recollections*, 40–41.
6. Egan, *Recollections*, 34.
7. *Ibid.*, 34; Watson, (ed.), *Trial of Thurtell and Hunt*, 7–8.
8. (London) *Times*, November 11, 1823, p. 3.
9. Watson (ed.), *Trial of Thurtell and Hunt*, 6–7; Egan, *Recollections*, 43; *The Fatal Effects of Gambling*, xviii–xx; *Times*, November 4, 1823, p. 2.
10. Watson (ed.), *Trial of Thurtell and Hunt*, 19–20; *The Fatal Effects of Gambling*, xvii–xviii; Egan, *Recollections*, 42–43.
11. *The Fatal Effects of Gambling*, x–xii.
12. As quoted in Watson (ed.), *Trial of Thurtell and Hunt*, 11.
13. Egan, *Recollections*, 34–35, 43–44.
14. *Ibid.*, 34–35; *Times*, November 11, 1823, p. 2.
15. Egan, *Recollections*, 35–38.
16. *Ibid.*
17. Watson (ed.), *Trial of Thurtell and Hunt*, 14.

18. *Ibid.*, 7, 14–19; *Report of the Proceedings on the Trial: The King, on the Prosecution of the County Fire Office, Versus Thomas Thurtell and Others* (London, 1824).

19. Egan, *Recollections*, 37, 39.

20. Watson (ed.), *Trial of Thurtell and Hunt*, 16.

Chapter Four
THE ROAD MENDERS' DISCOVERIES

1. The principal contemporary account of the discovery of the murderers of William Weare is George Henry Jones, *Account of the Murder of the Late Mr. William Weare* (London, 1824).

2. *The Fatal Effects of Gambling*, 56.

3. Jones, *Account of the Murder*, 1–2.

4. See Patrick Pringle, *Hue and Cry: The Story of Henry and John Fielding and Their Bow Street Runners* (London, 1955).

5. Jones, *Account of the Murder*, 2–3, 19–20.

6. (London) *Observer*, January 12, 1824, pp. 1–4.

7. John L. Bradley (ed.), *Rogue's Progress: The Autobiography of "Lord Chief Baron" Nicholson* (Boston, 1965), 150–51.

8. *Times*, November 3, 1823, p. 2; *The Fatal Effects of Gambling*, 5.

9. Jones, *Account of the Murder*, 4.

10. *Ibid.*, 5–9.

11. *Ibid.*, 9–10.

12. *Times*, November 1, 1823, p. 3.

13. *Ibid.*

14. *Ibid.*

15. Jones, *Account of the Murder*, 10–11; *The Fatal Effects of Gambling*, 6.

16. Jones, *Account of the Murder*, 10–11; *The Fatal Effects of Gambling*, 6.

17. Jones, *Account of the Murder*, 150–52, 173–75.

18. The following account of Hunt's confession comes from the *Times*, November 1, 1823; Jones, *Account of the Murder*, 11–17.

19. *Times*, October 31, 1823, p. 3.

20. *The Fatal Effects of Gambling*, 7.

21. *Ibid.*, 7–8.

Chapter Five
REVELATIONS AT THE ARTICHOKE

1. Unless otherwise noted, the following account of the inquest is taken from Jones, *Account of the Murder*, 18–44.

2. *Times*, November 3, 1823, p. 3.

3. *The Fatal Effects of Gambling*, 40–42.

4. *Ibid.*, 42–43.

5. *Ibid.*, 43–45; *Weekly Dispatch*, November 9, 1823, p. 359.

6. *Times*, November 3, 1823, p. 3.

7. *Ibid.*, November 4, 1823, p. 2.

8. *Morning Chronicle*, November 3, 2, 1823, both p. 3.

Chapter Six
THE WHITE-FACED HORSE

1. Unless otherwise noted, my account of the evidence is drawn from Jones, *Account of the Murder*, 45–78.
2. *Observer*, November 9, 1823, p. 2.
3. *The Fatal Effects of Gambling*, 71–72, 73.
4. *Times*, November 5, 1823, p. 3.

Chapter Seven
THE RUMORMONGERS

1. *Times*, October 31, 1823, p. 3.
2. See Richard D. Altick, *The English Common Reader: A Social History of the Mass Reading Public, 1800–1900* (Chicago, 1957), 318–47; Altick, *Victorian Studies in Scarlet*, 54–60.
3. Percy Fitzgerald, *Chronicles of Bow Street Police-Office* (London, 1888), II, 127, 141–42.
4. *Times*, November 5, 11, 13, 1823, pp. 2, 2–3, 2; *Morning Chronicle*, November 6, 1823, pp. 3, 4.
5. *Times*, November 14, 7, 11, 1823, all p. 2.
6. *Ibid.*, November 12, 15, 1823, pp. 3, 2.
7. As quoted in Watson, *Trial of Thurtell and Hunt*, 19.
8. *Times*, November 12, 1823, p. 3.
9. *Ibid.*, November 4, 1823, p. 3.
10. *Ibid.*, November 13, 1823, p. 2; *Morning Chronicle*, November 13, 1823, p. 3.
11. *Times*, November 6, 12, 8, 1823, pp. 3, 3, 2.
12. *Ibid.*, November 10, 1823, p. 3.
13. *Weekly Dispatch*, November 16, 1823, p. 366.
14. *Times*, November 6, 1823, p. 3.
15. *Ibid.*, November 10, 1823, pp. 2–3.
16. *Ibid.*
17. Charles Milnes Gaskell (ed.), *An Eton Boy: Being the Letters of James Milnes Gaskell from Eton & Oxford, 1820–1830* (London, 1939), 12.
18. *Times*, November 12, 14, 15, 1823, all p. 2.
19. Charles Hindley, *The History of the Catnach Press* (1887; rpr. Detroit, 1969), 69–71; Henry Vitzetelly, *Glances Back Through Seventy Years* (2 vols.; London, 1893), I, 10–11.
20. *The Hoax Discovered; or, Mr. Weare Alive* (London, [1823]), 4.
21. *The Gamblers: A Moral Poem* (London, [1824]), 8, 30.
22. Edward Fitzball, *Thirty-five Years of a Dramatic Author's Life* (London, 1859), II, 399–406.
23. *The Gamblers: A New Melo-drama, in Two Acts* (London, 1824).
24. *Times*, November 18, 1823, p. 2.
25. *Ibid.*
26. *Observer*, November 23, 1823, p. 1.

Chapter Eight
THE SECOND SOLICITOR

1. *Times*, November 13, 15, 1823, both p. 2.
2. *The Fatal Effects of Gambling*, 59.
3. *Times*, November 10, 1823, p. 2.
4. *Ibid.*, November 14, 1823, p. 2; Thomas Lloyd to [?], November 12, 1823, in Public Record Office, London, HO 20 2 XCIA 2166.
5. *Times*, November 15, 1823, p. 2.
6. *Ibid.*, November 17, 1823, p. 3.
7. *Ibid.*
8. *Ibid.*, November 19, 1823, p. 2.
9. *Ibid.*
10. *Ibid.*, November 20, 1823, p. 2; *Weekly Dispatch*, November 23, 1823, p. 373.
11. *Times*, November 25, 1823, p. 2.
12. *Ibid.*
13. *Ibid.*
14. Lloyd to [?], November 13, 1823, in Public Record Office, HO 20 2 XCIA 2166.
15. John Thurtell to Mrs. Walker, November 9, 1823, Lloyd to [?], November 10, 1823, both *ibid.*
16. Lloyd to [?], November 13, 1823, *ibid.*
17. Lloyd to [?], November 10, 1823, *ibid.*

Chapter Nine
THE FAIRNESS OF MR. JUSTICE PARK

1. *Times*, December 1, 1823, p. 2.
2. Jones, *Account of the Murder*, 78–79.
3. Serjeant [William] Ballantine, *Some Experiences of a Barrister's Life* (5th ed., London 1882), 125.
4. Watson (ed.), *Trial of Thurtell and Hunt*, 16–17.
5. Jones, *Account of the Murder*, 81.
6. *Ibid.*, 82–86.
7. Sir James Fitzjames Stephen, *A History of the Criminal Law of England* (London, 1883), I, 216–33.
8. Jones, *Account of the Murder*, 85–88.
9. Ballantine quotes his father in *Some Experiences*, 55.
10. Jones, *Account of the Murder*, 88–89.
11. Edward Herbert, "A Pen and Ink Sketch of a Late Trial for Murder, in a Letter from Hertford," *London Magazine*, IX (1824), 167.
12. *Ibid.*
13. *Times*, December 6, 1823, p. 2.
14. *Dictionary of National Biography* (London, 1963–64), II, 785–86, IV, 266–67, VIII, 804–805, XV, 1082–83, 1295, XIX, 608–609; James Grant, *The Bench and the Bar* (2nd ed.; London, 1838), I, 241–49, 264–300, II, 124–130, 201–204.
15. My account of the motion for postponement and Park's response is taken from Jones, *Account of the Murder*, 95–145.
16. *Weekly Dispatch*, December 14, 1823.
17. As quoted in *History of the Murder of Mr. Weare, and the Chain of Circumstances and Events, Connected with That Horrid Transaction* (London, 1824), 53–54.

18. As quoted *ibid.,* 55–56.
19. *Times,* December 8, 1823, p. 2.
20. *A Vindication of the Right Honorable Sir James Allan Park, Knt.* (London, 1823).
21. *Ibid.*
22. Joseph, Jekyll, *Correspondence of Mr. Joseph Jekyll* (London, 1894), 136.

Chapter Ten
EGAN'S INTERVIEWS

1. The account of Egan's interviews is taken from Egan, *Recollections,* 27–36.
2. *Weekly Dispatch,* December 7, 1823; Beaumont's denial and Egan's defense appear in Egan, *Recollections,* 29.
3. *Times,* December 11, 1823, p. 2.
4. Egan, *Recollections,* 2; *Times,* January 16, 1824, p. 2.

Chapter Eleven
THE TROUT IN THE MILK

1. Herbert, "Pen and Ink Sketch," 168.
2. *Ibid.,* 169.
3. Unless otherwise noted, my account of the trial is taken from Jones, *Account of the Murder,* 150–239.
4. Herbert, "Pen and Ink Sketch," 169.
5. *Ibid.,* 173.
6. *Ibid.*
7. *Ibid.,* 174–75.
8. *Ibid.,* 178.
9. *Ibid.*
10. Jones, *Account of the Murder,* 211–12.
11. Herbert, "Pen and Ink Sketch," 172.
12. *Ibid.*
13. *Ibid.*

Chapter Twelve
ANOTHER KEAN

1. Herbert, "Pen and Ink Sketch," 179.
2. My account of the trial, except as otherwise noted, continues to follow Jones, *Account of the Murder,* 240–327.
3. Herbert, "Pen and Ink Sketch," 182.
4. *Ibid.,* 183.
5. Egan, *Recollections,* 3.
6. Herbert, "Pen and Ink Sketch," 183.
7. Herbert, "Pen and Ink Sketch," 184.
8. Egan, *Recollections,* 4.

Chapter Thirteen
THE NEW DROP

1. Egan, *Recollections,* 4–7; *Times,* January 9, 1824, p. 3.
2. Egan, *Recollections,* 4–7; *Times,* January 9, 1824, p. 3.

3. Egan, *Recollections*, 7–8; *Times*, January 9, 1824, p. 3.

4. Egan, *Recollections*, 40.

5. Horace Bleackley, *The Hangmen of England* (London, 1929), 197–201.

6. Egan, *Recollections*, 8.

7. *Ibid.*

8. Egan, *New Series of Boxiana*, I, 267–303.

9. Herbert, "Pen and Ink Sketch," 184.

10. *Times*, January 9, 1824, p. 3.

11. Jones, *Account of the Murder*, 329; Egan, *Recollections*, 22.

12. *The Fatal Effects of Gambling*, 312–13; Egan, *Recollections*, 7. It was not until January 27 that Hunt learned that he would not share Thurtell's fate.

13. *Times*, January 10, 1824, p. 2.

14. *Ibid.*

15. Egan, *Recollections*, 10–11.

16. *Times*, January 10, 1824, p. 3.

17. Egan, *Recollections*, 11.

18. *Times*, January 10, 1824, p. 3.

19. *Ibid.*; Egan, *Recollections*, 12. The crowd's Victorian successors were less mannerly. See Albert Borowitz, *The Woman Who Murdered Black Satin: The Bermondsey Horror* (Columbus, 1981).

20. *Times*, January 10, 1824, p. 3; Camden Pelham, *The Chronicles of Crime; or, The New Newgate Calendar* (London, 1886), II, 89–90.

21. Egan, *Recollections*, 12.

22. *British Press*, n.d., quoted in Egan, *Recollections*, 23.

23. *Times*, January 10, 1824, p. 2.

24. *Morning Chronicle*, January 10, 1824, p. 3.

25. Egan, *Recollections*, 33.

26. Herbert, "Pen and Ink Sketch," 184.

27. *Blackwood's Edinburgh Magazine*, XV (1824), 194–95.

28. *Norwich Mercury*, January 17, 1824, as quoted in Jones, *Account of the Murder*, 340–44.

29. Jones, *Account of the Murder*, 333.

30. *The Fatal Effects of Gambling*, 331.

31. *The Fatal Effects of Gambling*, 332, 333. Undersheriff Nicholson had complied with Thurtell's request in refusing every application for a cast from his face, but the authorities at St. Bartholomew's did not regard themselves as bound by this restriction.

32. *Ibid.*, 333.

33. Henri de Latouche, *La Reine d'Espagne*, Act IV, Scene i; *The Fatal Effects of Gambling*, 334.

34. *The Life and Fortunes of John Pocock of Cape Town, 1814–1876; Compiled from His Journals and Letters* (Cape Town, 1974), 14–15.

Chapter Fourteen
THE FATAL EFFECTS OF THE FAST LIFE

1. *Times*, January 12, 1824, p. 2.

2. *Ibid.*, January 13, 1824, p. 2.

3. *Ibid.*

4. Hindley, *History of the Catnach Press*, 71.

5. The letter appears in *Notes and Queries*, 10th series, XII (1909), 283–84.

6. *The Hertfordshire Tragedy; or, The Fatal Effects of Gambling* (London, 1824).

7. Henry Mayhew, *London Labour and the London Poor* (1861–62; rpr. New York, 1968), I, 283.

8. *Notes and Queries,* 11th series, IV (1911), 244.

9. *The Fatal Effects of Gambling,* ix.

10. *A History of the Gaming Houses, and Gamesters of the Metropolis,* appendix to *History of the Murder of Mr. Weare,* 4.

11. John Wooll, *The Dangerous and Irresistible Progress of Habitual Sin, as Exemplified in the Murder of Mr. Weare, a Sermon Preached in the Chapel of Rugby School on Sunday November 2, 1823, by Rev. John Wooll* (Rugby, 1824), 12.

12. George Augustus Sala, *Things I Have Seen and People I Have Known* (London, 1894), II, 92–93.

13. *Times,* January 10, 1824, p. 3.

14. *Weekly Dispatch,* January 11, 1824.

15. *Ibid.,* January 18, 1824.

16. *Ibid.,* January 11, 1824.

17. *Weekly Dispatch,* December 19, 1823, as quoted in Ford, *Prizefighting,* 188.

18. *Times,* December 29, 1824, p. 3.

19. *Ibid.,* December 30, 1824, p. 2.

20. Dowling, quoted in Ford, *Prizefighting,* 189–90.

21. Alan Lloyd, *The Great Prize Fight* (New York, 1977).

22. Leon Radzinowicz, *A History of English Criminal Law and Its Administration from 1750* (London, 1956), II, 296.

23. Wade, *Treatise on the Police,* 108.

24. Henry Blyth, *Hell and Hazard; or, William Crockford Versus the Gentlemen of England* (Chicago, 1969); John Raymond (ed.), *The Reminiscences and Recollections of Captain Gronow* (London, 1964), 256.

25. Ashton, *History of Gambling,* 147–49.

26. Blyth, *Hell and Hazard,* 202.

Chapter Fifteen
PROBERT'S MARE

1. *Report of the Proceedings on the Trial,* 70–71.

2. *Times,* March 19, 1825, p. 4.

3. *Ibid.*

4. *Ibid.;* Henry's fate is unknown. The will of Alderman Thurtell, executed in 1842 and admitted to probate after his death four years later, does not mention his sailor son. Public Record Office, in Prob. 2038. Tom does not appear to have risen in the graces of his father, who created an income trust for Tom's wife, Sarah, to which Tom succeeded only on her death.

5. Egan, *Recollections,* 22.

6. *Times,* January 9, 1824, p. 3.

7. Egan, *Recollections,* 22.

8. *Sunday Times,* January 25, 1824, as quoted in Watson (ed.), *Trial of Thurtell and Hunt,* 46–47.

9. Unascribed newspaper clipping, dated January, 1824, in Thurtell-Hunt Collection, Aldenham School, Elstree.

10. Unascribed newspaper clipping, dated April 1824, clipping from *Sunday Times,* June 20, 1824, both *ibid.*

11. *Weekly Dispatch*, January 18, 1824, p. 30.

12. *Times*, April 6, 8, 1825, both p. 3. These two articles are the source for the account of Probert's trial and execution, which follows.

13. *Ibid.*, April 8.

14. Unascribed newspaper clipping, dated April 13, 1825, in Thurtell-Hunt Collection.

15. *Times*, June 20, 1825, p. 3.

16. Probert had, at the suggestion of his brother-in-law, earlier considered a solicitation of his jurymen to join in a proposed petition for clemency. William Probert to the Reverend Horace Cotton, April 21, 1825, in the collection of the author.

17. *Times*, June 20, 1825, p. 3.

18. Horace Bleackley (ed.), *Trial of Henry Fauntleroy and Other Famous Trials for Forgery*, Notable British Trials (Edinburgh, 1934), 41.

19. *Times*, June 20, 1825, p. 3.

20. *Ibid.*, June 21, 1825, p. 3.

21. *Ibid.* After Probert's death a watercolor prison portrait of the condemned man (now in the collection of the author) was given to Cotton.

22. Unascribed newspaper clippings, n.d., in the Thurtell-Hunt Collection.

23. *Annual Register, 1825*, Appendix to Chronicle, 338.

24. *Times*, March 3, 1825, p. 3.

25. *County Herald*, July, 1825, as quoted in an unascribed newspaper clipping, n.d., in Thurtell-Hunt Collection.

26. *Times*, June 23, 1825, p. 3.

Chapter Sixteen
THE SURVIVAL OF HUNT

1. Jones, *Account of the Murder*, 337–38.

2. *Ibid.*, 339–40.

3. W. Branch Johnson, *The English Prison Hulks* (London, 1957), 1–7, 13–14, 177–79.

4. *Weekly Dispatch*, February 1, 1824, p. 45.

5. Jones, *Account of the Murder*, 340.

6. The *Weekly Dispatch* printed Hunt's confession in its issues of February 1, (pp. 44–45), February 8 (pp. 52–53), and February 15 (p. 61), 1824. My account is derived from that source.

7. Needless to say, Bill Probert did not share the public's enthusiasm for the confession. Prior to his execution, he declared that "the confession of Hunt was in many of its parts utterly false, particularly those which related to [Probert's] wife; he protested that he believed the confession . . . was got up by another person at a time when public curiosity was much excited." *Times*, June 21, 1825, p. 3.

8. Watson (ed.), *Trial of Thurtell and Hunt*, 45.

9. Charles Bateson, *The Convict Ships, 1788–1868* (Glasgow, 1959), 211, 294–95, 329.

10. *Exeter Alfred*, March, 1824, as quoted in unascribed newspaper clipping in Thurtell-Hunt Collection.

11. *Dublin Warder*, 1825, as quoted in unascribed newspaper clipping *ibid.*

12. *Times*, April 30, 1825.

13. John Alexander Ferguson, *Bibliography of Australia* (Sydney, 1941), I, 358.

14. Bateson, *Convict Ships*, 198–99.

15. *The Full Particulars of the Sudden and Awful Murder of Hunt!* reprinted in Geoffrey

Chapman Ingleton (ed.), *True Patriots All; or, News from Early Australia* (7 vols.; Sydney, n.d.), 105–106. Perhaps the publisher is the same disreputable firm that in 1823, under the name W. Chubb, of the Strand, issued *The Hoax Discovered; or, Mr. Weare Alive;* Bateson, *Convict Ships,* 294–95.

16. Archives Office, New South Wales, AO 4/4009A, reel 2662.

17. *Ibid.,* AO 4/3511, reel 1036.

18. C. M. H. Clark, *A History of Australia* (London, 1962), I, 296–302.

19. Tighe Hopkins, *The Romance of Fraud* (New York, 1914), 102.

20. Archives Office, New South Wales, AO 4/1818, reel 902.

21. *Ibid.,* AO 4/4086, reel 918, Ticket of Leave No. 32/1070.

22. Roger Therry, *Reminiscences of Thirty Years' Residence in New South Wales and Victoria* (1863; rpr. Sydney, 1974), 99.

23. Public Record Office, HO 10/33.

24. Therry, *Reminiscences,* 99.

25. Archives Office, New South Wales, AO X645-6, reel 591, AO 4/4442, reel 480, pp. 143–44, Conditional Pardon No. 43/217.

26. Therry, *Reminiscences,* 99. The present Bathurst courthouse was built in 1878. Therry states that Hunt served as court keeper for at least twenty years.

27. Registry of Births, Deaths, and Marriages, New South Wales, no. 157, vol. 79.

28. Therry, *Reminiscences,* 100.

29. Registry of Births, Deaths and Marriages, New South Wales, baptismal certificates, dated August 23, 1982, relating to Joseph Henry and Angela Mary Hunt, issued at the application of the author.

30. Therry, *Reminiscences,* 100.

31. James T. Ryan, *Reminiscences of Australia* (Sydney, 1894), 129–30.

32. Registry of Births, Deaths, and Marriages, New South Wales, death certificate, dated June 9, 1982, relating to Joseph Blaine Hunt, issued at the request of the author.

Chapter Seventeen
A RETURN TO HERTFORDSHIRE

1. Walter Thornbury, *Haunted London* (London, 1880), 166.

2. *Notes and Queries,* 6th series, XII (1885), 136, 8th series, IV (1893), 216.

3. Jessie Dobson, "The College Criminals: 3. John Thurtell," *Annals of the Royal College of Surgeons of England* (May, 1952), 324–31.

4. Rayner Heppenstall, *Reflections on the Newgate Calendar* (London, 1975), 210.

5. J. R. Avery, *The Elstree Murder* (Elstree, 1962), last page (unnumbered).

6. John Edwin Cussans, *History of Hertfordshire* (London, 1879–81), III, 279.

7. Gordon S. Maxwell, *The Fringe of London* (London, 1925), 140–41.

8. *Observer,* January 12, 1824, p. 4.

9. Egan, *Recollections,* 33–34.

10. Herbert, "Pen and Ink Sketch," 184–85.

11. *Ibid.,* 185.

12. Jones, *Account of the Murder,* 294–95.

13. F. B. Maggs, "The Radlett Murder," (Paper read to the Radlett Literary Society, December 2, 1946, in Thurtell-Hunt Collection).

14. *Ibid.*

Chapter Eighteen
BLOCKHEADS IN A DARK LANE

1. Wilfred Whitten [John O'London], "The Literature of a Crime," in his *The Joy of London and Other Essays* (London, n.d.), 57; Maxwell, *Fringe of London*, 146. On the Cenci murder, see Borowitz *Gallery of Sinister Perspectives,* 11–20.

2. Kathryn Moore Heleniak, *William Mulready* (New Haven, 1980), 3–35; Marcia Pointon, "Painters and Pugilism in Early Nineteenth-Century England, *Gazette des Beaux-Arts* (October, 1978), 131–140; Richard Redgrave, *A Century of Painters of the English School* (2nd ed.; London, 1890), 267–80; Anne Rorimer, *Drawings by William Mulready* (London, 1972), 7–12; Frederic G. Stephens, *Memorials of William Mulready, R.A.* (New York, 1890), 23–24, 63–68, 91–92.

3. William Mulready to Sir John Swinburne, January 11, 16, 1824, both in Swinburne (Capheaton) MSS, Northumberland Record Office, Newcastle-upon-Tyne, ZSW 627.

4. W. P. Frith, *My Autobiography and Reminiscences* (3rd ed.; London, 1887), I, 183.

5. "The Murder of Mr. William Weare, of Lyon's Inn," *All the Year Round,* December 8, 1866, p. 522.

6. Alexander Brodie (ed.), *Reminiscences of Solomon Alex. Hart, R.A.* (London, 1882), 111.

7. *Times,* December 2, 3, 1823, both p. 2.

8. Trevelyan, *British History in the Nineteenth Century,* 171.

9. William Cobbett, *Rural Rides* (New York, 1932), 235.

10. C. Kegan Paul, *Memories* (London, 1899), 338.

11. Charles Lamb, *The Complete Works and Letters of Charles Lamb* (New York, 1935), 945, 876–77.

12. Reginald L. Hine, *Charles Lamb and His Hertfordshire* (London, 1949), 12–13.

13. H. J. C. Grierson (ed.), *The Letters of Sir Walter Scott, 1823–1825* (London, 1935), 160.

14. J. G. Cochrane (ed.), *Catalogue of the Library of Abbotsford* (Edinburgh, 1838), 296.

15. *The Journal of Sir Walter Scott* (New York, 1891), 148.

16. *Ibid.,* 401.

17. Washington Irving, *Journals and Notebooks,* ed. Walter A. Reichart (Madison, 1970) III, 270, 419–20.

18. John Forster, quoted in Keith Hollingsworth, *The Newgate Novel, 1830–1847* (Detroit, 1963), 37.

19. William Toynbee (ed.), *The Diaries of William Charles Macready* (London, 1912), I, 35.

20. Alfred McKinley Terhune and Annabelle Burdick Terhune (eds.), *The Letters of Edward FitzGerald* (Princeton, 1980), IV, 217.

21. Charles Richard Sanders and Kenneth J. Fielding (eds.), *The Collected Letters of Thomas and Jane Welsh Carlyle* (Durham, 1976), V, 299.

22. Herbert Jenkins, *The Life of George Borrow* (1912; rpr. Port Washington, 1970), 368.

23. John Wilson [Christopher North] *et al., Noctes Ambrosianae* (Philadelphia, 1843), I, 254–66.

24. Shelton Mackenzie (ed.), *The Odoherty Papers by the Late William Maginn, LL.D.* (New York, 1855), II, 226–29.

25. Thomas De Quincey, "On Murder Considered as One of the Fine Arts," in *The English Mail-Coach and Other Essays* (London, 1961), 49, 72.

26. *Ibid.,* 89–90. See A. S. Plumtree, "The Artist as Murderer: De Quincey's Essay 'On Murder Considered as One of the Fine Arts,'" in Robert Lance Snyder (ed.), *Thomas De Quincey: Bicentenary Studies* (Norman, 1985), 140–63.

27. John Mitford, "The Owl," in Whitten, *Joy of London*, 62–63.

28. Edward Robert Bulwer Lytton, first earl of Lytton, *The Life, Letters and Literary Remains of Edward Bulwer, Lord Lytton, by His Son* (New York, 1884), I, 259–66, 270–4.

29. Hollingsworth, *Newgate Novel*, 39.

30. Edward Bulwer Lytton, *Pelham; or, Adventures of a Gentleman* (1828; rpr. Boston, 1893), I, 95, II, 31, 235–36.

31. Victor Alexander George Robert Lytton, second earl of Lytton, *Life of Edward Bulwer, First Lord Lytton by His Grandson the Earl of Lytton* (London, 1913), I, 389.

32. George Borrow, *Lavengro*, in Clement Shorter (ed.), *The Works of George Borrow* (London, 1923), III, 3–4.

33. Clement K. Shorter, *The Life of George Borrow* (New York, n.d.), 66, 73.

34. *Times*, January 10, 1824, p. 3.

35. [George Borrow], *Celebrated Trials, and Remarkable Cases of Criminal Jurisprudence from the Earliest Records to the Year 1825* (London, 1824), VI, 534–55.

36. George Borrow, *The Zincali; or, An Account of the Gypsies of Spain*, in Shorter (ed.), *Works of George Borrow*, X, 19–20; Borrow, *Lavengro*, 261, 285–86.

37. Borrow, *Lavengro*, 286.

38. George Borrow, *The Romany Rye*, in Shorter (ed.), *Works of George Borrow*, VI, 134–39.

39. William Makepeace Thackeray, *Vanity Fair: A Novel Without a Hero*, in *The Works of Thackeray* (New York, 1903), III, 368; Charles Dickens, "The Out-and-Out Young Gentleman," in *Sketches by Boz* [and other sketches] (London, 1957), 506.

40. Charles Dickens, *Miscellaneous Papers* (New York, n.d.), II, 124, 125.

41. Charles Dickens and Wilkie Collins, *The Lazy Tour of Two Idle Apprentices* (New York, n.d.), 270.

42. Charles Dickens, *The Life and Adventures of Martin Chuzzlewit* (London, 1882), Vol. II of *The Works of Charles Dickens*, 259, 348–49.

43. Joyce Emmerson Preston Muddock [Dick Donovan], *Thurtell's Crime . . . : The Story of a Strange Tragedy* (London, [1906]).

44. Thomas Burke, *Murder at Elstree; or, Mr. Thurtell and His Gig* (London, 1936), 93, 23.

45. Philip Lindsay, *The Swell Yokel* (London, 1955).

46. Sydney Smith, quoted in Maxwell, *Fringe of London*, 150; Richard Whateley (ed.), *Bacon's Essays with Annotations* (Boston, 1863), 132. For phrenological studies of Thurtell, see *Medical Adviser and Guide to Health and Long Life*, January 17, 24, 1824, pp. 97–100, 114–15. Alexander Smith, "A Lark's Flight," in his *Dreamthorp: A Book of Essays Written in the Country* (Garden City, 1934), 100.

47. Walter de la Mare, *Early One Morning in the Spring* (New York, 1935), 204–206.

48. Review of P. Cunningham, *Two Years in New South Wales*, in *Quarterly Review*, XXXVII (1828), 15.

49. *Observer*, November 2, 1823, p. 3; *Times*, November 3, 1823, p. 3.

50. Pierce Egan, *Life in London*, (London, 1869), xiii–xiv.

51. Thomas Carlyle, "Jean Paul Richter," in *Critical and Miscellaneous Essays* (New York, n.d.), II, 105; Carlyle, "Boswell's *Life of Johnson*," *ibid.*, 410; Carlyle, "Goethe's Works," *ibid.*, III, 35–36.

52. As cited under *gigman*, in *Compact Edition of the Oxford English Dictionary* (1971), I, 1141.

53. George Borrow, *The Romany Rye*, in Shorter (ed.). *Works of George Borrow*, VI, 227, 229.

54. Thomas Carlyle, *The French Revolution*, Standard Classics (New York, n.d.), III, 318–19.

SELECTED BIBLIOGRAPHY

REPORTS, ACCOUNTS, AND DOCUMENTS OF THE CASE

An Account of the Last Moments and Execution of William Probert, William Sargent, Alias Baker, and Harper, for Horse Stealing, and Smith, for Burglary, at Newgate, on Monday, June 20, 1825. Gateshead: Stephenson, 1825.

An Account of the Trial and Sentence of John Thurtell and Joseph Hunt, etc. N.p., 1824.

Altick, Richard D. *Victorian Studies in Scarlet: Murders and Manners in the Age of Victoria.* New York, 1970.

Annual Register, 1823–25.

Atlay, J. B. *Famous Trials.* London, 1899.

Avery, J. R. *The Elstree Murder.* Elstree, 1962.

Ballantine, Serjeant [William]. *Some Experiences of a Barrister's Life.* 5th ed. London, 1882.

Benson, Capt. L. *The Book of Remarkable Trials and Notorious Characters.* London, n.d.

Birkenhead, Earl of. *More Famous Trials.* London, n.d.

Birmingham, George A. *Murder Most Foul!* London, 1929.

[Borrow, George]. *Celebrated Trials, and Remarkable Cases of Criminal Jurisprudence from the Earliest Records to the Year 1825.* Vol. VI of 6 vols. London: Knight and Lacey, 1825.

Bradley, John L., ed. *Rogue's Progress: The Autobiography of "Lord Chief Baron" Nicholson.* Boston, 1965.

Brice, A. H. M. "The Murder in Gill's Hill Lane." In *Look upon the Prisoner: Studies in Crime.* London, n.d.

Cobbett, William. *Rural Rides.* New York, 1932.

The Confession and Execution of John Thurtell at Hertford Gaol. London: Pitts, 1824. Reproduced in Charles Hindley, *Curiosities of Street Literature.* London, 1871.

Darwin, Bernard. "The Murder of William Weare." In *Stronger Than Fiction: Great Stories of True Crime.* New York, 1947.

Dilnot, George. *Triumphs of Detection.* London, n.d.

Dobson, Jessie. "The College Criminals: 3. John Thurtell." *Annals of the Royal College of Surgeons of England* (May, 1952), 324–31.

Drynan, Jim. "A Tale of Murder." *St. Bartholomew's Hospital Journal* (August, 1969), 306–13.

Egan, Pierce. *Account of the Trial of John Thurtell and Joseph Hunt and Recollections of John Thurtell.* London: Knight & Lacey, 1824.

Fairburn's Edition of the Trial of John Thurtell and Joseph Hunt, etc. London: Fairburn, 1824.

The Fatal Effects of Gambling Exemplified in the Murder of Wm. Weare, and the Trial and Fate of John Thurtell, the Murderer, and His Accomplices, to which is added: *The Gambler's Scourge, a Complete Exposé of the Whole System of Gambling in the Metropolis.* London: Kelly, 1824.

Fitzgerald, Percy. *Chronicles of Bow Street Police-Office.* 2 vols. London, 1888.

Full Account of the Atrocious Murder of the Late Mr. Weare, etc. London: Sherwood, Jones, 1823.

A Full, True and Particular Account of the Trial of Thurtell & Hunt for the Murder of Mr. Weare, at Hertford, in Oct. Last. Gateshead: Stephenson, 1823.

The Gamblers: A Moral Poem. London: Chapman, [1824].

Gaskell, Charles Milnes, ed. *An Eton Boy: Being the Letters of James Milnes Gaskell from Eton & Oxford, 1820–1830.* London: 1939.

Hardwick, Michael. "Thurtell and Hunt." In *The Verdict of the Court,* edited by Hardwick. London, 1960.

Heppenstall, Rayner. *Reflections on the Newgate Calendar.* London, 1975.

Herbert, Edward. "A Pen and Ink Sketch of a Late Trial for Murder, in a Letter from Hertford." *London Magazine,* IX (1824), 165–85.

The Hertford Genuine Edition of the Trial of John Thurtell and Joseph Hunt, etc. Hertford: Staughton, 1824.

Hertfordshire County Records. Sessions Books, 1799–1833. Hertford, 1939.

The Hertfordshire Tragedy; or, The Fatal Effects of Gambling. London: Catnach, 1824.

History of the Murder of Mr. Weare, and the Chain of Circumstances and Events, Connected with That Horrid Transaction, followed by *A History of the Gaming Houses, and Gamesters of the Metropolis.* London: Jones, 1824.

The Hoax Discovered; or, Mr. Weare Alive. London: W. Chubb, [1823].

Horrid Effects of Gambling Exemplified in the Atrocious Murder of Mr. William Weare. London: Hodgson, 1824.

Jekyll, Joseph. *Correspondence of Mr. Joseph Jekyll.* London, 1894.

Jones, George Henry. *Account of the Murder of the Late Mr. William Weare.* London: Sherwood, Jones, 1824.

Knapp, Andrew, and William Baldwin. *The Newgate Calendar.* Vol. IV of 4 vols. London: Robins, 1828.

The Life and Fortunes of John Pocock of Cape Town, 1814–1876; Compiled from His Journals and Letters. Cape Town, 1974.

The Life, Trials and Execution of John Thurtell, etc. N.p., 1824.

Logan, Guy B. H. *Great Murder Mysteries.* New York, 1931.

————. *Masters of Crime: Studies of Multiple Murders.* London, 1928.

————. *Rope, Knife and Chair.* New York, n.d.

————. *Verdict and Sentence.* London, 1935.

Madame Tussaud & Sons Catalogue. Christmas edition, 1878.

Megroz, Phyllis. "Thurtell and Hunt: The Brutal Affair in Gill's Hill Lane." In *Sixty Famous Trials,* edited by Richard Huson. London, n.d.

"The Murder of Mr. William Weare, of Lyon's Inn." *All the Year Round,* December 8, 1866, pp. 516–22.

Narrative of the Murder of Mr. Weare. London: Edgerley, 1823.

A Narrative of the Mysterious and Dreadful Murder of Mr. W. Weare, etc. London: McGowan, 1824.

Pelham, Camden. *The Chronicles of Crime; or, The New Newgate Calendar.* Vol. II of 2 vols. London, 1886.

Postgate, Raymond. *Murder, Piracy and Treason.* New York, 1925.

Report of the Proceedings on the Trial: The King, on the Prosecution of the County Fire Office, Versus Thomas Thurtell and Others. London: Glindon, 1824.

Sala, George Augustus. *Things I Have Seen and People I Have Known.* Vol. II of 2 vols. London, 1894.

"Thurtell, Hunt, and Probert, and the Murder of William Weare." In *New Wonderful Magazine.* Vol. II of 2 vols. London, n.d.

Thurtell-Hunt Collection. Private collection of publications and playbills. 1823–25. Aldenham School, Elstree, England.

The Trial of John Thurtell and Joseph Hunt, etc. London: Hodgson, 1824.

The Trial of John Thurtell and Joseph Hunt, etc. London: Sherwood, Jones, 1824.

The Trial of Thurtell & Hunt. London: Dickinson, 1824.

The Trial of Thurtell & Hunt for the Wilful Murder of Wm. Weare, etc. London: Baldwin, Cradock and Joy, 1824.

Verbatim Report of the Proceedings on the Trial of John Thurtell and Joseph Hunt, etc. London: Dickie, 1824.

A Vindication of the Right Honorable Sir James Allan [sic] Park, Knt. London, 1823.

Watson, Eric R., ed. *Trial of Thurtell and Hunt.* Notable British Trials. Edinburgh: Hodge, 1920.

Williams, Montagu. *Later Leaves.* London, 1891.

Wooll, John. *The Dangerous and Irresistable Progress of Habitual Sin, as Exemplified in the Murder of Mr. Weare. A Sermon Preached in the Chapel of Rugby School on Sunday, November 2, 1823, by Rev. John Wooll.* Rugby: Rowell, 1824.

CONTEMPORARY NEWSPAPERS AND PERIODICALS

Blackwood's Edinburgh Magazine

Gentleman's Magazine

London Magazine

Medical Adviser and Guide to Health and Long Life

Morning Chronicle

New Monthly Magazine and Library Journal

Norwich Mercury
Observer
Times
Weekly Dispatch

THE CASE IN ART AND LITERATURE

Bigland, Eileen. *In the Steps of George Borrow*. London, 1951.

Birrell, Augustine. *William Hazlitt*. London, 1926.

Brodie, Alexander, ed. *Reminiscences of Solomon Alex. Hart, R. A.* London, 1882.

Bulwer Lytton, Edward. *Pelham; or, The Adventures of a Gentleman*. 2 vols. 1828; rpr. Boston, 1893.

Bulwer Lytton, Edward Robert, first earl of Lytton. *The Life, Letters and Literary Remains of Edward Bulwer, Lord Lytton, by His Son*. 2 vols. New York, 1884.

Bulwer Lytton, Victor Alexander George Robert, second earl of Lytton. *The Life of Edward Bulwer, First Lord Lytton by his Grandson the Earl of Lytton*. 2 vols. London, 1913.

Burke, Thomas. *Murder at Elstree; or, Mr. Thurtell and His Gig*. London, 1936.

Carlyle, Thomas. *Critical and Miscellaneous Essays*. Standard Classics. 4 vols. New York, n.d.

————. *The French Revolution*. Standard Classics. 3 vols. New York, n.d.

Cochrane, J. G., ed. *Catalogue of the Library of Abbotsford*. Edinburgh, 1838.

Dearden, Seton. *The Gypsy Gentleman: A Study of George Borrow*. London, 1939.

De la Mare, Walter. *Early One Morning in the Spring*. New York, 1935.

De Quincey, Thomas. "On Murder Considered as One of the Fine Arts." In his *The English Mail-Coach and Other Essays*. London, 1961.

Dickens, Charles. *The Life and Adventures of Martin Chuzzlewit*. London, 1882. In *The Works of Charles Dickens*, 30 vols.

————. *Miscellaneous Papers*. 2 vols. New York, n.d.

————. "The Out-and-Out Young Gentleman." In his *Sketches by Boz* [and other sketches]. London, 1957.

Dickens, Charles, and Wilkie Collins. *The Lazy Tour of Two Idle Apprentices*. New York, n.d.

Doyle, Arthur Conan. *Through the Magic Door*. Toronto, n.d.

Eaton, Horace Ainsworth. *Thomas De Quincey*. 1936; rpr. New York, 1972.

Egan, Pierce. *Boxiana; or, Sketches of Modern Pugilism*. 3 vols. London, 1818–21.

————. *New Series of Boxiana*. 2 vols. London, 1828–29.

————. *The Finish to the Adventures of Tom, Jerry and Logic*. London, 1889.

————. *Life in London*. London, 1869.

Fréchet, René. *George Borrow*. Paris, 1956.

Frith, W. P. *My Autobiography and Reminiscences*. Vol. I of 2 vols. 3rd ed. London, 1887.

Froude, James Anthony. *Thomas Carlyle: A History of the First Forty Years of His Life, 1795–1835*. 2 vols. New York, 1882.

Goldberg, Michael. *Carlyle and Dickens*. Athens, Ga., 1972.

Gordon, Mrs. [Mary]. *"Christopher North": A Memoir of John Wilson.* New York, 1875.

Grierson, H. J. C.. ed. *The Letters of Sir Walter Scott, 1823–1825.* London, 1935.

Hazlitt, William. "The Fight." In *William Hazlitt, Essayist and Critic: Selections from His Writings,* edited by Alexander Ireland. London, [1889].

Heleniak, Kathryn Moore. *William Mulready.* New Haven, 1980.

Hindley, Charles. *The True History of Tom and Jerry.* London, n.d.

Hine, Reginald L. *Charles Lamb and His Hertfordshire.* London, 1949.

Hollingsworth, Keith. *The Newgate Novel, 1830–1847.* Detroit, 1963.

Howe, P. P. *The Life of William Hazlitt.* London, 1947.

Irving, Washington. "Buckthorne; or, The Young Man of Great Expectations." In *The Complete Tales of Washington Irving,* edited by Charles Neider. Garden City, 1975.

———. *Journals and Notebooks.* Edited by Walter A. Reichart. Vol. III of 4 vols. to date. Madison, 1970.

Jenkins, Herbert. *The Life of George Borrow.* 1912; rpr. Port Washington, 1970.

Kaplan, Fred. *Thomas Carlyle: A Biography.* Ithaca, 1983.

Kinnaird, John. *William Hazlitt: Critic of Power.* New York, 1978.

Knapp, William I. *Life, Writings and Correspondence of George Borrow.* 2 vols. New York, 1899.

Lamb, Charles. *The Complete Works and Letters of Charles Lamb.* New York, 1935.

Lindsay, Philip. *The Swell Yokel.* London, 1955.

Locker-Lampson, Frederick. *My Confidences: An Autobiographical Sketch Addressed to My Descendants.* London, 1896.

Maclean, Catherine Macdonald. *Born Under Saturn: A Biography of William Hazlitt.* London, 1943.

Macready, William Charles. *The Diaries of William Charles Macready, 1833–1851.* Edited by William Toynbee. 2 vols. London, 1912.

Maginn, William. "The Lament for Thurtell." In *The Odoherty Papers,* edited by Shelton Mackenzie. 2 vols. New York, 1855.

Maxwell, Gordon S. *The Fringe of London.* London, 1925.

Muddock, Joyce Emmerson Preston [Dick Donovan]. *Thurtell's Crime . . .: The Story of a Strange Tragedy.* London, [1906].

Pearson, Hesketh. *The Fool of Love: A Life of William Hazlitt.* New York, 1934.

Plumtree, A. S. "The Artist as Murderer: De Quincey's Essay 'On Murder Considered as One of the Fine Arts.'" In *Thomas De Quincey: Bicentenary Studies,* edited by Robert Lance Snyder. Norman, 1985, 140–63.

Pointon, Marcia. "Painters and Pugilism in Early Nineteenth-Century England." *Gazette des Beaux-Arts* (October, 1978), 131–40.

Real Life in London. 2 vols. London, 1823.

Redgrave, Richard, and Samuel Redgrave. *A Century of Painters of the English School.* 2nd ed. London, 1890.

Rickett, Arthur. *The Vagabond in Literature.* 1906; rpr. Port Washington, 1968.

Rorimer, Anne. *Drawings by William Mulready.* London, 1972.

Sadleir, Michael. *Edward and Rosina, 1803–1836.* Boston, 1931. Vol. I of *Bulwer: A Panorama,* 1 vol. to date.

Scott, Sir Walter. *The Journal of Sir Walter Scott.* New York, 1891.

Sanders, Charles Richard, and Kenneth J. Fielding, eds. *The Collected Letters of Thomas and Jane Welsh Carlyle.* Vol. V of 12 vols. Durham, 1976.

Shorter, Clement, ed. *The Works of George Borrow.* 16 vols. London, 1923.

Smith, Alexander. "A Lark's Flight." In his *Dreamthorp: A Book of Essays Written in the Country.* Garden City, 1934.

Stephens, Frederic G. *Memorials of William Mulready, R. A.* New York, 1890.

Terhune, Alfred McKinley, and Annabelle Burdick Terhune, eds. *The Letters of Edward FitzGerald.* 4 vols. Princeton, 1980.

Thackeray, William Makepeace. *Vanity Fair: A Novel Without a Hero.* New York, 1903. Vols. I–III of *The Works of Thackeray,* 32 vols.

Whateley, Richard, ed. *Bacon's Essays with Annotations.* Boston, 1863.

Whitten, Wilfred [John O'London]. "The Literature of a Crime." In his *The Joy of London and Other Essays.* London, n.d.

Wilcox, Stewart C., *Hazlitt in the Work Shop: The Manuscript of "The Fight."* Baltimore, 1943.

Wilson, John [Christopher North] *et al. Noctes Ambrosianae.* 4 vols. Philadelphia, 1843.

BACKGROUND SOURCES

Altick, Richard D. *The English Common Reader: A Social History of the Mass Reading Public, 1800–1900.* Chicago, 1957.

Ashton, John. *The History of Gambling in England.* 1898; rpr. Montclair, 1969.

Badcock, John [Jon Bee]. *The Fancy.* 2 vols. London, 1826.

Bateson, Charles. *The Convict Ships, 1788–1868.* Glasgow, 1959.

Bleackley, Horace. *The Hangmen of England.* London, 1929.

Blyth, Henry. *Hell & Hazard; or, William Crockford Versus the Gentlemen of England.* Chicago, 1969.

Borowitz, Albert. *A Gallery of Sinister Perspectives: Ten Crimes and a Scandal.* Kent, 1982.

———. *The Woman Who Murdered Black Satin: The Bermondsey Horror.* Columbus, 1981.

Boulton, William B. *The Amusements of Old London.* 2 vols. 1901; rpr. New York, 1969.

Clark, C. M. H. *A History of Australia.* 4 vols. London, 1962.

Collison, Robert. *The Story of Street Literature.* London, 1973.

Cozens-Hardy, B., and E. A. Kent. *The Mayors of Norwich, 1403–1835.* Norwich, 1938.

Cussans, John Edwin. *History of Hertfordshire.* 3 vols. London, 1870–81.

Doyle, Arthur Conan. *Rodney Stone.* Garden City, 1930.

Ferguson, John Alexander. *Bibliography of Australia.* 7 vols. Sydney, 1941–69.

Fitzball, Edward. *Thirty-five Years of a Dramatic Author's Life.* Vol. II of 2 vols. London, 1859.

Ford, John. *Prizefighting: The Age of Regency Boximania*. Newton Abbot, 1971.

Goodman, Jonathan. *Bloody Versicles: The Rhymes of Crime*. Newton Abbot, 1971.

Grant, James. *The Bench and the Bar*. 2 vols. 2nd ed. London, 1838.

Grombach, John V. *The Saga of the Fist*. South Brunswick, 1977.

Hibbert, Christopher. *George IV, Regent and King*. New York, 1973.

Hindley, Charles. *The Life and Times of James Catnach*. London, 1878.

————. *The History of the Catnach Press*. 1887; rpr. Detroit, 1969.

Hopkins, Tighe. *The Romance of Fraud*. New York, 1914.

Hughes, Robert. *The Fatal Shore*. New York, 1987.

Ingleton, Geoffrey Chapman, ed. *True Patriots All; or, News from Early Australia*. Sydney, n.d.

Jack, Ian. *English Literature, 1815–1832*. Oxford, 1963.

Johnson, W. Branch. *The English Prison Hulks*. London, 1957.

Lloyd, Alan. *The Great Prize Fight*. New York, 1977.

Low, Donald A. *Thieves' Kitchen: The Regency Underworld*. London, 1982.

Mayhew, Henry. *London Labour and the London Poor*. Vol. I of 4 vols. 1861–62; rpr. New York, 1968.

Miles, Henry Downes. *Pugilistica: Being One Hundred and Forty-four Years of the History of British Boxing*. 3 vols. London, 1880–1906.

Newton, H. Chance. *Crime and the Drama; or, Dark Deeds Dramatized*. London, 1927.

Partridge, Colonel S. G. *Prisoner's Progress*. London, n.d.

Priestley, J. B. *The Prince of Pleasure and His Regency, 1811–1820*. London, 1971.

Radzinowicz, Leon. *A History of English Criminal Law and Its Administration from 1750*. 4 vols. London, 1948–68.

Raymond, John, ed. *The Reminiscences and Recollections of Captain Gronow*. London, 1964.

Reid, J. C. *Bucks and Bruisers: Pierce Egan and Regency England*. London, 1971.

Ryan, James T. *Reminiscences of Australia*. Sydney, 1894.

Selections from the Fancy; or, True Sportsman's Guide. Barre, 1972.

Shaw, George Bernard. *Cashel Byron's Profession*. New York, 1904.

Shoolbred, C. F. *The Law of Gaming and Betting*. 2nd ed. London, 1935.

Steinmetz, Andrew. *The Gaming Table*. 2 vols. 1870; rpr. Montclair, 1969.

Stephen, Sir James Fitzjames. *A History of the Criminal Law of England*. 3 vols. London, 1883.

Tarr, Laszlo. *The History of the Carriage*. New York, 1969.

Therry, Roger. *Reminiscences of Thirty Years' Residence in New South Wales and Victoria*. 1863; rpr. Sydney, 1974.

Thornbury, Walter. *Haunted London*. London, 1880.

Trevelyan, George Macaulay. *British History in the Nineteenth Century (1782–1901)*. London, 1922.

Turnor, Lewis. *History of the Ancient Town and Borough of Hertford*. Hertford, 1830.

Wade, John. *A Treatise on the Police and Crimes of the Metropolis.* 1829; rpr. Montclair, 1972.

Walford, Edward. *Greater London.* 2 vols. London, 1883–84.

White, R. J. *Life in Regency England.* London, 1963.

Wignall, Trevor C. *The Story of Boxing.* London, 1923.

Willis, W. R. "The Romance of the Road." In *Bygone Hertfordshire,* edited by William Andrews. London, 1898.

INDEX

Abbott, Lord Chief Justice Charles, 210–11, 214
Addis, James, 39, 40–41, 52–53, 55, 148, 162–63, 235
Altick, Richard, 3
Andrews, Thomas: description of, 109; pretrial publicity, 112–13; argument for postponement, 118; Thurtell's evaluation of, 138; defense strategy, 149–50; cross-examination of witnesses, 157–58, 161–64; question of legality of trial, 179; mentioned, 142
Anne, Queen, 9
Annison, William, 101, 210–11
Aram, Eugene, 235
Avery, J. R., 236–37

Ballads, 253, 255
Ballantine, Serjeant William, 104
Barton, Bernard, 254
Bates, Thomas, 53
Bateson, Charles, 229
Beaumont, Barber: arson conspiracy, 28, 29, 36, 86, 168; as Thurtell's enemy, 30; attempted murder of, 87, 112, 225, 245; meeting with Hunt in prison, 97, 99; letter to Thurtell in prison, 137, 138
Beeson, John, 50, 149–50, 169
Belasco, Abraham, 25–26
Belasco, Israel, 25
Belcher, Jem, 15, 190
Belcher, Tom, 26
Bellingham, John, 197

Bentham, Jeremy, 223
Bingham, Richard, 68, 70, 76–77, 248
Blackwood's Magazine, 194, 257–58
Blaxland, Gregory, 230
Bleackley, Horace, 184
Bolingbroke, Nathaniel, 195
Bolland, William, 109, 142, 163, 214
Borrow, George, 4, 20, 21, 257, 263–66, 275
Boxing: association with Thurtell-Hunt case, 2, 82, 83; debate on morality of, 2; underworld connections of, 2–3, 12; prohibition of, 6–7; sponsorship of, 7; and barriers between social classes, 7–8; Hickman-Neat bout, 13, 16–18, 27; locations for, 15; writings about, 15–16, 256; Thurtell's associations with, 25–27; effect of Thurtell-Hunt case, 202–207; decline of, 204–207; negative attitude of Washington Irving, 256
Bradbee, Mr., 211–12
Broadsides. See Street literature
Broderick, Mr., 107, 109, 142, 152, 164
Broughton, Jack, 6–7
Browning, Robert, 253
Buckingham, Edward, 65
Bulmer, William, 40
Bulwer Lytton, Edward, 5, 208, 257, 262–63
Bunn, George, 228
Burke, Edmund, 113
Burke, Thomas, 269–70
Burn, Jem, 205–207

Burrough, Mr. Justice James, 86, 205–
    207
Butler, John, 69–70
Byron, George Gordon, Lord, 8

Calas, Jean, 171
Carlyle, Jane, 257
Carlyle, Thomas, 5, 272–75
Carter, Jack, 26
Castlereagh, Lord, 35
Catnach, James, 89, 90, 199
Cenci, Beatrice, 3–5, 250
Chapbooks, 3, 229–30
Chelmsford, Lord, 110
Cheshire, Thomas, 184, 190–91
Chitty, Joseph: injunction against per-
    formance of *The Gamblers*, 93, 110;
    Thurtell's defense counsel, 109, 142;
    postponement arguments, 113–14;
    Thurtell's evaluation of, 138; question
    of legality of trial, 179, 180
Chubb, W., 90, 229
Clarence, Duke of, 8
Clarke, William, 68–69, 70, 162, 171,
    248
Clutterbuck, Robert: murder investiga-
    tion, 33–34, 37, 157, 160, 161, 241;
    admonition to Hunt at preliminary
    hearings, 44; publication of Hunt's
    confession, 49–50; during inquest, 54,
    60; exhumation of Weare's body, 77;
    denial of Pearson's access to Thurtell,
    95; Hunt's confession, 144, 145; en-
    dorsement of pamphlet about trial,
    199
Cobbett, Richard, 253
Cobbett, William, 253
Cogswell, Benjamin, 65
Coleridge, Samuel Taylor, 260
Collier, John Payne, 24
Collins, Wilkie, 268
Colton, Reverend Mr., 186, 214
Cooper, George, 14
Corder, William, 235
Cotton, Reverend Horace, 218
Cousens, William, 215–16
Crayon, Geoffrey, 8
Cribb, Tom, 13, 15
Crockford, William, 208, 209

Cruikshank, George, 16, 223
Cruikshank, Robert, 16
Cumberland, Duke of, 6–7

Dallas, Lord Chief Justice Robert, 86
De la Mare, Walter, 272
De Quincey, Thomas, 258–60
Despard, Colonel Edward Marcus, 98
Dickens, Charles, 5, 218, 266–69
Disraeli, Benjamin, 208
Dobson, Jessie, 235
Dodson, Mary, 21, 22, 27–28, 30, 269
Donovan, Dick, 269
Douglas, J. E., 20
Dowling, Vincent, 207
Dyer, Sir James, 172

Edgerly, Joseph, 89, 112
Egan, Pierce: acquaintance with Thur-
    tell, 4, 5, 21; description of fights, 7,
    17; life of, 15–16; publication of *Box-
    iana*, 15, 250; publication of *Life in
    London*, 16; reporting style, 16; de-
    scription of Thurtell, 20, 24–27, 29;
    recollection of Hunt, 23; description
    of Weare, 24; prison interviews with
    Thurtell, 135–41; description of gal-
    lows for execution, 184–85; descrip-
    tion of execution, 190; appearance of
    Thurtell's dead body, 192; assessment
    of Thurtell after execution, 193; *Recol-
    lections of John Thurtell*, 213; reconstruc-
    tion of crime, 241–42; works owned
    by Sir Walter Scott, 255; opinion of
    Bulwer Lytton and gift of Thurtell's
    caul, 263; symbolism of gigs, 273–74
Elizabeth I, 171
Elliott, W. J., 241
Evans, George William, 231

Fauntleroy, Henry, 218
Fean, Mr., 211–12
Fenton, Francis Tarrant, 95–100, 118,
    142, 189
Ferguson, John Alexander, 229
Field, Robert, 51, 55, 70–71, 77, 162,
    171
Fielding, Henry, 32
Fighting. *See* Boxing

Fitzball, Edward, 91
FitzGerald, Edward, 257
Fitzgerald, Percy, 80–81
Fleet, John, 69, 164
Ford, Richard, 257
Forster, John, 257
Foster, Charles, 33, 35, 164
Four Inside, 198
Foxen, James, 184
Franklin, T. W., 158, 180, 182–83, 186–89, 190, 194–95
Fraser, William, 234–35
Freeman, James, 37, 39, 242
Frewin, James, 215
Frith, W. P., 251–52

Gamblers, The, 90–92, 110–12, 137, 198
Gambling: association with Thurtell-Hunt case, 1–2, 80–85; debate on morality of, 2; underworld connections of, 2–3; prohibitions and restrictions, 8–10; aristocratic clubs, 9–10; swindlers, 10–12; effects on fashionable youth, 11–12; street literature pertaining to, 90; effect of Thurtell-Hunt case, 207–208; decline of, 208–209
Gaskell, James Milnes, 88, 253
Gas-light Man. *See* Hickman, Tom
George IV, 8, 9
Giddens, John, 21
Gigs: use as literary image, 4, 5, 81, 273–75; Freeman's evidence about, 39, 161; appearance on day after murder, 40; white-faced horse, 40, 68, 147, 161, 165; on murder night, 40–41, 68–69, 227, 244; Hunt's hiring of, 45–46, 65–66, 149; removal of corpse from Probert's pond, 48; used in melodrama theater, 91–92; in prosecution's opening statement of trial, 147–48; Probert's testimony concerning, 154; description by Thomas Wilson, 161; Addis' testimony about, 162–63; use for conveyance of Thurtell's body for dissection, 195; neologisms built on word *gig*, 274–75
Godwin, William, 262
Grant, James, 109

Gurney, John, 109, 115, 118, 142, 144–49, 159
Gwillim, Amanda, 29

Hackman, James, 240
Hale, Lord, 175–76
Hale, Mary, 244
Halls, Thomas, 211–12
Harding, James Duffield, 252
Harding, William, 69
Hardwick, Michael, 237, 239
Harmer, Mr., 142, 144, 174, 224
Hart, Solomon, 252
Haydon, Langdon, 173
Haydow, Thomas, 62
Hazlitt, William, 4, 16–19
Heenan, John, 207
Helme, John, 112
Henry VIII, 8
Heppenstall, Rayner, 236
Herbert, Edward: description of pretrial scene, 107–108; description of defendants at trial, 142–43; description of Probert, 152–53; description of Elizabeth Probert, 159; description of witnesses, 161–63; description of Thurtell, 166, 173, 180; description of jury delivering verdict, 179; assessment of Thurtell after execution, 193–94; reconstruction of crime, 242, 244; satires of, 258; article on Thurtell's hanging, 264
Herrington, John, 32, 39–40
Hertfordshire Tragedy, The, 198–99
Heward, James, 33, 52, 54, 55, 89
Hickman, Tom, 13–18, 27
Holroyd, Mr. Justice George, 104, 113, 115, 116
Hood, Thomas, 275
Hopkins, Tighe, 231
Hudson, Josh, 26, 29, 185
Hunt, Joseph: life of, 23–24; underworld connections, 24; vocal talents, 24, 61, 141, 224, 228; Thurtell's talk of revenge to, 30; arrest of, 35; testimony at preliminary hearings, 41–42, 44; first confession, 45–49, 144–45; location of Weare's body, 50; comment to Field about murder night, 51; viewing of

Weare's corpse, 52; testimony at inquest, 54–58, 62–63; complicity in crime, 61; hiring and return of gig, 65–66, 71, 149; actions on day of murder, 69–70; imprisonment of, 77, 94, 96, 182, 183; gambling associations, 84; arson prosecution, 86, 97; appearance at trial, 108–109, 143, 179; legal advisers at trial, 110, 142; motion for postponement of trial of, 144–45; promise of immunity, 144–45, 147, 174, 176; use of confession during trial, 148; circumstantial evidence against, 149; reaction to Probert during trial, 152; Thurtell's defense, 169–71; his defense, 174; request for permission to address jury, 178; guilty verdict, 179; before Thurtell's execution, 187, 188, 189; application for reprieve, 222–23; confessions following reprieve, 223–28, 244–45; rumors of death on convict ship, 228–30; sentence to life in Australia, 228–33; marriage, 232; children, 232–33; death, 233; Herbert's reconstruction of murder night, 242, 244; character of, 244–46. *See also* Thurtell-Hunt case
Hunt, Richard, 32, 39–40, 163

Irving, Washington, 8, 256

Jackson, "Gentleman" John, 8, 204
Jay, George, 95, 99, 101–102, 139, 142
Jekyll, John, 120
Jones, George Henry, 33, 41, 112, 157, 160, 161, 199, 252
Jones, Thomas, 232–33

Kay, Thomas, 68, 103–104, 253
Kean, Edmund, 173, 267
Kelly, Captain, 225
Kelly, Thomas, 195, 200–201
Kemble, Fanny, 257
Kent, George, 204–205
King, William, 71
King v. *Fleet*, 114, 116
King v. *Jolliffe*, 114, 116
King v. *Mead*, 113, 116

Lamb, Charles, 254
Lamb, William, 105
Landseer, Sir Edwin, 252
Langan, Jack, 185, 258
Latouche, Henri de, 196
Lawrence, Sir Thomas, 252–53
Lemming. *See* Lemon
Lemon, 24–25, 84–85, 191
Lindsay, Philip, 270–71
Literature. *See* Melodrama theaters; Street literature; and names of specific authors
Lloyd, Reverend Thomas, 95–102, 104, 194, 213
Lockhart, John Gibson, 258

Mackinlay, George, 20, 173–74, 177
Macready, William Charles, 257
Maggs, F. D., 247, 248
Maginn, Dr. William, 258
Maloney, Mary, 66–67
March, Stephen, 65–66, 165
Marshall, Sir John, 257
Martin, Jack, 25, 26, 29, 256–57
Mason, John Finch, 33, 44, 144, 160
Maxwell, Gordon, 237–38, 250
Mayhew, Henry, 200
Mayne, Richard, 209
Melbourne, Lord, 105
Melodrama theaters, 3, 91–93, 198–99
Mendoza, Daniel, 8
Meredith, Mary, 215
Meredith, Mrs., 215, 216
Meredith, William, 215, 216
Mitford, Reverend John, 260–62
Mitton, Madame Anna, 257
Moncrieff, W. T., 16
Montague, Mrs. Basil, 257
Muddock, Joyce Emmerson Preston (Dick Donovan), 269
Mulready, William, 143, 153, 250–51
Mumford, James, 140–41
Murray, John, 257

Neale, Ned, 205–207
Neat, Bill, 13, 15–18, 27
Newgate Calendar, 171, 175
Newspapers: pretrial publicity, 3, 79–89, 106–107, 111–12, 115, 117; publica-

tion of Hunt's first confession, 49–50; reaction to inquest verdict, 64; circulation of dailies and weeklies, 79–80; libels against Thurtell, 85–86; on restriction of legal advisers to Thurtell, 97–98; Park's criticism of pretrial publicity, 106–107, 117; reactions to postponement, 117–19; restrictions on liberty of press, 119–20; attack by Thurtell, 136–37; assessments of Thurtell after execution, 192–95; on boxing, 202–205

Nicholls, Charles, 31–33, 52

Nicholson, Renton, 36

Nicholson, Undersheriff, 111, 159, 183, 189, 192, 195

Noel, John: solicitor for Probert, 23, 60, 157; as counsel for investigation, 37, 41–45; suggestion of Weare as victim, 37; publication of Hunt's confession, 49–50; at inquest, 54; Hunt's statement to, 63; Weare's appointment with, 67; Thurtell's reaction to prosecution, 77; association with gambling, 82; Hunt's immunity, 144, 145

Noyes, Anne, 40, 42, 47, 73, 74

Noyes, Caroline, 29–30, 87

Noyes, Elizabeth, 23. See also Probert, Elizabeth

Noyes, Thomas, 40, 55, 72, 161, 224

Oliver, Tom, 15

O'London, John (Wilfred Whitten), 250

Otway, Rear Admiral William, 20

Painter, Ned, 21, 25

Palmer, William, 267–68

Pamphlets. See Street literature

Park, Sir James Alan: arson prosecution, 28, 86, 104; description of, 104–105; address to grand jury panel, 105–107; postponement of trial, 110–17; comments on pretrial publicity, 111–12, 176; reactions to postponement, 117–20; Thurtell's opinion of, 140; motion for postponement of Hunt's trial, 144–45; Thurtell's request for adjournment, 163–64; charge to jury at end of trial, 175–78; comments on circum-

stantial evidence, 175–76; review of evidence, 176–77; ruling on legality of trial, 179; address to Thurtell on order for execution, 180; Probert's trial for horse stealing, 214; statement on behavior of confederates, 245; slur by Charles Lamb, 254

Parkes, Joe, 17

Paul, Kegan, 253

Pearson, Charles: arrest of, 95–96; request to see Thurtell in jail, 95; bail for, 96–97; Thurtell's preference for, 99, 100, 137, 140; writer of Thurtell's defense speech, 194

Peel, Sir Robert, 99, 101, 222

Pelham, Camden, 191–92

Perceval, Spencer, 197

Percy Anecdotes, 171, 175

Phillips, Charles, 77, 110, 142, 166, 171, 178

Pidcock, John, 164

Platt, Thomas Joshua, 109–10, 113, 142, 150–52, 161, 164

Plays. *See* Melodrama theaters

Pocock, John, 197

Poetry, 260–62

Prizefighting. *See* Boxing

Probert, Elizabeth: during murder weekend, 42, 47, 52–53, 60; information provided during investigation, 73–76; Caroline Noyes living with, 87; testimony during trial, 148, 159–61; Weare's watch, 149, 161; Thurtell's comments on her testimony, 170; husband's death sentence, 218

Probert, William: appearance, 23; life of, 23; business frauds with Thurtells, 27; arrest of, 33; layout of home and property, 34–35; actions on murder weekend, 41, 46–47, 51, 55, 69–70; testimony at preliminary hearings, 41; Sunday visit to Nicholls, 52; viewing of corpse, 52; preliminary statements at inquest, 54; testimony at inquest, 58–61; complicity in murder, 61–62, 148, 156–57; imprisonment during investigation, 77; on Thurtell's murder plans, 88; grant of immunity, 107–108, 145–47; appearance at beginning

of trial, 108–109, 144, 152–53; defense attorneys, 110, 142; testimony at trial, 153–58; criminal record, 158; Thurtell's defense, 169–71; Thurtell's ridicule of his testimony, 178–79; rumors following murder trial, 213–14; trial for horse stealing, 214–18, 245; execution of, 218–20; burial, 221; Hunt's account of their meeting, 224; tourism at cottage, 234–35; site of cottage, 240; Herbert's reconstruction of murder night, 242, 244; character of, 244–46. *See also* Thurtell-Hunt case
Probett, Stephen, 65–66
Pugilistic Club, 7, 204

Radzinowicz, Leon, 208
Randall, Jack, 16, 27, 212
Reay, Martha, 240
Redgrave, Richard, 251
Reni, Guido, 4
Rexworthy, William, 37, 52, 145, 150
Richards, Mr., 185–86
Richter, Jean Paul Friedrich, 274
Rogers, Mary, 232
Rooke, Benjamin, 52, 54–58, 61, 63, 145
Ruthven, George Thomas Joseph, 35–36, 41, 43, 53–54, 65, 152, 165, 241–42
Ryan, James T., 232–33

Sala, George Augustus, 202
Sayers, Tom, 207
Scott, Sir Walter, 254–55
Shorter, Clement, 264
Simmonds, Constable Henry, 32, 35, 152
Slack, Jack, 6–7
Slack, Richard, 65
Slattery, Jonathan, 231
Smeeton, George, 15
Smith, Alexander, 271–72
Smith, Philip, 31–32, 39, 239
Smith, Sydney, 271
Snowden, John, 210–11
Spring, Tom, 13, 21, 185, 207, 258
Stanmers, James, 215
Stott, C. A., 237
Strange, Elizabeth, 69

Street literature, 89–90, 119–20, 199–202, 229–30, 253, 255
Sullivan, John L., 207
Sutton, High Sheriff Robert, 99, 103, 183, 186, 190, 194
Swinburne, Sir John, 251

Taddy, Serjeant, 28
Talleyrand, 208
Tetsall, Charles, 29, 72–73
Thackeray, William Makepeace, 1, 266
Theaters. *See* Melodrama theaters
Therry, Roger, 231–32
Thesiger, Frederick, 110, 142, 144–45, 158, 178
Thistlewood, Arthur, 98
Thoreau, Henry David, 148–49
Thornbury, Walter, 234
Thurtell, George, 264
Thurtell, Henry, 22, 211–12
Thurtell, John: boxing and gambling associations, 1, 2, 21–27, 80–85, 168, 204; appearance of, 4, 21; personality of, 4, 25–26, 271; acquaintance with writers, 4, 18, 19, 21, 264, 265; as boxing trainer, 18, 19; early life, 19–20, 167; naval service, 20–21, 85–86, 155, 177; business dealings, 21–22, 27, 168; arson conspiracy and prosecution, 27–29, 36, 86–87, 137, 138, 210; personality disintegration, 29–30; grudge against Weare, 30, 45, 177–78; arrest of, 35–36, 43; evidence of conversation with Weare, 37; actions on murder night, 40–41, 68–69, 73; testimony at preliminary hearings, 42–44; inquest verdict against, 61; Weare's watch, 73, 74; imprisonment of, 77–78, 94, 96, 138; preparation of defense, 77–78; newspaper libels against, 85–86; alleged murder attempts, 87–89, 112, 224–25, 228, 245, 256–57; access to legal advisers, 94–102, 118–19; choice of legal advisers, 99–100, 137, 140; prison letter to Mrs. Walker, 100–101; exhibited to witnesses before trial, 103–104; appearance at trial, 108–109, 143, 179, 180; defense attorneys, 109–10, 138, 142; prison interviews

with Egan, 135–41; attack on press, 136–37; defense, 136, 138–39, 166–74, 178, 194, 272; relations with parents, 139, 186; opinion of Mr. Justice Park, 140; circumstantial evidence against, 149, 171–72; reaction to Probert during trial, 152; description of murder based on Probert's testimony, 155–56; request for adjournment of trial, 163–64; damning admissions following murder, 164; eloquence mentioned in Park's charge to jury, 175; comments while jury out, 178–79; verdict of guilty, 179; postponement of execution, 180; before execution, 180–83, 185–87; request for contempt for Hertford execution practices, 183–84; execution of, 187–92, 271–72; newspaper assessments after execution, 192–95; purported hope of last-minute rescue from execution, 192; dissection of body, 195–96; viewing of corpse by crowd, 195–96; phrenologists' findings, 196–97; forgiveness of Probert, 212; view of Probert's future after murder trial, 212–13; Hunt's account of their meeting, 224; Hunt's account of murder, 225–28; skull of, 235–36; judgment on skill as criminal, 247–49; skeleton used in anatomical studies, 251–52; influence on works of George Borrow, 263–66; compared with William Palmer, 267–68; essayists' views of, 271–72. *See also* Thurtell-Hunt case

Thurtell, Thomas (father), 19, 21, 22, 27, 64, 101, 139, 194–95

Thurtell, Tom (brother): bankruptcy of, 22, 69; business frauds with brother John, 27; arson conspiracy and prosecution, 27–28, 48, 70, 210–11, 224; arrest of, 35; on murder weekend, 41, 55; acquittal at inquest, 62; testimony against brother John, 71–73; woman friend of, 87; visit to brother before execution, 186; letter from brother on day of execution, 189

Thurtell-Hunt case: boxing and gambling associations, 1, 2, 177–78; im-

pact on literature, 1, 3–5, 250, 254–75; popular appeal of, 1; underworld ramifications of, 2–3; freedom of the press issues, 3; pretrial publicity, 3, 79–90, 106–107, 111–12, 115, 117, 119–20; right to counsel issues, 3, 94–102, 118–19; images of case, 4; discovery of murder weapons, 31–32, 39–40; preliminary police investigation, 32–37; preliminary hearings, 37–49; Hunt's first confession, 45–49; location of corpse, 49–51; newspaper publication of Hunt's first confession, 49–50; inquest, 52–62, 62–64; police investigation following inquest, 65–71; Tom Thurtell's testimony against brother, 71–73; exhumation order, 76–77; symbolism of, 80–81; hoax theory, 90; melodrama theaters pertaining to, 91–93, 198–99; grand jury proceedings, 104–20; appearance of defendants at trial, 108–109, 142–43; lawyers for the prosecution, 109, 142; defense attorneys, 109–10, 142; postponement of trial, 110–17; press reactions to postponement, 117–19; case for the prosecution, 142–65; motion for postponement of Hunt's trial, 144–45; Probert's immunity, 145–46; prosecution's opening statement, 146–49; defense strategy for Thurtell, 149–50; Probert's testimony, 155–58; Elizabeth Probert's testimony, 159–61; adjournment request by Thurtell, 163–64; case for defense, 166–74; Hunt's defense, 174; Park's charge to jury, 175–78; argument on illegality of trial, 179; verdict, 179; order of execution, 180; preparation for Thurtell's execution, 183–85; execution of Thurtell, 187–92; street literature associated with, 199–202; effects on boxing, 202–207; effects on gambling, 207–208; Hunt's account of murder, 225–28; current landmarks, 234–41; reconstruction of crime, 241–44; unanswered questions, 241–49; characters of Probert and Hunt, 244–46; Thurtell's skill as criminal, 247–49; murder as gangland slay-

ing, 249; impact on artists, 250–53;
impact on schoolchildren, 253; in literary correspondence and diaries, 254–
57; satires of, 257–60; poetry based
on, 260–62; impact on fiction, 262–
71; impact on essays, 271–75
Tom and Jerry, 16
Trevelyan, G. M., 1, 253

Upson, John, 145, 164

Victoria, Queen, 209
Vizetelly, Henry, 89–90
Voltaire, 171

Wade, John, 9–10, 208
Wadeson, Samuel, 173
Walker, Mrs., 87, 100–101, 215
Wallace-Hadrill, Reverend David, 237–
41
Walmesley, Joseph, 174
Ward, Thomas Abel, 53, 77, 150–52, 251
Wardle, James, 53, 160
Watson, Eric, 20, 27, 104
Weare, Richard, 67–68, 162
Weare, William: underworld connections,
24–25; Thurtell's hatred of, 30, 177–
78; conversation with Thurtell, 37;
Noel's suggestion of murder of, 37;
Hunt's first confession, 45–49; discov-
ery of body of, 50–51; burial, 62–63;
funeral, 62; movements on day of
murder, 66–67; watch, 67, 73, 149,
164; association with Noel, 82; murder
as gangland killing, 84–85; character
of, 147; Hunt's account of murder of,
225–28; residence, 234; burial site,
240–41. *See also* Thurtell-Hunt case
Webb, William, 200, 234, 255
Whately, Archbishop Richard, 271
Whitten, Wilfred, 250
Wild, Jonathan, 3, 235
William IV, 8
Williams, Boiled Beef, 198
Williams, Charles Frederick, 110, 142
Williams, Llewellyn, 91
Wilson (prison governor): Hunt's singing
for, 141; security of prisoners, 142;
during trial, 144, 146; treatment of
Thurtell before execution, 180, 182,
183, 188, 189, 190, 191; appreciation
from Thurtell's father, 194; Hunt's re-
prieve, 223
Wilson, Thomas, 68, 161
Winter, Thomas, 73
Winter, Tom (boxer). *See* Spring, Tom
Wontner, John, 184
Woodruff, Susan Anne, 40, 52, 163
Woods, James, 87–88, 112, 224–25, 269
Wooll, Reverend John, 201
Wormald, Thomas, 235
Wyatt, Benjamin, 208